Honor,
Courage,
Commitment

Honor, Courage, Commitment

Navy Boot Camp

J. F. Leahy

Naval Institute Press ■ Annapolis, Maryland

Naval Institute Press
291 Wood Road
Annapolis, MD 21402

ISBN 13: 978-1-55750-536-1

Library of Congress Cataloging-in-Publication Data
Leahy, J. F., 1946-
Honor, courage, commitment : Navy boot camp / J. F. Leahy.
   p. cm.
Includes bibliographical references and index.
ISBN 1-55750-536-5 (alk. paper)
1. Naval education—United States. 2. Sailors—Training of—
United States. 3. United States. Navy—Recruiting, enlistment, etc.
I. Title.
V433 .L43 2002
359.5'0973—dc21   2002019761

Printed in the United States of America on acid-free paper ∞

09 08   9 8 7

For the Red Ropes past, present, and those to come
The Navy and the nation are forever in your debt
Keep pushing, shipmates

Contents

Foreword

Honor, courage, commitment—these words were adopted by Navy leadership in early 1993 to replace our previous watchwords. This change was made by a group led by the Secretary of the Navy, the Chief of Naval Operations, the Commandant of the Marine Corps, myself, and a dozen other leaders and civilian advisers and was a response to some troubling conduct. In the end there was a general agreement that honor, courage, and commitment were aptly chosen (they had been serving the Marine Corps well for many years already). I agreed to this change, but I left the meeting fully aware that the easy part was done. The really difficult task of making these words truly meaningful to sailors (and therefore to our Navy) lay ahead. In order for them to have real and lasting impact on our Navy these words must be taught with clarity and intensity.

In truth, the previous watchwords—integrity, tradition, and professionalism—had great potential, but they had never been taught to sailors or even well-publicized in the Navy. Instead they were relegated to the occasional quarterdeck banner or command logo, rarely seen and even more rarely used to inspire, motivate, or provoke sailors to contemplate the importance of naval service and their own personal conduct, both on and off duty. Although these are fine-sounding words with noble connotations, they are, in fact, just words. And as every ethics and values teacher knows, memorizing words isn't enough. To be effective they must be learned in the context of naval heritage and tradition. Jack Leahy has identified one place—Recruit Training Command, popularly known as "boot camp"—where every waking moment is dedicated toward instilling those values into fifty thousand or more young men and women every year.

Preparing sailors to live and fight at sea in a shore-based training environment has always been challenging and, as Jack Leahy's work will make clear to you, it hasn't gotten any easier. Although this book is a recording of the comments of recruits and their trainers with minimal amplifying commentary by Leahy, it illuminates the three main ingredients of the recruit training experience in an honest and straightforward way: recruits, recruit division commanders (RDCs), and the boot camp itself—Great Lakes Naval Training Center.

I believe recruit training is better now than at any time in my memory. Recruit training works. That it does work is attributable exclusively to RDCs, the "Red Ropers." I join in the sentiments contained in Jack's dedication: "For the Red Ropes— past, present, and those to come—the Navy and the nation are forever in your debt." We are! We have been, and God willing, we always will be.

We were in their debt following Pearl Harbor when, outnumbered and outgunned, sailors demonstrated great valor and sacrifice all across the Pacific, taking fearsome losses, holding the line, remaining outwardly confident of victory through the darkest hours of that conflict. And in October 2000, when young sailors—most in their teens and early twenties—working under the most horrific situations imaginable, saved the USS *Cole* in Yemen. And most recently, we were in their debt in February 2002 when the USS *Theodore Roosevelt* set the all-time Navy record for continuous time away at sea, launching nearly one hundred long-range air missions every day. We are in their debt today for, as you read this book, young men and women— trained by these recruit division commanders—are guarding our freedom somewhere, everywhere, in this troubled world.

No sailor, ever, *ever*, forgets his boot camp company commander (now RDC). My memories of BM1 Jones (Company 649, San Diego, 1965) are crystal clear these many years later. Known and addressed only as Mr. Jones (in the training style of the day), he was small, wiry, and tough. He was intense and profane. Most impressive, he was omnipresent. He was present at reveille and taps, and every moment in between. There were regular sightings during the mid watch as well. He was, in a salty and perverse kind of way, extremely witty and wise. On one occasion during an outbreak of spinal meningitis we were all given preventive medication daily to take after meals. When BM1 Jones found several of the yellow pills on the head floor he was enraged, and we all began to anticipate the rifle drills or other such punishment in store for us. Instead he made us all take a sheet of stationery and write a brief letter. Beginning "Dear Mom and Dad," he dictated a short note on the facts of the meningitis outbreak and the several deaths that had already occurred. His dictation noted that the Navy was conscientiously providing lifesaving medicine to us every day and concluded by informing them that we threw our medicine away instead of taking it as ordered. He had us conclude "With love, your son" and sign our names. He then collected the letters and stamped the addressed envelopes. He apparently never mailed the letters, but nearly all our mothers received a strange letter we wrote later that night attempting to explain. No more discarded medicine was ever found on the deck.

Strangely, I intensely disliked and feared him, but somehow I respected and trusted him at the same time. These many years later I realize that he was the very epitome of duty and reliability; his commitment to prepare us was beyond doubt. We might not have been happy in his charge, but we learned respect for authority, loyalty to the institution, and the absolute importance of following orders.

In my mind's album are many snapshots of boot camp that have not faded over the years. In one, BM1 Jones is marching off with a half dozen other company commanders from our battalion, all in dress uniforms, to take the E-7 examination. That small group departing in military formation was the symbol of all Navy authority and structure for me. While I knew nothing about the advancement system or the near mystical importance of selection to chief, I knew there was something special about that scene. Over the years, all the negative feelings gave way to respect and even affection for BM1 Jones. Wherever you are today, Boats—good luck and smooth sailing, shipmate.

I laughed when I read the debate about the differences between today's recruits and earlier generations, whether they are "less fit" or "smarter" than before. That debate has been going on in the Chief's Mess and Wardroom since Noah first set sail. Truth, like beauty, has to be in the eye of the beholder, I'm afraid. It is hard for me to accept either assertion. In my day, for example, beyond the perpetual marching and rifle drills in preparation for pass-in-review, there was very little physical activity, and my RDC never led or participated in it. Today there is a real effort to include regular, meaningful physical activity, and the RDCs—like Chief Marty Zeller at the gas house—are required to lead from the front. So if recruits are less fit, the Navy has taken some steps to meet the deficiency. As to whether or not today's youngster is smarter, I am skeptical. The brightest have been exposed to lots of technology and are exceptionally competent, but most, even some with college degrees, write poorly and may not understand basic civics or geography. The most obvious differences over earlier generations are diversity and the near certainty of extensive media exposure to popular culture. There are many other differences: More are married or single parents, and there are fewer stigmas attached to failure and more propensity to openly question authority. But in the all-important categories of motivation and potential, the similarities with earlier generations of recruits likely outnumber the differences. Like the recruits of my day, most are just young folks looking for a place to fit in and succeed.

Jack's work captures the frustrations and the pride shared by all the players in the recruit training experience. It is both thought provoking and reassuring to listen to the recruits as they are by turns fearful, playful, irreverent, proud, or confident and to hear their RDCs speak in a straightforward manner about the challenges they contend with as they turn recruits into sailors. Bravo Zulu, Jack. Bravo Zulu, Division 005. Bravo Zulu, Recruit Training Command, Great Lakes, Illinois.

John Hagan
Master Chief Petty Officer of the Navy (Retired)

Preface

It was one of those Cape Cod evenings that make me wish I weren't a midwesterner. Four old friends, Navy shipmates nearly thirty years ago, had finally reconnected through the magic of the Internet. Mary Ann and Jack King had opted for Navy careers, married, and retired after twenty years; Jim Rose and I had returned to civilian lives after four years' service. Over excellent seafood risottos at Barolo's in Hyannis, we reminisced, and as often happens among sailors, the talk turned to our earliest Navy experiences. What were things like now, we wondered? In the long summer twilight we talked of pranks played and watches stood, of liberty runs and inspections, of boot camps and company commanders, and things both silly and significant, until, as often happens, one of us remarked, "You know, somebody ought to write a book."

And so I did.

The timing, if not perfect, was at least favorable. My long-planned retirement from a major research and development organization was imminent. And even though I'd hung up my navy white hat in 1970, in a way I'd never strayed far from the fleet. I had spent nearly a decade as a civilian consultant in the intelligence community, often enough side by side with sailors. I'd visited and worked in over forty countries—many more than I had ever seen on active duty—and I had developed a dozen or more technical manuals, some still in use throughout the fleet. Anytime my boss had a project evenly slightly nautical, he'd remind me of my Navy roots.

Those roots stretched back to a dark winter night in 1966, and to a Roman Catholic seminary in Baltimore. I'd been called in yet again by the rector, who gently reminded me that sneaking off to date nurses at Bon Secours Hospital was not career-enhancing, at least not in the eyes of the celibate Paulist fathers. Wearily, he gave me thirty dollars—I resisted the temptation to ask for pieces of silver—and a train ticket home. He reminded me that my draft status would soon revert to 1-A, and said that if I wanted to avoid stomping through the bush in Vietnam, I might consider other, more sociable arrangements as quickly as I could. I did—and three weeks later arrived in Navy boot camp. It was three years before I got to Vietnam.

I did have a leg up on the other recruits, though: Having just emerged from an authoritarian, hierarchical, highly structured life, I couldn't see what all the fuss was about at Recruit Training Command, Great Lakes. Sharing living spaces, toilet facilities, and showers with eighty other guys my age, while being yelled at constantly, seemed natural enough to me. I muddled through the mildly challenging physical exercises and, I suppose, departed at least marginally more fit than when I arrived. After eight weeks of hiding behind stanchions every time a working party was called, I passed from boot camp into the fleet. The dress blue uniform was a distinct advantage when courting student nurses, I happily discovered.

I pondered all this as I flew home to Ohio after my visit to Cape Cod. Surely, there must be dozens of books on Navy boot camp, I thought. I had devoured Tom Rick's excellent work *Making the Corps*, of course, but that was about Marines and Parris Island. Surely someone had taken the time to tell the story of Navy recruit training, particularly in view of the recent changes in public policy dictating complete gender integration at all levels of training. I decided to find out.

I returned to the university where I teach part-time and researched the literature. I was surprised to find that outside of some recent newspaper and magazine articles, there appeared to be few recent books on Navy recruit training. A flurry of e-mails and, finally, a book proposal to Navy Public Affairs at the Pentagon provoked an encouraging response. "If the Naval Institute agrees to publish the book, we'll grant you access." Concurrent conversations with the U.S. Naval Institute Press were also encouraging, in a catch-22 sort of way. "If the Navy grants access first, we'll be delighted to publish the manuscript." Bill Dermody of the public affairs staff at the Naval Training Center, Great Lakes, had the most encouraging advice of all: "Gee, what you really need is someone with enough horsepower to cut through the bureaucracy and get this show on the road. Why not give Mike McCalip a call?"

Command Master Chief Petty Officer Mike McCalip is the senior enlisted sailor at Great Lakes. As the CMC, Mike is the command's enlisted leader, but he's much more than that. As one sailor told me, "He's not the top guy in the Navy, but I bet he's got his phone number." His billet, competitively staffed with the active participation of the chief of naval personnel, is a key post, much sought after in the fleet. His cadre of seven hundred recruit division commanders man the "Quarterdeck of the Navy," the first port of call for the Navy's newest sailors. Part of a staff of twelve hundred, they are the backbone of an operation that converts fifty-three thousand green, scared kids into fleet sailors each year. Mike is a tough, no-nonsense, fleet-minded warrior of the old school. And, like good chief petty officers everywhere, Mike makes things happen.

Did he ever. Master Chief McCalip quickly arranged meetings for me with Capt. Ed Gantt, the commanding officer of Recruit Training Command (RTC), and the members of his wardroom. With their enthusiastic support, I was soon granted unlimited access to RTC for as long as needed. No area was off limits; I could come and go freely, observe anything, participate when I felt comfortable, interview whoever was willing to chat, and record whatever I thought significant. "This is a place where old sailors make new sailors," Mike said over coffee one day. "It's where we pass on our culture, our 'sailorness.' Capture that, and you've captured the essence of the place." I couldn't have said it better.

You'll find no bayonet charges, pugil sticks, or hand-to-hand combat at Great Lakes. Navy boot camp differs greatly from that of the other services, because the Navy mission is different. It's the rare sailor (SEALS, Seabees, and Special Boats Units excepted) who will ever have to rely on physical strength to overcome an enemy in single combat. The Navy trains the way it fights. These days, most sailors are technicians or operators; they maintain weapons systems, operate communications systems, or manage dozens of logistical tasks afloat and ashore. And so today's sailor undergoes solid aerobic conditioning to sharpen reflexes and develop the stamina necessary to stay fit for extended periods in cramped, stressful, but often sedentary, pursuits. The system aims to provide basically trained, physically fit, mentally tough sailors, conditioned to keep warships on station for extended periods, yet ready to fight at a moment's notice. Every waking moment is dedicated to that goal.

Together, Master Chief McCalip and I decided that the boot camp story could best be told by following a typical division "from bus to bus"—that is, from the moment the recruits first arrived until they departed for the fleet, nine weeks later. Since Great Lakes is now the Navy's only boot camp, and trains both male and female recruits, it made sense to focus on a gender-integrated division. (Because only 18 percent of Navy recruits are female, four of every five divisions are still all-male.) We agreed that Division 01-005, the first gender-integrated division to form after the start of the new fiscal year on 1 October, would fit the bill. These are the stories of the recruits of that division, as they told them to me. All names are real, and—except for minor editing to smooth the transition between speech and the written page—the stories are told in their words. With the exception of those who operate under the presumption of confidentiality, such as chaplains, physicians, or psychologists, all participants gave formal permission for me to quote them directly in this book.

For sixty-five days and nights I followed these young men and women as they adapted to Navy life. I completed nearly two hundred fifty hours of formal interviews, over ninety of which were tape-recorded and are now part of the oral history archive at the Naval Institute. I solicited nearly three hundred pages of handwritten "reaction papers" from recruits, most composed during their fifth through eighth week of training. Many recruits kindly shared personal letters to and from their families at home. Cdr. Bob Rawls, RTC's director of military training, permitted me to read and copy hundreds of letters he has received, from both recruits and graduates in the fleet, during four years at Great Lakes. And after the recruits recognized that I was "tame" and wouldn't add to their distress, they talked openly and at length, and I treasure these informal, unrecorded moments as touching the heart of their boot camp experience.

Journalistic integrity requires two disclosures. The first concerns the nature of my participation with Division 005, which was a lot like that of a parent at an amusement park. I shadowed the recruits as they marched to the gun range, obstacle course, gas chamber, or firefighting deck, and observed them closely (and often enough, with heart in mouth) as they endured the "attractions." I'd then scoot around and meet them at the exit. I spent a great deal of time with them on the drill deck or in the classrooms, quietly observing their interactions with their division commanders and instructors. And, like any parent, I'd spend the evening talking with them, getting to know them better and soliciting their reactions to the day's activities.

The second issue concerns language. Backstage at Recruit Training Command, in staff areas not usually accessible to recruits, are signs reminding that "Profanity Is Not Quality Leadership." I was both embarrassed and chagrined to learn that the Navy, where I once learned to curse like a sailor, had decided that offensive language had lost its ability to shock. Most of the staff did very well in containing the use of profanity, and after a while the recruits did too. The rare use of profanity that did occur has been edited out of this manuscript. However, the book retains the necessary terms specific to the Navy. For readers unfamiliar with Navy jargon, a glossary is provided at the end of this book.

You can read this story from many perspectives. If you're an old sailor, you can look at today's recruits and today's boot camp and say, "Gosh, I remember that," or "Man, it wasn't like that back when I went through there." The French tell us that the more things change, the more they stay the same. It matters not whether it was five years ago or fifty, you can walk back through the gates of Recruit Training Command, and the years strip away. Yogi Berra caught the flavor of it: It's déjà vu all over again.

If you're someone interested in the subject of gender integration in the military, you may gain some insight from the experiences of the forty-five women quoted throughout this book. Except for first reference, where name, age, and hometown are provided, I've chosen to refer to all recruits by their last name only, and to all petty officers and chief petty officers by their rating or title. Complete gender integration is taken for granted in today's Navy. You might find it interesting to try to deduce which speakers are men, and which are women. (A complete roster can be found in the appendix.)

If you're someone concerned about recruiting shortfalls in an age where flipping burgers pays more than military service, or about lowered educational standards in the all-volunteer force, you can take heart from the many special programs designed for recruits with special circumstances. Division 005 was a line division, randomly assembled from recruits who arrived on 3 October, but Master Chief McCalip provided an excellent overview of special programs for recruits with more challenging circumstances (see chapter 6).

If you're a young man or woman considering a career in the Navy, you may be wondering what boot camp is like, and worried that you might not be cut out for military service. If so, take heart: Everyone who arrived on the night of 3 October felt just like you. They were worried, scared, even terrified, and had the bus been making round trips to the airport, most would have gladly signed up for the return trip. There were some rough moments, and not every minute was fun, but they succeeded and made it to the fleet, and you can too.

Finally, if, like my university colleagues, you're interested in research methodology and sociological fieldwork, you can approach this book as a participant-observer recording of contemporaneous oral history, in a performance-based, criterion-referenced, stratified-age, and interest-defined cohort, deduced from an emic perspective. Come on, I dare you.

And as for me? Well, it was all of that, of course, but really— really it was a labor of love.

Acknowledgments

If words are bullets in the battle for truth, then a book is a crew-served weapon. No writer—even in a day of word processors, spell checkers, and instant access to millions of facts through the Internet—ever truly works alone.

This book was really written by hundreds of sailors. From recruits to captains, each had a story to tell, and I've tried to capture the essence of their experiences at Recruit Training Command. I am immensely grateful for their cooperation, and I'm honored to have known each of them.

There are others whose contributions are less visible, but certainly no less valuable. Without their help, this book would have remained an old sailor's dream.

Ready! (The Pre-Research Stage)

Mary Ann D. King, Commander USN (Retired), Jack King, LTJG, USN (Retired), and Jim Rose (Lieutenant, USNR 1973–77) for scouring the Internet to find lost shipmates, and for igniting the spark that caused this book to be written.

Cdr. Rob Newell, USN, LCDR Ike Skelton, USN, Lt. Wendy Snyder, USN, Ms. Donna Grace Schwenter, Ms. Kay Este, and Mr. Bill Dermody, all of the Navy Public Affairs organization, for their enthusiasm and cooperation in facilitating this project.

CMDMC (SW/SS/PJ) Mike McCalip, command master chief petty officer at Recruit Training Command, for opening the doors and shining the light that allowed me to experience RTC as few outsiders have ever been privileged to see it.

Aim! (The On-Station Research Phase)

Lt. Oudrey Hervey, public affairs officer at Recruit Training Command, who demonstrated, time and again, the best qualities of an effective PAO: Patience, Accessibility, and Openness.

QMCS (SW) Jeff Atkinson, leading chief petty officer at MCPON Hall. Senior Chief Atkinson knows boot camp inside out. He's a sailor's sailor. He called me "shipmate" one day, and I felt good for the whole afternoon.

AOC (AW) Mike Lucas, whose ninth division won the coveted and rarely awarded designation as a Chief of Naval Operations (CNO) Commended Division, a distinction recognizing excellence at RTC Great Lakes. I'd work for Chief Mike Lucas in a minute—and that's about the highest compliment an old black shoe can pay to an Airedale.

GM1 (SW) Philip Olensinski, who when asked what a gunner's mate was doing in a Public Affairs Office, smiled and replied, "Well, shooting off my mouth, of course."

DC2 (SW) Matt Mogle, photographer, facilitator, and all-round good guy. Matt's unofficial motto is "Journalism is just another form of damage control." The brief credit lines on the photographs in this book, which sound so sterile and bloodless, really mean that Matt spent countless hours clambering over obstacles to capture the perfect shot. Thanks, Matt.

Seaman Recruit Megan A. Wirsch, recruit yeoman for Division 005. A very special thank-you to Megan who, in addition to all the other miseries of boot camp, was assigned to assist me during her Service-Week period, and who transcribed dozens of audiotapes. I haven't found an error yet, Megan!

The many men and women of RTC who, although not individually named, contributed both formally and informally to this story.

And, finally, to my own "ship's company":

To Margaret, who has endured my sea stories, these twenty-five years past, and who cheerfully read and corrected draft after draft of this manuscript.

To John Joseph, who volunteered his time to sort and collate more than seven hundred photographs.

To Dennis, who drew on his experiences as a high school teacher to provide keen insight into the minds, music, and manners of today's young people.

To Mike, without whose computer skills I'd have been forced to draft this manuscript with a quill pen, and who cheerfully performed tedious Internet research, ensured that all legal releases were complete and accurate, and cross-indexed names and events.

And, finally, to Alamo J. Puppytoes, resident Jack Russell terrier, who kept this, the loneliest of pursuits, ever exciting. He thought the "Dog Song" was really about him.

With a crew like this, how could a writer ever go wrong?

Honor,
Courage,
Commitment

1
In the Beginning

I came home one afternoon, and saw an ad that said, "Government Jobs—Train to Be an Air Traffic Controller." That had to be better than working in a factory in Springfield, Missouri, for the rest of my life. I called the "800" number. Forty-five minutes later, two Navy recruiters knocked on my door.

I first went down to the Navy recruiting office in San Bernardino, California, with my friend. He had been talking about joining the Navy for, like, three years. I just went along for the ride. He decided not to come . . . But here I am.

Our daughter's college grades kept slipping. The school said she could get her softball scholarship back if she could just raise her grades to 2.0. She came bopping in one day and said, "Well, Mama, I made a 1.9." I said, "That's it, child. We've been paying for school, your car, your living expenses, everything, and it's just not working. It ends right now, and you're going to have to figure out something else to do." And the next thing you know, she went and joined the Navy.

I was born in Burma. I came to this country as a refugee just a few years ago. America is a wonderful country. I want to be a real American.

From colonial days to the present, young Americans have borne arms to defend freedom and our way of life. Each year, over fifty thousand volunteer to serve their country by enlisting in the U.S. Navy. Eighty-one of them arrived at the Navy's Recruit Training Command in Great Lakes, Illinois, on the evening of 3 October 2000. This is their story.

If you had passed them on the street, you'd probably not have noticed them. They looked, dressed, and spoke like any other kids you'd be likely to meet in your hometown. One had delivered pizza in a sprawling Californian suburb, another grew up on a ranch in northern Montana. One worked at Wendy's, another at McDonald's. Their average age was twenty, yet several had just graduated from high school, and one was nearly thirty-five. A few had parents or close relatives in the military, but most had no connections with the service at all. All were drug free—the military has zero tolerance for drug abusers and screens extensively before enlisting recruits—although a few just smiled when asked privately if they had ever taken a puff in school or on the playground. Some liked heavy metal music and sported tattoos whose symbolism was lost on an older generation; others loved country music and all things western; still others listened to rap, hip-hop, or other artifacts of urban culture. Good kids, every one of them. They might have been your kids or mine.

In an age of gender integration in the military, they were almost equally divided: forty-four young men and thirty-seven young women. They hailed from large cities and small towns in thirty states. One was a college graduate, a few had attended college for a few semesters, yet another left school in the ninth grade. Most were children of the working class; their parents were electricians, truckers, policemen, shopkeepers. Their ethnic and religious identities varied: black and white; Hispanic and Asian; Catholic, Protestant, Muslim, Buddhist, and nonbelievers. Three are named Smith, and two named Williams. They've names like Jones and Johnson and Jackson; one was named Gray, and another named Grayer. They are the Navy's future, they are America's future. They are America.

Thomas Kelly, 25, Pueblo, Colorado

I was a trucker before I enlisted in the Navy. My wife is twenty-three, and my daughter is five. My wife developed a chronic bone disease called osteogenisis imperfecta, or brittle-bone disease. I joined the Navy to provide a better life for them. I wanted good medical care for my wife, even if it meant being away from home for a while. As an over-the-road trucker, I'm used to that, anyway. I've lived all my life in Pueblo, so I'm looking forward to a change. I have a family tradition of serving in the Navy; my grandfather was a sailor in World War II, and my older brother was in the

Navy during Desert Storm. He got out about four years ago, but he encouraged me to look into the Navy.

My recruiter was Petty Officer Cliff Martin, in Pueblo. I went into his office one day, and he gave me a lot of details about Navy benefits. I'm a pretty big guy, I'm six foot six and weigh about a hundred and ninety pounds, so Petty Officer Martin suggested that I look into the master at arms rating. The master at arms force is the police department of the Navy, and he suggested that even if I only spend four years in the service, afterward I'd be qualified to apply to the FBI, the Border Patrol, or maybe the Texas Rangers. I figured boot camp would be a good experience. As long as you do what you're told, you'll be all right. I knew I'd run into a lot of guys with similar interests. I'm into country music, rodeo, and western things. I've driven trucks all over the western United States. I knew I'd be older than most of the guys, but didn't think that would be much of a problem. What really motivated me is getting the benefits of military service, especially, as I said, the medical benefits for my wife. My mom works at Fort Carson, Colorado, and she told me about how well the military treats its members. My master at arms school will be at Lackland Air Force Base in San Antonio, and it's long enough that I can bring my wife and daughter down there for awhile. So I said fine, sign me up, and on 3 October I reported to the processing station in Denver. By that afternoon, I was on my way.

Rebecca Anne Freeman, 21, DeQuincy, Louisiana

Well, my mom was telling you about what happened when I got my grades, that last time. I graduated from South Beauregard High School in Longville, and went on to play college softball at Pensacola Junior College in Florida. I was an outfielder on the Lady Pirates team. I'm an active person, and, to be honest, college wasn't working out for me. I felt I was taking classes just to take them— I didn't have a major and I didn't know what I was going for, I was just going to school to play softball. So, when things sort of fell apart, I asked my dad, who was in the Marines, and he suggested that I talk to the recruiters in Baton Rouge. I talked to a really nice guy named Avery Vaugh. I didn't know very much about the Navy or the kinds of things that they do. My mom really thought it would be better if I went into the Air Force, because she didn't want me to be on a ship all the time. My uncle had retired from the Air Force. I talked to both recruiters, and chose the Navy because it seems to have more to offer. I want to be a rescue swimmer, one of the *people who jump out of helicopters to help pilots if they have an accident. I like to help people, and that seemed to be a good way to do it. As I say, I'm really sports-minded. I'm worried about a lot of things about boot camp, including meeting new people and having the officers yelling at me all the time, but the physical part of it ought to be fun.*

Eric Alan Hopkins, 18, Shelbyville, Indiana

I come from a family where military service is expected. I have lots of uncles who were in the service, and I guess we've had a member of our family in every major war that America's been in. Right after graduation, I was sitting at home, watching TV, and, out of the blue, I got a call from the Navy recruiter. I told him that I might go on to college, and he was really nice and said that he wouldn't bother me if I already had plans. But I said, what the heck, send me a couple of pamphlets and let me read them first. I really liked what they had to say, more so than the other services. I had nearly signed up with the Indiana National Guard, but their recruiter was more like, "Here, take this National Guard football, take this National Guard pencil," and he was really beginning to turn me off with his sales pitch. The Navy recruiter, Petty Officer Drew Dobbins, was really straightforward. He told me about a lot of special programs for electronics and the nuclear field, and about the different bonuses and benefits. He had me take some tests, and I did really well, so he told me that I could have my choice of programs. I was thinking about advanced electronics and computers, but they brought in a nuclear specialist, and he convinced me that that was the best choice I could make. To be honest, when I was a kid, I was more interested in the Marine Corps or the Army. But the recruiter was so straightforward and laid back, and wasn't pushy about things, that I liked it better than the other choices. I guess I could have gone on to college because my grades were high enough, but my dad's health isn't all that good, and I thought this was a better choice for me and my family.

Robert Gildersleeve, 24, Birmingham, Alabama

I come from a pretty straight family. My mother is a registered nurse and my dad is a police officer in Roosevelt City. I have three uncles who retired from the Army, and my dad got out of the Air Force in 1974. I've thought about the military since I was in high school. I was going to go to Alabama State in Montgomery right after high school, and be in the marching band. I was in marching band in high school and liked it a lot. But things didn't develop quite the way I wanted, and I sort of lost interest and jumped into the work field. From the time I was eighteen, I've had a lot of jobs holding jackhammers and that sort of thing. Awhile ago, I had a baby girl—she's just two years old now—and I started thinking that "this life is not me—I can do better than this." My mind started to steer toward the military. I told my mom one night that I was thinking of joining the service. She said to me, "Robert, how many times have I heard you say that? If you're going to do it, go do it." So I went down and talked to the recruiter, and the more I learned, the better it looked.

Now, I was a little bit suspicious of recruiters, see. Back, oh, three or four years ago, I talked to the Army recruiter, and, oh, didn't he make the Army sound good! He told me that I'd have a nice desk job, tracking missiles and such, and that it was clean, good work. But I checked with my uncle who retired from the military. I read the job description and the MOS [military occupational specialty] to my uncle and he said, "That recruiter is lying! You'll be out in a field in a tent where it's cold and rainy, and you'll have this little machine, and every time Saddam Hussein fires one of his missiles, you're going to be the first one to get hit. You see, the Army guys, they just told you what you wanted to hear, so you'd join up with them, you know?" But Petty Officer Johnson, he told it straight. I was DEP [Delayed Entry Program] for a month and a half, and he kept in touch all the time, till it was time for him to come and pick me up and take me down to the military entry processing station in Montgomery. I'm looking forward to boot camp. I'm older than some guys, but I can march pretty good, and know all the commands from being in the marching band in high school. I'm going to be an aviation apprentice when I graduate, and I'm looking forward to getting down to Pensacola, which isn't far from my family and daughter in Birmingham.

Kelly, Freeman, Hopkins, Gildersleeve, and all their new shipmates had similar experiences after deciding to enter the Navy. All were transported by their recruiters to one of sixty-five military entry processing stations (MEPS) around the country. There they were tested, screened for drugs, and presented with a formal contract outlining their obligations and what the Navy promised in return. Most enlisted for four years, although those who were accepted for advanced training made a six-year commitment. Many would receive substantial bonuses after completing initial training. All were introduced to the time-honored military tradition: hurry up and wait.

Arturo (Artie) Guiterrez, 18, Imperial, California

After my friend decided not to join up, they told me to be ready to go by myself real early Tuesday morning. Petty Officer Del Angel picked me up, and we left at three A.M. and went down to San Diego, to the MEPS station. We were supposed to be done there by eight o'clock, but they didn't come for us until ten. We went over to the airport, and we had to hang around for a couple more hours. There were three of us, and we got separated at the airport, so we had to run around there at the end, looking for each other. It was my first flight, and it was fun. When you first go up, it kind of sucks you in; it's like a roller-coaster ride. We stopped at Denver, and we had to run like crazy because we were late getting there, and it was raining.

Mary A. Smith, 21, Denison, Texas

I left my mom's at three in the morning, too. We stayed up all night, packing my bags, and I pretty much had my whole family call, and I think I got maybe thirty-five minutes of sleep the entire night. My recruiter was supposed to be at my house at four o'clock, but I called him and told him to hurry up and come over before I changed my mind. My bags had pretty much been packed beside the front door, but I kept finding other things and packing and repacking just to keep busy. He came and got me, and took me to the processing station in Dallas. I got another physical, and waited around for awhile, then got on the plane with a lot of guys who were coming to the Navy, and we were all really nervous. I didn't know what to expect. I don't have any friends in the Navy, and I didn't know what was going to happen, and nobody wanted to tell us anything. One funny thing happened at the MEPS station, though. They started calling me Smith Comma Mary, because there are so many Smiths, I guess, and the Navy has called me that ever since.

Jesse James Mathis, 19, Forest, Mississippi

I was on the delayed entry program, so I had been running an asphalt machine doing highway construction work all summer. It was pretty hot when I left Mississippi, so I was wearing a tank top and no socks. When the recruiter came and picked me up at the house, he took me to the MEPS station at Jackson, Mississippi.

Me and a bunch of old boys there, we checked into a hotel and went across and ate at Denny's. Then we went and got us a bottle of whiskey and about four cases of beer. There were about six of us, all coming into the Navy. We drank awhile there at the Best Western, and swam in the pool till, oh, one o'clock or so, and just partied the rest of the night. I was tired that next morning, but we all went back over to the MEPS station, did our paperwork, then we just stood around and played pool and talked and stuff. They finally called all the people who were going to boot camp, and took us over to the airport in Jackson. We flew on Northwest up to Memphis, and then we changed planes for O'Hare. I fell asleep on the plane to Chicago, so I missed the food and was pretty hungry and cold by the time we got to Chicago.

Schely Rasco, who thought air traffic control sounded interesting, also arrived at Chicago's O'Hare Airport that afternoon. It had been her first flight. Adding to her nervousness, the recruiters in Kansas City had placed her in charge of a detachment of seven other recruits. The plane was crowded, and she wasn't able to sit with anyone she'd met at the military entry processing station. She was among the last to leave the airplane, and by the time she did so, the others had lined up outside the gate, and saluted her. Laughing, they set off to find the United Services Organization (USO) center.

Marschel (Schely) Rasco, 24, Springfield, Missouri
It was a real mess. I've never flown at all, so I didn't know what to expect at O'Hare. It's huge, and we really didn't know where we were supposed to go. We flew in on American Airlines, and we had to get to the United terminal. Then we had to find the USO. It's up on a mezzanine above the ticket counters. We were wandering all over the place, looking for the stairs. Some of the guys wanted to stop and get something to eat, but I kept the group together. Finally, I asked a man where it was, and he pointed to this little unmarked door off to the side. We'd still be there if I hadn't asked, I guess.

FC2(SW)* David Mesmer of the receiving detachment at O'Hare airport, explains: "The Navy contracts with the USO to use their lounge. Each recruiter is supposed to give his detachment detailed directions on how to find us. When they arrive,

*Petty Officer Mesmer is a fire controlman, second class (E5), with surface warfare qualifications.

we go through the list of prohibited items, to give them a chance to dump cigarettes, snacks, and anything else they can't take out to the base. We have a big-screen TV, drink and snack machines, and telephones for recruits while they wait. There are usually a couple of USO volunteers to help when we're busy. Many recruits arrive in the afternoon, although they can arrive at any time, depending on the airlines. We expect most in the early evening, but we can send small groups out to the base by van or taxi, when we need to."

The recruits met and socialized while awaiting the first bus to Great Lakes. Although there was no guarantee that they'd be assigned to the same division, those on the same bus had a better than even chance of staying together for the nine and a half weeks of boot camp. Rasco soon encountered others who would become part of Division 005. One was Devon Caldeira.

Devon (Dee) Caldeira, 19, Park Slope, Brooklyn, New York

I started meeting people right after we got to the airport. A bunch of us from Fort Hamilton, New York, had come together—Perez in our division is from Brooklyn too, East New York—and we all caught the bus over to Newark Airport. All the time I was on the bus, I was thinking about my family, and my house, and if I was making the right decision to come to the Navy, you know? When I was on the plane, I was looking around to see as much of New York as I could, looking down to see if I could see my house, even though I knew I couldn't. I was just thinking about my family, my sister and my brothers, and maybe if I get to the airport I could change my mind, but once you're on the plane, it's a one-way street and you can't come back. We got to Chicago, and I still wasn't sure this was what I wanted to do.

Division 005 included recruits from thirty states, the largest contingent (15) coming from California.

Marleane Paes, 18, Rialto, California

I grew up about ten miles west of San Bernardino. When I got up that last morning at home, I thought I was just dreaming. I had a lot of regrets, because it was my last day at home, and I really didn't want to leave. When Petty Officer Fuentes came to pick me up, I was really nervous, but I knew that I had to go. Once I got down to San Diego, they held me back for four days, because they thought that they had some incorrect tests for me, but it turned out that the results were right, after all. But I met up with two other people there at the MEPS station during those four days, so it was better. We flew over here together, the three of us, and the other girl, Jennette Zaragoza, wound up in 005, too. I was so scared, because I had never been on an airplane, and everyone was telling me to calm down, and not worry about the turbulence and all. When we got to Chicago, we went to the USO office as we were told, and we walked in the door in a little group. There were other people coming up to the office right at the same time we were. They made us empty out all food, all the stuff that they won't allow. I talked to this nice girl from Missouri—it turns out it was Rasco, and we'd be in the same division and all.

By five thirty, the lounge was full. AME1(AW)* Myron Harris, a fifteen-year Navy veteran, entered the lounge. One of a cadre of experienced petty officers—he had "pushed" six recruit divisions during his tour at Great Lakes—Harris would escort the new recruits from the airport to Recruit Training Command. Standing in front of the reception desk, Harris, who had no need for the public address system, addressed the now silent recruits.

"All right people! Listen up! From now on, there's no talking, understand? When I give you the word, I want you to get up, get your gear, hold that gear in your left hand, and if you have orders, hold those orders in your right hand. Is that understood? And let's get one thing straight right now. The only acceptable answers are 'yes, Petty Officer,' 'no, Petty Officer,' or 'I don't understand, Petty Officer.' Now, is that *clear*?"

"Yes, Petty Officer!"

"Very good, then. Line up outside in the passageway. I want the males to fall in to the right, and the females to the left. When I tell you, and only when I tell you, you will proceed down that passageway, down the ladder, and out onto the main deck of the terminal. You will stop as soon as you get out on that main deck, and you will wait for me, is that understood? Now, move out!" Several recruits chuckled at the unfamiliar nautical terms, but did as ordered. Petty Officer Harris was not amused. Later he explained, "Well, at some point they have to start boot camp. We've decided that the bus ride is as good as anywhere to get them into the right frame of mind. It gives them something to think about, going out there, too."

*Petty Officer Harris is an aviation structural mechanic—safety (E6), with aviation warfare qualifications.

Harris followed the last recruit down the ladder, and moved to the head of the line of waiting recruits. Quickly he led them to a large motor coach parked at the curb.

Jennifer Arcia, 19, Silt, Colorado
Oh my gosh, I was scared. This man was yelling at us, and he didn't even know who we were. He broke everything down into little pieces. "First you open the door, then you go down the steps, then you open the door at the bottom, then you go out." I thought, is this what boot camp is going to be like?

Petty Officer Harris continued, "Board the bus in single file, move to the back, and take the first available seat. Keep your belongings on your lap, and fold your hands on top of them. Place nothing on the floor, and nothing in the rack overhead. Now, do it."

"Every single thing we do, we do for a reason," Harris remarked later. "We make them keep their belongings in their laps, because, every time we'd made a bus run, someone forgot something. Or they'd get worried about contraband, and we'd find knives, drugs, you name it—up on the racks. These buses make three or four runs an evening, we'd have a mess every night. And lining up the way we did topside—well, that puts the females up front in the bus where I can see them and keep them out of harm's way."

Jennifer Buki, 19, Erie, Pennsylvania
The bus ride from the airport was completely silent, like, we weren't allowed to even talk to the person next to us. Couldn't talk, couldn't do anything; you looked around and you saw no faces that you knew, whatsoever, and you were wondering, like, is this person going to be my friend and am I ever going to see this person again. It's just, like, a total cultural shock, and you don't know what to do, or where to stand or whatever, to avoid getting yelled at.

The bus was equipped with video monitors. A videotape *The Days Are Long But the Weeks Fly By* gave the recruits a hint of what to expect on arrival. The recruits remained silent, lost in their own thoughts, as the bus fought the early evening rush-hour traffic on the hour-long journey toward boot camp. The base is located thirty-eight miles north of downtown Chicago and twelve miles south of the Wisconsin state line. Their anticipation and anxiety grew as the bus pulled off Interstate 94, and headed east on Illinois 137. It took only a few minutes more to arrive at Great Lakes.

Woodrow (Woody) Carpenter, 23, Lebanon, Missouri

That's when I got worried. I had been looking out the window, trying to figure where we were going, but it was dark and raining a little. But when we pulled up and turned in that gate, I figured, well, this is it.

Turning left into the base, the bus stopped at Building 1405, the Recruit In-Processing Center. Dedicated to the Golden Thirteen, the first African Americans to be commissioned as naval officers, the modern, red-brick center opened in June 1987. It replaced a rabbit warren of wooden barracks, which had served as the gateway to the Navy since the early days of World War II. For the recruits of Division 01-005 (generally shortened to 005), boot camp was about to begin.

2
The Recruit Division Commanders

While the new recruits were flying to Chicago, six senior Navy petty officers crowded around their boss's desk. MMCS(SW)* John Tucker consulted the master training schedule.

Senior Chief Tucker

Okay, then. Here's what the schedule says. Chief Zeller, you'll team up with Kent and Russell again, and you'll be Division 005. You all have worked together before, right? And Senior Chief Nelson, you'll have Chief Brown and Petty Officer Redekop as your partners, and you'll be Division 006. Russell, did I hear you say that you'll do the pickup? Now that summer surge is about done, things should go faster than last time. It looks like you'll be ready to bring them over here around 0230. Kent and Redekop—why don't you guys go topside when we're done here and make sure your compartments are ready for the new divisions?

The recruit division commanders (RDCs) had mustered in Senior Chief Tucker's office, just east of the quarterdeck in Ship Eight. To add nautical flavor to boot camp, the Navy has named each of its thousand-person barracks after a famous warship. The large brown and white sign outside formally identified the tan and white barracks as the USS *Abraham Lincoln*, but that name was rarely used in casual conversation. One of fifteen such buildings constructed during the Vietnam War, Ship Eight housed twelve recruit divisions and was staffed by two officers and thirty-six senior petty officers. MMCS(SW) John Tucker was the ship's leading chief petty officer (LCPO).

*Senior Chief Tucker is a senior chief machinist's mate (E8) with surface warfare qualifications.

Senior Chief Tucker *I've been ship's LCPO since March. I went to boot camp here, myself, over in Ship 13, in the spring of 1986. I've been in the Navy for fifteen years. After I finished boot camp, I attended service school across the street. When I finally left Great Lakes, I went aboard the USS* Santa Barbara *(AE28) in August 1986. We left on deployment that very same day; I remember I had only four or five hours to find a place to park my truck for six months. I stayed aboard the* Santa Barbara *for four years, and made it to MM2 before I left. I came back up here as an instructor. Everybody thinks teaching is easy, but we lit off that 1,200-pound steam plant and secured it three times a day. In a lot of ways, that was more work than sea duty. We were selling a lot of our frigates to other countries at the time, so I taught a lot of foreign Navy people, both enlisted and officers. That was a great job. After a shot at UDT [Underwater Demolition Team] training school in California, I went aboard the USS* Mount Vernon *(LSD 39) as LPO of the forward engine room in June 1994. I made chief there, and came up here for the third time in 1998. I pushed six divisions on the street here, and I became LCPO in March when I was promoted to senior chief. When I leave here, I'll go back to sea, so I'm always concerned about the quality of sailors we're producing at Great Lakes. Someday, my life might depend upon them.*

The recruit division commanders who would lead Division 005 over the next nine weeks introduced themselves.

FCC(SW)* Martin D. Zeller, Kansas City, Missouri
I came into the Navy in 1985. Unlike Senior Chief Tucker, I attended boot camp in Orlando, Florida. After boot camp, the Navy offered me a job as an electronics technician, fire controlman, or sonar technician, and I preferred being in the thick of things in fire control. I was selected for fire controlman schools, for a total of fourteen months. My first ship was the USS La Moure County *(LST 1194) based at Little Creek, Virginia. A couple years after that, in 1989, I got a real great assignment for a fire controlman—I was assigned to the USS* Iowa, *one of the last four commissioned battleships. I was only on board a short time, and the Navy decided to mothball the battle wagons. That was just a couple months after the accident in the gun turret, where so many guys were killed. I pulled shore duty in my hometown, and worked at the MEPS at*

*Chief Zeller is a chief fire controlman (E7) with surface warfare qualifications.

Kansas City, Missouri. After three years there, I went back to sea aboard the Arleigh Burke *(DDG 51). Without a doubt, duty aboard the* Burke *was the best duty I've ever had. So, all in all, I've been around on three different classes of ships over the last fifteen years, all in the weapons departments. This is my third recruit division at Great Lakes.*

PR1(AW)* Dan Kent, Detroit, Michigan

Like the senior chief, I attended boot camp here at Great Lakes. I graduated back in August 1980. I wanted to be a gunner's mate, but my recruiter was in aviation, so he pushed me that way. He told me that we got to jump out of airplanes, and I said sign me up. I went to Parachute Rigger School at Lakehurst, New Jersey. Now, in those days, all PRs had to jump out of an airplane with the first parachute we packed. It was a great motivator for getting things right the first time, mainly because if you didn't, there wouldn't be a second time. I survived, and was assigned to a couple East Coast aviation squadrons, and one at Lemore, California. I was in VS24, on the Nimitz, *VF102 aboard the USS* America, *and VFA94 on the* Abraham Lincoln *and the* Kitty Hawk. *But my all-time best duty station was as an instructor at the Navy's SERE (Survival, Escape, Resistance, and Evasion) school at Rangley, Maine. We spent a lot of time outdoors. I was a member of the "opposing force," we wore Soviet uniforms, and it was kind of like acting. It was very different from anything else in the Navy, and lots of fun. I've been here for three years. Division 005 is my ninth and last division. I was a battle station facilitator for a year, between my sixth and seventh divisions. There have been a lot of changes since my first push in 1998. The biggest change has been in the way that integration is handled. My first division was an all-female division, and we'd integrate only to go to class and drill. Now they're totally integrated except for sleeping and hygiene.*

DC1(SW)** Lela Russell, Omaha, Nebraska

I've been in the Navy for eleven years. I went to boot camp at Orlando, Florida. Although Omaha is not as big as a lot of cities, like every town, there are drugs and gangs and poverty. I didn't want any part of it, so I came into the Navy to get away from all

---

*Petty Officer Kent is an aircrew survival equipmentman, first class (E6), with air warfare qualifications.
**Petty Officer Russell is a damage controlman, first class (E6), with surface warfare qualifications.

that. I had two daughters, I was going to night school for electronics, and working a full-time job during the day and keeping house, and I said to myself, there has to be something better than this. My original goal was to come in as an electrician, but when I was in boot camp, I really liked the fire-fighting part of things, too. So I wasn't real sure what to do. The first ship I was on was the USS Holland (AS 32), based in Charleston, South Carolina. The Holland is a sub tender, and when you first report aboard they take you to the department head, and he told me I was going to damage control. After about a year or so there, I went aboard the USS Santa Barbara (AE28). I must have reported aboard shortly after the senior chief transferred off. The Santa Barbara is a fuel and ammo ship, and being a damage controlman on that kind of ship is a very hairy experience. I spent four and a half years on the Santa Barbara, and went to the USS John F. Kennedy (CV-67) for a couple years, and finally to Sigonella, Sicily, where I was the LPO of the base fire department. It's rare, even today, to find a female fire chief on a Navy base, and almost unheard of to have one overseas, with local civilians reporting to her. That was quite an experience. After I had been there for two years, I got a message that they wanted me to screen for an RDC position. I didn't particularly want to leave—I enjoyed being the head of the fire department—but my detailer told me that duty here would really help my chances for making chief, and I hadn't been ashore much at all. I've been here since July, and this is my second push.

It's easy for recruits to forget, sometimes, that their division commanders have "been there and done that" themselves. All three Red Ropes (a common nickname for the recruit division commanders, from the red aiguilette worn on the left shoulder) had vivid memories of their own boot camp experience.

Senior Chief Tucker *When I was here as a recruit, I was a flag bearer. Back in those days, it was all male, of course. We were just a regular, street division. Now, my company commander was also a machinist mate. He was an aggressive guy, a power lifter, and the other guy, who was also in an engineering rating, was an aerobics instructor. So, right there I got exposed to physical fitness and good health, and I've kept that up ever since. The company commander was really a disciplined guy. He never let anyone into his office, but he took an interest in me, and took the time to speak to me about the machinist mate rating. I was on watch one after-*

noon, and he even let me sit down for about thirty minutes, and he talked about our rating and what the job is like, how hot and sweaty and dirty it can get. That guy really motivated me, by telling me how important the job was, and, how, because of the ship's engineers, the ship always sails on time. Engineers are the guys that get things done.

Chief Zeller *I was the mail petty officer in boot camp, but halfway through I got fired for taking my own mail to the mailbox without permission. That's when I learned that privileges come with responsibilities, and that you can't take advantage of your authority to treat yourself better than others. My company commanders were both first-class petty officers. One was a hull technician, and one was a machinist's mate. These were some tough sailors. They ran a tight ship. I guess they might have difficulty in today's environment, because both of them were very aggressive guys.*

Petty Officer Kent *I was a third-class recruit petty officer. I was the swimming petty officer, basically the captain of our swim team. My company commander's style would be considered politically incorrect these days. You know, they say you'll never forget your company commander's name, or what he said, or how his voice sounded. Well, I can still hear his voice today, twenty years later. And I find myself repeating the same phrases that he used. But, as Chief Zeller says, I'm not sure that they'd be all that successful in today's Navy. The philosophy back then was more toward intimidation than education.*

Petty Officer Russell *I was the laundry PO. My company commander was a Petty Officer Knowles. She was a great role model for us. In those days, boot camp was segregated by gender, we were all females, and she told us what life was like for women in the Navy. And she didn't pull any punches, she told it like it is. I think that she and I have the same techniques. I'm like Kent, I find myself saying the same stuff that she said to me. I was older than many of the recruits when I came in, I was twenty-two, and she was a great inspiration to all the female recruits, but especially to me.*

It's clear that the recruit division commanders really love their work. Even a cursory discussion of the challenges and rewards of working with the Navy's newest sailors reveals how passionately the RDCs feel about their assignments. Many have accepted single-status assignment, away from family and loved ones, just so that they might influence the next generation of sailors.

Senior Chief Tucker *I asked for these orders. I'm physically active, and think that we ought to portray that to the recruits. What the recruits see in their RDCs, that's the Navy for them. If they see the Navy as someone who doesn't portray what we want the Navy to be, they'll carry that attitude out in the fleet forever. Not only that, but when they get out of the Navy after four or five years, their attitude will represent the Navy in all those small towns. This is it. There is no better job for an enlisted man. I've 36 staff members, and 1,100 young people under me. There is no other place in the Navy where I could have all that.*

Chief Zeller *This is my third division, and I'm learning every step of the way. Watching these recruits evolve into young sailors, watching that esprit de corps develop, oh yeah, it's worth it. I'd take these orders again in a minute if I had it to do over.*

Petty Officer Kent *I'd do it all over again too, no question. I had two or three reasons for coming to Great Lakes. I wanted to be close to home on my last tour, but that's just a personal thing. Mostly, I enjoy teaching, and this is my third instructor tour. And this place is where you can have the biggest impact. With nine divisions, I've influenced at least a thousand sailors, and that's great.*

Petty Officer Russell *I'd do it again in a New York minute. Working with these recruits is the best thing I've ever had a chance to do in the Navy.*

3
Reporting Aboard

As the bus ground to a halt outside Building 1405, the recruits quickly filed off and entered the building. They found themselves in a large assembly area, just east of the quarterdeck. Immediately, they were instructed to form four ranks of ten recruits each.

AZ1(AW)* Bill Sparks stepped forward. Firmly, he explained how to stand at attention. "Hold your hands in front of you. Close your fist like you were holding a roll of dimes. Turn your hands till your thumbs face upward. Drop your hands till your thumbs are along the seam of your pants. From now on, that's how you'll stand when anyone is addressing you. Is that clear? *Is that clear?*"

"Yes, Petty Officer!"

"Now, I'm going to call out your name. When you hear your name, or something that *sounds* like it might be your name, you will respond with your Social Security number. I want to hear individual digits. I don't want to hear "forty-seven" or "sixty-three" or "ninety-two." I want to hear one through nine, only. And oh is a letter, zero is a number. If your Social Security number ends in "four thousand," I want to hear four-zero-zero-zero and no other variation. Jones! *Jones!*"

Jennifer Jones, 19, Claremont, California
When I got off the bus, the first thing I did was, like, totally screw up! . . . You come inside, and you line up, and they ask you your name and Social Security number and stuff, and I moved! I

---

*Petty Officer Sparks is an aviation maintenance administrationman, first class (E6), with air warfare qualifications.

totally screwed up, and I had been there for, like, maybe twenty seconds! He totally yelled at me, and told me I was wrong, blah-blah-blah, and made me an example, and everyone else got to go on, and I had to stay. I was scared, but I was the first person and I was supposed to be the example, and I was the first name he called out and I totally blew it.

Ashleigh Pankratz, 18, Great Falls, Montana

Well, we all went single file out of the bus and went into this hall-way, and we all lined up, and we were all given specific instruc-tions, but some of the recruits messed it up, so they got their butts chewed, big time. I was standing there like, oh my gosh! I was shaking at first, because this guy was just yelling at everybody, and then he's telling you to have everything out, and he gives you ten seconds, and it takes like thirty seconds to do stuff, but they expect you to do things, and give you things that you can't do, just to push you harder.

Nerve-wracking as the first moments might have been, they were a relief to a few recruits, who, having arrived early in the day, had to wait for a full busload to begin processing.

Leah Taylor, 18, Anchorage, Alaska

I had met one other recruit when I was at the MEPS station at Anchorage, so we flew down together. We got to Chicago early in the morning, and the civilian at the USO said that most people don't arrive till the middle of the afternoon. So they called a taxi and we rode out to the base. The taxi took us right to the reception building. I guess they weren't expecting anyone that early in the day, because they put us in this big classroom and left us alone most of the time. They gave us bag lunches, but mostly we just sat and talked to each other when no one was looking. There were recruits working in there, and they told us that it wasn't bad, that there would be lots of yelling and screaming, but that they really couldn't do anything mean to us in that building, just make us feel bad. About eight o'clock the first bus got there, and we got in line with everyone else. We felt okay because we had a chance to lay our heads down while we waited, but the new people were pretty tired.

After positive identification by Social Security number, the recruits were directed to a small room containing pay phones, and were permitted to make a short "safe arrival" call. If they couldn't reach next of kin, they were to call their recruiter, who would relay the message in the morning. Reaching voice mail counted as a completed call.

Pankratz   *We all started lining up, and we got one phone call only, and if you reached an answering machine, that was it. That's all I got, an answering machine, and I just wanted to start crying. I wanted to go home, right then.*

The recruits continued in-processing. They were issued "Smart Cards"—debit cards that doubled as identification while in boot camp. Recruits with unacceptable footwear were issued new athletic shoes, and each recruit was issued a preliminary uniform with underclothes, running shorts, and a Navy sweat suit. Although pleased to receive their first "Navy uniform," the recruits didn't yet appreciate that the "Smurf suit" (nicknamed after the bright blue TV cartoon characters) branded them as newly arrived rookies. They boxed their civilian clothes, and delivered them to a Federal Express agent in the clothing issue area. By midnight many of the recruits were visibly fatigued.

Jeanette Zaragoza, 18, Riverside, California
Well, I had been up most of the day before, and hardly slept at all at the hotel by the MEPS station. Then we were up before dawn, and processed all day, and then flew from California to Chicago. Some others took a nap on the way over on the bus, but I was so scared I couldn't do anything but watch the videotape and wonder if I had done the right thing. So, with all the processing, I was getting really tired, and they kept us going.

QMCS(SW)* Jeff Atkinson is the leading chief petty officer for the General Inquiries Office at Recruit Training Command. He has pushed divisions on the street, spent a couple of years as a ship's leading chief, and now handles hundreds of inquiries from parents and families of recruits. Atkinson knows boot camp, inside and out. "Everybody thinks the first thing the Navy takes from you is your hair. No—the first thing we take from you is sleep. *Then* we take your hair." There were other things that the Navy would take from the recruits that evening.

*Senior Chief Atkinson is a senior chief quartermaster (E8), with surface warfare qualifications.

Jones *After they gave us our sweats, they divided the guys and girls, and we had to pee in a cup again, and that was lame! And it was embarrassing too, it was the first time that I was in a room with a bunch of other girls, and we're all peeing, and there's an RDC trying to make us hurry up, and it's like, hey, I'm doing the best I can. And everyone is really scared about that part of it, anyway. That was the third time I had to do that . . . We had to do it twice at MEPS and then once at RTC. I understand that they don't want any drug addicts, but still, three times in one day?*

It was after 0200 when the last of the detachment finished "ditty bag" (preliminary clothing issue), records processing, and urinalysis. The recruits mustered again, this time with loaded seabags, for their first meeting with Petty Officer Russell, who had drawn "pickup" duty at the afternoon's meeting. Shouldering their seabags for the first time, the recruits began the long trek across base to Ship Eight. They'd be assigned lockers and bunks, deposit their seabags, eat, and have a quick opportunity to wash up before returning to the processing center.

Tafaswa Fletcher, 18, Bridgeport, Connecticut
I couldn't believe that we had to carry all that stuff at once. When I picked up the seabag and put the straps on my shoulders, it nearly pulled me over. DC1 Russell tried to get us to march in step, but it was no use. We couldn't even keep together as a group. And we walked and walked and walked. We only had a couple minutes after we got there, and then Petty Officer Russell took us to breakfast. I hadn't eaten since lunch the day before, but I had trouble eating, I was so nervous and scared. They didn't give us much time, we were out and marching back to the processing center within a couple minutes.

The recruits returned to Building 1405 at 0500. Those who had been unable to complete the urinalysis tests earlier were sequestered until nature took its course. The recruit's height and weight and percentage of body fat were checked, using accurate digital scales.

"It's funny," remarked Petty Officer Russell, "how many people had either gained weight or shrunk since they were measured at MEPS the day before. Especially the ones that are just borderline for being overweight or for body fat. Not that anyone would accuse the recruiters of cheating, but, still, when you have a recruit whose body fat is 28 percent, and the limit is 23 percent, well . . ."

Even overweight recruits would lose a little at the next stage of processing. By 0700 civilian barbers had arrived, and the recruits lined up for the traditional boot camp haircut. Most female recruits had wisely visited their hair stylists before leaving home, and, with few exceptions, all met the length and style guidelines.

"We tell them to get G.I. Jane haircuts before coming," said Russell. "See those tokens that the recruits are handing to the barbers? They get paid by the number of haircuts they give. It's OK for the guys, but what woman wants to walk around with a thirty-second haircut?" The recruits agreed.

Freeman *I used to have spiked white hair, but I got it cut right before I left home. I figured I'd have enough trouble at boot camp, without having to worry about that, too.*

The male recruits had no such inhibitions.

Michael Collins, 25, Amarillo, Texas
I had long hair when I came here. I remember running my hand through it on the plane coming up and figuring, well, it won't be that way soon. And it wasn't. I couldn't have been in the chair for a minute, and I was as bald as a cue ball.

Newly shorn, the recruits filed into a classroom. Definitions of the Navy's core values were displayed on the walls. Every event that these recruits experienced over the next nine and a half weeks would be tied to these values.

Honor. "I will bear true faith and allegiance . . ." Accordingly, we will conduct ourselves in the highest ethical manner in all relationships with peers, superiors, and subordinates. We will be honest and truthful in our dealings with each other, and with those outside the Navy. We will be willing to make honest recommendations and accept those of junior personnel. We will encourage new ideas and deliver the bad news, even when it is unpopular. We will abide by an uncompromising code of integrity, taking responsibility for our actions and keeping our word, and we will fulfill or exceed our legal and ethical responsibilities in our public and personal lives twenty-four hours a day. Illegal or improper behavior or even the appearance of such behavior will not be tolerated. We are accountable for our professional and personal behavior. We will be mindful of the privilege to serve our fellow Americans.

Courage. "I will support and defend . . ." Accordingly, we will have courage to meet the demands of our profession and the mission when it is hazardous, demanding, or otherwise difficult; to make decisions in the best interest of the Navy and the nation, without regard to personal consequences; and to meet these challenges while adhering to a higher standard of personal conduct and decency. We will be loyal to our nation, ensuring that the resources entrusted to us are used in an honest, careful, and efficient way. Courage is the value that gives us the moral and mental strength to do what is right, even in the face of personal or professional adversity.

Commitment. "I will obey the orders . . ." Accordingly, we will demand respect up and down the chain of command, and care for the safety and the professional, personal, and spiritual well-being of our people. We will show respect toward all people without regard to race, religion, or gender, and treat each individual with human dignity. We will be committed to positive change and constant improvement. and will exhibit the highest degree of moral character, technical excellence, quality, and competence in what we have been trained to do. The day-to-day duty of every Navy man and woman is to work together as a team to improve the quality of our work, our people, and ourselves.

At 0730, DCCS(SW)* Tom Vogt strode to the front of the room. Leading chief of the in-processing division, Vogt explained the meaning of these core values and their importance in the lives of every sailor. He then led the recruits through the "Moment of Truth."

"Lots has been written about the 'Moment of Truth,'" he said, when asked later. "It's something that VIPs like to see when they come here. But it's not as dramatic as they make it out to be. We simply tell the recruits, 'Hey, now's the time to set the record

---

*Senior Chief Vogt is a senior chief damagecontrolman (E8), with surface warfare qualifications.

straight. If there's something that you didn't tell us before, and it can affect your eligibility to join the Navy, now's the time to get it out on the table.' We tell them that the majority of stuff that we hear at 'Moment of Truth' is no big deal: somebody got a speeding ticket on the way to the MEPS, or they got caught smoking a joint in the bathroom in middle school, or something. But we do find people who admit concealed felonies, or those who are in the country illegally, or have done other things which would bar them from serving in the military."

Senior Chief Vogt read from a list of things that the Navy counselors standing in the rear of the room would be interested in exploring further. A handful of recruits stood and, each escorted by a counselor, left the room. Most returned within a few minutes, but one or two were not seen again.

"We have a separation and segregation building," Senior Chief Vogt continued. "If we identify a recruit who doesn't belong here, we'll administratively process them immediately, and get them back home as quickly as we can. But they never mix with the other recruits after we've identified them at 'Moment of Truth.'"

The recruits remained in the classroom for the remainder of the morning. At intervals, specialized screening teams for nuclear propulsion, communications, and intelligence questioned the recruits. Much of the time, though, they were allowed to put their heads down on their desks and catch up on the rest that they had missed during the previous night.

Michelle Gray, 19, Baltimore, Maryland
I was really getting tired, and we hadn't done anything physical yet. It was just hurry up and wait, all the time. We spent a lot of time in lines waiting to do something. There were lines for clothing issue, lines to get our Smart Cards, everything. I was wondering if we'd ever get any time to ourselves when we were in boot camp.

Marketta Hardin, 24, Springfield, Tennessee
I had a chance to talk to the girls near me. We were seated by divisions, so Pierce and Taylor and a couple others were right near me. The petty officers didn't seem to mind if we talked softly, as long as there wasn't anything else going on.

After a sack lunch, the recruits left the in-processing center and marched to the adjacent medical screening facility. They were interviewed about the general state of their health, had their eyes examined, and were issued any necessary prescriptions. Complete dental x-rays were taken and processed. The recruits were separated by gender, and each recruit received a complete, and private, medical examination. Once they had passed the medical screening, the recruits returned to Building 1405, and by midafternoon they were ready to leave the in-processing center.

Jessica (Blair) Hooton-Hetrick, 22, Colorado Springs, Colorado
Well, it was actually a lot better than I thought it would be. I mean, you've seen movies about boot camp, right? But the people were polite and professional, and there wasn't the 'herd' thing, you know? I was surprised, I really was.

Fletcher *I had signed up to be a hospital corpsman, so I was watching to see what they were doing, especially in medical. Most of them looked like they were real young, and I thought, gee, in a couple months, that might be me doing the physicals. That was kind of neat, seeing all that.*

Kelly *It surprised me that they were going to issue us new glasses. I had brought my own with me, but they said that everyone had to have the same kind for boot camp. I looked around, and saw a couple recruits with these big brown, ugly frames. I thought, man, they could do better than that. But that was the kind of glasses we were going to wear while we were at Great Lakes.*

By early Wednesday afternoon the division had completed preliminary processing. Because of a federal holiday the following Monday, they would have a slightly extended P-Week (processing week) cycle. Most were so terrified that they wouldn't notice the difference.

4
Orientation

Chief Zeller and Petty Officer Kent had relieved Petty Officer Russell at noon. Together, they mustered the recruits in a classroom, introduced themselves, and gave the recruits an overview of what to expect during the next few months. After Monday's holiday, they'd have a week of preparatory time, and the division would then be commissioned and begin a highly structured, eight-week training cycle. Recruits who showed acceptable progress would remain with the division and participate in Battle Stations, an exhaustive (and exhausting), twelve-hour test of every element of their training, in late November. Those who did not would be set back in training, and spend a few extra weeks—perhaps even a month—in boot camp. A training setback—generally referred to as an ASMO, for the assignment memorandum upon which the order was written—was an event dreaded by every recruit, and one to be avoided at all costs.

"We also try to give them an overview of the vocabulary of recruit training, even before we leave Building 1405," remarked Petty Officer Kent later. "Simple things, like the use of the words 'male' and 'female' rather than 'men' or 'women,' or 'guys and gals,' or whatever they had used before coming here. We explain that the floor is now the 'deck,' the walls are the 'bulkheads,' and the restrooms are now the 'heads.' Otherwise, we might have some unfortunate social errors when they need to use the facilities."

After a quick period of instruction on the grinder (the large paved area where drill is performed) outside Building 1405, the RDCs led the recruits back to barracks. Geography favored Division 005, since Ship Eight is near the center of the base. Constrained by railroad tracks to the east and west, and bisected by

Buckley Road (Illinois 137), the base is about a mile and a half long, and a quarter-mile wide. Chief Zeller aptly describes it as being "like Manhattan, but without the subway." As the weather turned colder, the recruits would appreciate their proximity to the galley, schoolhouse, and drill halls. Those on the far edges of the base could count on an additional ten- to fifteen-minute march each time they moved from building to building. The new recruits did not yet appreciate their good fortune.

Shannon Pierce, 19, Swainsboro, Georgia

Chief Zeller had us muster on the grinder, after we'd been at Building 1405 since early that morning. I had no idea where we were, or where we were going. He just told us to fall in, and to try to keep in step. We went through a tunnel, and on the other side I saw barracks up and down the lefthand side of the street. I remembered them from the night before. . . . I knew we were going the same way as we did with our seabags. Finally we came to Ship Eight.

The Navy is committed to complete gender integration. With the exception of sleep and hygiene, the recruits would perform all daily activities together. Male recruits were assigned to Compartment D-01 on the second deck of Ship Eight, and shared the eighty-person compartment with the men of Division 006. The female recruits likewise shared an eighty-person compartment with their counterparts of 006, one floor above. The male compartment would be used as Division 005's "house," and when integrated, the division would work together in D-01. The female space topside, Compartment D-02, would serve as Division 006's home port. Ten other divisions berthed in Ship Eight. The senior recruits lost no time in making their new shipmates feel right at home.

Freeman   *Right after we got to Ship Eight, a guy asked us if we had seen Chuckie. I told him I didn't think we had anyone named Chuckie in our division. He laughed. I hope not, he said. He's a ghost. He told me that back in the old days, there was lots of sickness on the base. There was this recruit named Chuckie, and he was supposed to go on watch. I don't know if he was on the compartment watch or ship's watch or quarterdeck or what. But anyway, this guy got all dressed up in the uniform of the day, with his guard belt and flashlight with the red lens and everything. And as he was going to stand his watch, he died of the sickness.*

But the thing is, he still is trying to stand his watch. People say that they have seen him, late at night, dressed up in the old uniform with the leggings and jumper with no stripes. They say he is wearing a watch cap, and his eyes are bright red with the fever. If you see him, you're not supposed to stop him, because he's been trying to get to his watch all these years.

When he told me that, I was afraid to go into the head for a while, till someone else told me that was just a story they tell new recruits to shake them up. If my division ever finds that dude again, he'll have red eyes and won't make it to his watch for a while!

After evening chow, the RDCs made preliminary selection of recruit petty officers, who would assist with administrative tasks. Recruit petty officers derive their authority from the commanding officer, via the RDCs, and serve at their pleasure. Chief Zeller chose Seaman Recruit Michael Collins, of Amarillo, Texas, to be the first recruit petty officer in charge (RPOC), and Jennifer Jones of Claremont, California, as his primary assistant (AROC). As training progressed, others in turn would get an opportunity to lead the division.

Reveille sounded at 0400 the following day. Because the recruits had yet to be declared "fit for full duty" by the medical unit, no physical training was scheduled for the morning. After breakfast, the recruits returned to the in-processing area for the bane of all military recruits, their preliminary inoculations.

Upon arriving at the clinic, the recruits were again segregated by gender. Each recruit was questioned about possible allergies. Six single-file lines were formed, three for each gender. Each line passed through a gantlet of six medical corpsmen, three per side. Wearing protective clothing, including a plastic face mask, each corpsman stood adjacent to a table, with dozens of hypodermic needles and syringes neatly arrayed upon it.

Megan Wirsch, 19, Auburn, California

On shot day, after various kinds of poking and prodding, I got six shots in a twenty-second period. All I can say is ouch! The first five weren't so bad, but the last one really burned. Some of us took it better than others. As for me, I was bleeding and I felt like I wanted to cry. It was just as if I had walked through a hazing and been beaten up. It was kind of scary, but the funny thing is that I wasn't scared in line. But I really wanted to cry after I was through the line. Things were moving fast, but I'm not sure if it made things

easier or harder. Luckily, though, I am positively allergic to peni-
cillin, so when everyone else got a shot in the butt, all I had to do
was wear a sign saying that I was allergic. But I'd take that any day
over a shot in my caboose. Some of the males looked really pale
and we females were sure some of them would pass out. But of
course, all the guys had to act macho.

If the males were indeed "acting macho," they were hiding
their anxiety well.

Paul Parker, 18, Coffee Springs, Alabama

Getting those shots was an experience I'll never forget. First of all,
they put the division in lines of ten to fifteen people. Then they told
us to remove our shirts and roll up the sleeves of our tee-shirts. We
walked into a room, and each one of us gave them our Smart
Card. They put your name into the computer to show that you had
received your shots. We lined up in single file, with three corpsmen
on each side. Each one of them gave one shot, three in each arm,
for a total of six. We went into another room, males in one line
and females in another. My arms were throbbing from those six
shots. They took six males at a time, and six females, into separate
rooms. They lined us all up in front of a stretcher and said, 'Pull
down your pants.' All six guys pulled down our pants and bent
over for the final shot. I was scared when they said, 'Drop your
pants,' because I don't remember ever having a shot in my butt
before. So I was worried and had a good reason to be. That last
shot hurt.

To help the recruits "digest" the inoculations, the division
mustered on the north parade ground. It was time to learn how
to march. Chief Zeller remarked later, "There's not a whole lot of
strenuous stuff you can do during P-days. They don't get cleared
for physical training until all the medical tests get read, usually
on the morning of their 1-1 day [the first day of the first week of
training]. This group got an extra couple P-days, while we
waited for enough female recruits to arrive to fill up Division
006. We'd be competing against 006 as we went through training. So, from our perspective, it was great to get some extra drill
time in, to get a leg up on our brother division. And, besides, it
got their minds off their sore backsides."

The recruits spent most mornings drilling on the grinder
between Ships Nine and Ten or on the north parade ground

near the front gate. Afternoons were spent in lectures on the Uniform Code of Military Justice, Navy core values, and orientation to the various morale and welfare programs provided by the chaplains. But, mostly, they marched. And marched. And then they marched some more.

Dayna Scorsone, 18, Fort Gibson, Oklahoma

I remember our first attempt at marching, when Petty Officer Russell picked us up from Building 1405. "Get three abreast and keep up" was all she said. We all scurried like lost mice to get where we thought we should be. After being yelled at and straightened up, we start marching to our compartment. Getting in step was, and still is, the hardest part. All of us have different length legs and trying to understand that 1 and 3 mean your left foot—we were stepping all over each other. I recall almost losing my shoe and saying "I'm sorry" every time I stepped on another recruit's ankle. Even after a couple of days of marching everywhere we go, we would still get out of step for one reason or another. After the first few days, we learned how to sleep while marching! You could look around and see at least three recruits marching with their eyes closed. It's pretty amazing. I think that marching involves a lot of discipline and self-control. Teamwork is also involved. The first thing is to step off on the left foot at the same time. Most of the females have shorter legs than the males, and with short legs we have to put forth more effort in keeping up with the division. At the back of the division, we are all suffering.

Lawanda Leitner, 34, Detroit, Michigan

It took awhile, but I finally came to terms with the fact that there are some people who just shouldn't try to march. There is always someone walking up the back of your heels. And there are days when the cadence changes all of a sudden, and you can hear all the feet shuffling to try to get back on the step. It helps when we have a cadence caller who can sing, or at least keep a beat. It was nice the first time Petty Officer Kent sang cadence for us. The whole division was marching on air the whole day because he finally sang with us. He had told us that he would never sing on the street until the division's marching was solid. And when he began his cadence call, we repeated everything as loud and clear as we could, just so that he would keep singing with us. It made me feel good because it gives us a chance to show everyone that we do have it within ourselves to be a real team.

Arron Betton, 19, Los Angeles, California
Well, I never liked walking anywhere, if I could help it. I'm from L.A., and we drive where we need to go, you know? But if I'm getting paid to do it, I guess it's okay. It reminds me of JROTC in a way. I know how to march and to do all the steps and things, so the marching isn't really a problem for me. It took me awhile to get used to all the people we have in the division, though. I love it myself; it's cool, so sweet when everyone does their part right. I can say that I'm glad that I took JROTC while I was in high school. It put me a little step up on a lot of people who have never marched before. When I'm marching with the division, it sets my attitude for the day in a way. If we're all in step and doing the moves correctly, it puts me in a great mood. Because we're all in uniform, looking good, and people look at us and say, 'Man, those guys are good!' But if we're out of step, and people talking and being stupid, yelling at each other, then that ticks me off because if two people mess up, the rest of us get messed up, and we look like we don't know what we are doing at all. That makes me feel dirty and low. We are supposed to be representing the Navy and then we look bad. So it can go both ways.

Not everyone welcomed the elongated P-day interval. The recruits were still in sweat suits at the beginning of their formal training cycle.

From Seaman Recruit Megan Wirsch's first letter home *Mom! All I can say is that those who are sick in bed are actually the lucky ones, because we all stink! I can't even explain, Mom, how bad we all smell. We all know what the problem is, and where the nasty odor is coming from. Imagine, Mom, eighty or ninety new recruits, all scared, tired, and really confused, and marching all over the base. All of us, dirty and sweaty and stinky.*

Now, Mom, even worse, imagine our clothes. Remember that these aren't just ordinary clothes, these are Navy blue sweat suits with the Navy logo on the front and sides of the pants. Half the time we wear sweatshirts, and the rest of the time we wear tee-shirts. We call them our Smurf suits, and they soak up anything and everything. Of course, it gets better. Since we only get one set, there hasn't been an opportunity to wash them yet, and we've had them on for nearly a week now. Marching all over and practicing on the grinder really works up a sweat, and since our showers are three minutes long, you can just guess how many layers of dirt have been building up since we got here. I think this will be a memory I will never forget.

Petty Officer Kent says that when you drive through the gate here, there is a real difference in the smell. That would be us, the "Stinky Smurfs."

I do have to defend those who just smell bad because they haven't had a chance to wash their Smurfs yet. But there are extra-stinky Smurfs, who might want to wash out their socks and stuff a little more often. Some of them can clean out the room when they take off their Navy boots.

Well, Mama, it's a good thing my nose is all clogged up, or boot camp would be worse than it is. Even after yesterday, when we got to take showers as long as we liked, it was pretty bad. Now we just notice when we don't smell, and not when we do!

Seaman Recruit Wirsch was not the only recruit with a stuffed-up nose. By the end of their first week at Great Lakes, most recruits suffered from an upper respiratory infection, intestinal discomfort, or, for the truly unlucky, both. Each compartment—usually empty during training hours—housed a half-dozen or more recruits who had been declared "sick in quarters" (SIQ). And some were even less fortunate.

Stephanie Bruce,18, Social Circle, Georgia

If there is one thing in boot camp that is certain, it is that everybody has the Ricky Crud. You've got people coughing, sneezing, throwing up, and passing out almost every day. At night, you can hear sirens as ambulances go to the different barracks. I got really, really sick right after I got here. I made a trip three days in a row to Building 1007 [USS Tranquility, the branch dispensary, located across Illinois St. from Ship Eight]. I was coughing badly, running a fever, and just felt bad in general. Those three days I was SIQ, but the fourth day they said I was FFD [fit for full duty]. Two or three days later I was still feeling bad, maybe a little worse. So, I went back to Tranquility, and they said my temperature was 105 degrees and my pulse was 137 beats per minute. Right then, the doctors called for an ambulance, and I was driven to the Naval Hospital. Over there, they gave me a private room with a TV, telephone, and real bathroom. A female doctor came and said I had pneumonia. She was really nice; she went and bought me lunch from the McDonalds they have downstairs. She knew I was a recruit, so she bought it with her own money. I called my mom, like, a thousand times while I was there. She wanted to get on a plane to come up and take care of me, but I told her things were great in the hospital. I got to watch TV, talk on the phone, sleep and eat all the time. It was like a mini Ricky-vacation. Too bad I got ASMOed for it. That was the only drawback to it, that and being sick, but at least I got ASMOed into Division 005, and that was really nice.

In her short time at Great Lakes, Seaman Recruit Bruce had experienced the full spectrum of medical care available to recruits. She had received her basic physical examination and immunizations at Building 1523. Upon becoming ill, her division's medical yeoman escorted her to Building 1007, a recently constructed clinic and dispensary, centrally located just south of the recruit chapel. Ten-oh-seven, as it's called (the formal name USS *Tranquility* is rarely used) provides triage, urgent care, medication, and follow-up for recruits and staff. The U.S. Naval Hospital, Great Lakes, is the focus for military medicine in the north-central states. The nine-story general hospital is located at Camp Barry, on Mainside, just east of Recruit Training Command.

Wirsch   *Every body calls us "recruits," right? They ought to call us "acutes." Everybody around here now has, or had, or is in the process of getting, the Ricky Crud. Everybody started feeling run-down right after we got our shots, and nobody has really felt good since. I think I must be the host carrier, because I've been sick so many times. I've been hugging the throne in the head ever since I got here. And with eighty females in one compartment, and everybody sick, you just hope there's one open when you need it most. I've always been healthy, but during the short time I've been here I've had pink eye in both eyes at the same time. I had it so bad that I woke up in the morning with my eyes glued and crusted shut. Then I got the flu. When I went to the doctor, I got some Sudafed. Everyone in the division had the Ricky Crud at the same time, with swollen throat, earpain, headaches, and painful sinuses. Body aches you don't count, because they never stop, even when you are healthy.*

Mary Smith   *Chief Zeller made me the medical yeoman. Sometimes I don't know if that is good or bad. One of the things that I do is to set up everyone's appointments at medical. There are days when*

I've filled out twenty chits for sick call. I hate it when I have to go over there myself for anything. The waiting room is full of people coughing, sneezing, people with fevers, whatever. If something serious happens to you, they will see you right away, but with a million recruits on base, and everyone sick, if you just show up running a fever, you wind up in this big waiting area right inside the door till someone can look at you.

Gildersleeve *Well, I hurt my knee the first days we were here. I was on crutches for a couple days, then on LLD [light limited duty]. I went over to medical every other day, and they were pretty good. They knew what they were doing. Everyone complains about the long wait but if you are a "Rick on a Stick" [a recruit on crutches], it's good to sit down and not be marching and drilling and stuff.*

Because of the crushing workload, the recruits had little time to chat with the medical officers and enlisted corpsmen who provide medical care on base. Every category of provider is in short supply: dentists, nurses, physician's assistants, pharmacists, psychologists, physical therapists, and, most critically, physicians.

Lt. Robert J. Houser, MSC (Physician's Assistant)
Our job here is to take care of recruits. We see some staff, but mostly recruits. The volume here can be anywhere between fifty and a hundred patients, per provider, per day. It's overwhelming. They stack up like cordwood on the weekends. All the way down the hall.

Lt. Rowland J. Rivero, MD
We can't do much triage using corpsmen. With the number of patients every day, there's always the chance that someone will triage incorrectly. So most recruits who make sick call will see either a nurse, a physician's assistant, or a physician. We had 177,000 sick-call patients last year. With 53,000 different recruits here in a typical year, the average recruit lands here three or four times. Now, those are just averages. Some recruits we never see, others seem to be here every day.

Lieutenant Houser *We see everything from out-and-out malingering to life-threatening conditions. We've got a bad one right now— he presented with pneumonia, and now he's over in the hospital* with acute respiratory failure. But when you consider that we have a total population larger than a lot of cities, and most of the people are involved in physical activities all day long, it's really not all that unusual, I suppose.

The last fatality we saw had Marfan syndrome, and experienced sudden cardiac arrest. The MEPS station does a fair job of screening, but the motto of the physicians here is "We're like the little scrubbing bubbles—we work harder so they won't have to." The MEPS stations do a fair job at best. They are under a lot of stress to get recruits here. The Navy is shorthanded. The recruiters pressure the MEPS stations, and they pressure the contract physicians. We had a kid arrive with a glass eye last year. We've had a dwarf (achondroplastic presentation). He had to jump to get up on the examination table. He had some kind of unofficial waiver for his height, from the XO of his recruiting district. We see kids with multiple retained hardware, pins in their joints, plates in their skulls. We've seen a hermaphrodite, full-fledged Cushing's syndrome—you name it, we get it. Some are so blatant, so obvious, it's just a waste of taxpayers dollars sending them here.

Dr. Rivero *Those are just the physical conditions we see. From a psychiatric perspective, we are one of two entry points for the Recruit Evaluation Unit upstairs. Either the RDCs or we refer recruits to the psychiatrists and psychologists on a daily basis. The RDC can fill out a preliminary form to get them upstairs; they generally don't need us here in the clinic to look at them before they go topside. But just last night, I had one. I had a young lady come in here, who said she fell down the stairs in the barracks. I looked at her back, and she had bruises up and down her spine. It wasn't a fall pattern, she didn't have bruises to her extremities, and she didn't try to catch herself falling, no bump on the head—just a banged-up back. She was in hysterics when she came in; she was having a psychiatric episode right then. Personally, my hunch is that she was being abused at home, and when she came here to escape that, the first thing she ran into was a bunch of guys screaming in her face, and she broke down.*

This might surprise some people, but I'd say that 98 percent, maybe 99 percent of the kids we see in here have legitimate medical problems. Malingering happens, but not nearly as much as you might expect. Now, that doesn't mean that they'd all have wound up in the ER at their local hospital. It might not be all that serious, but you have to remember that this is a controlled environment. These kids can't run down to the drugstore for a bottle of aspirin.

So we have standard cold packs, analgesics, decongestants, all in small enough packages that there's really no danger of abuse. But still, on any given day you'll see a couple that are malingering. Maybe 10 percent of the ones we see have no visible pathology, but they do have pain, and it's fairly easy to tell when it's real.

Lieutenant Houser *Well, you have to understand, too, that the ones that stick out in our minds are the ones that are exceptions to the norm. When you are seeing fifty, sixty, maybe even a hundred patients on a duty day, you only remember the really unusual ones.*

Dr. Rivero *There's a protocol that we follow as to whom we treat here and who goes over to 200H [Building 200H, Naval Hospital, Great Lakes]. If a kid is decompensating over a seventy-two-hour period, if he's getting worse and not better, then it's time to get them over to a specialist. We really can't treat a recruit as an out-patient; it's not like when you're out in private practice and you say, okay, take this medication and come back tomorrow and see me. When we don't feel comfortable with how things are going, they head over to Mainside. If we suspect meningitis, if we even suspect that we suspect meningitis, they're across the street, stat. We don't have the facilities for spinal taps here, nor are we set up for isolation. And we've pretty much decided that anything that requires intubation, other than an out-and-out emergency, should go across the street. Naval Hospital, Great Lakes is, in every sense of the word, a teaching general hospital.* There's no place better to send them, at least in this region, if things are heading downhill.*

Lieutenant Houser *I know everyone talks about contagion, but I really don't think it's worse than any other place where you have large age cohorts together. The one big difference, though, is proximity. In a college dorm, you'd usually have people in separate rooms, with separate toilet facilities, whatever. These recruits are with each other all day, every day. You pull kids from every corner of the country, and from whatever foreign countries, you expect people to be exposed to viruses they've never seen before. Couple that with the fact that all these kids are sleep-deprived, and their immune system heads south. I can't tell you how many times I've heard a kid say, "I've never been sick like this before," and the answer is, hey, you've never been in boot camp before, either.*

*The Navy's only school for hospital corpsmen is attached to the hospital.

Dr. Rivero *Well, this place is a stress factory. You come here, your cortozol levels get all screwed up, and cortozol is vital to fighting infection. Add that to sleep deprivation, strange bugs, incipient malnutrition because you're stressed out and have zero appetite, and you wind up with infection.*

Lieutenant Houser *A lot of the recruits have been programmed or influenced by other recruits that their shots are going to make them sick. We have very few cases of allergic reaction to immunizations, either immediately over at 1523 or over here. All the immunizations we do here are common; in fact, most are required before you can enter public schools or college. The only immunization that the Navy gives that is a little unusual is yellow fever, and we don't do that one here. They'll get that at their first active-duty station. But, hey, you go through the tunnel, you get your shots, you come back to the barracks, somebody coughs or whatever, twenty-four hours later you have a headache, sniffles, your joints ache, and, ah! it must have been the shots. But it really isn't.*

Dr. Rivero *It's really amazing that, for many of these recruits, we're the first providers they've ever seen. Well, maybe the MEPS station is the very first doctor, but we know that they only see them for a couple minutes. We see thousand of recruits who have never, ever seen a dentist; their teeth are already rotting out of their heads. We see lots of female recruits who have never seen a gynecologist. They usually claim that they couldn't afford medical care, but, hey, the way things work in this country, you can always get adequate medical care. You may wind up waiting for awhile down at your local county general, but you'll get seen eventually.*

Lieutenant Houser *I'll tell you one thing that is interesting. About 15 percent of our recruits are female. At last count, 57 percent of all sick-call visits in this building were female. We're taking more than half of our resources—and we're shorthanded in every category you can think of—and dedicating them to 15 percent of our population.*

Dr. Rivero *We see recruits at two extremes. There are those who come over here every chance they get, and always have an excuse why they are here. And then there are those who keep on plugging, tough it out, walk around with fractures and keep going till they just physically can't, and then they drop. There are recruits whom*

I truly admire. There was one recruit who came in here after Battle Stations, he was hurting so bad he couldn't even limp right, and I took x-rays, and what do you know? Three fractures, two in one foot and one in the other. One broken metarsal on one foot, two on the other. When did it start hurting? Second event. He ran Battle Stations all night on two broken feet. There are kids like that out there, and you really have to admire their dedication. Their judgment might be questionable, though.

Lieutenant Houser *But, you know, a lot of those that keep on pluggin' are female, too. Recruits with pelvic stress fractures or stress fractures to the humus, and they keep on going. Amazing. It's been my experience that female recruits—at least a portion of them—have more ability to grin and bear it through pain than the average male recruit does.*

Dr. Rivero *I think a lot of problems could be corrected with wellness education, I really do. These kids smoked, most lived sedentary lifestyles until they hit here, some abused alcohol, and few had any idea of balanced nutrition. So if they don't get anything else out of this place, I hope that they leave with healthier lifestyles than when we got them.*

One area of interest to both Dr. Rivero and the recruits was nutrition. Navy food has a well-deserved reputation among the military services as a notch above the rest. While the thought of balanced meals may not have resonated with the younger recruits, the meals at Galley 928 were always hot, nutritious, and usually quite tasty.

Leitner *My college degree is in nutrition, so I was very interested when I first got here to see what the Navy would serve, and how they would prepare it. By and large, I thought it was okay. It's certainly not terrific, but it's acceptable. It's can be bland at times, but it's wholesome and filling.*

Parker *Navy food is no different than any other cafeteria food, I guess. The food tastes similar to lunchroom food when I was in school. And, just like in junior high, there are people going up and down the line, making sure that everyone behaves.*

Leitner *For me, the best meal of the day is breakfast. I'm usually pretty famished by the time we get over to the galley. I'd really like the opportunity to sit and chat while eating, to have some time to relax, but with all the recruits lined up, we don't get much time at all. And I haven't had a chance to talk at a meal since we got here.*

Wirsch *Well, the food is okay, I guess. I have a problem with finding something to drink, though. I observe my church's ordinances about not taking caffeine, so I skip the soda pop and coffee and tea. I usually just have water, or "Ricky bug juice," which is what everyone calls the red, Koolaid-like stuff that they have in the machines. The milk can be good at breakfast, but it's never very cold.*

Betton *The food is good, but not great. They pretty much have all the same stuff I used to eat at home. Now, I never did eat breakfast at home, so eating three meals here instead of two really helped my performance. Staying with a good attitude can be hard, though, especially when you can't recognize what the food is. The servers will tip you off sometimes, they get to eat before everyone else, and if something isn't tasting right, you know not to take it. It took me awhile to get used to everything they have here. I think they should let you have more food at each meal, though. As it is now, you can't go get seconds, because they don't want people to overeat, I guess. But everyone here is an adult, if you have to get your weight down, then it should be your own decision as to what to eat, and not some RDC or MAA telling you how much you can take for your meal.*

Leitner *One bad thing about the menus here is that they are so predictable. You see the same dishes every couple of days. I'm older than everyone else in the division, so it may be that my tastes are a little more grown up. But we see fast-food kinds of things more often than we see regular foods, I think.*

Darrin Johnson, 31, Lubbock, Texas

I don't mind the Navy food at all. I just wish we could have snacks in the machines in the lounge upstairs. The machine is there, but it's not connected or working.

Leitner *In boot camp your system is totally mixed up from the changes in time you eat every day. We can be finished dinner by*

1700 some days; most of us are famished by bedtime. And any kind of food, even food from the galley, is contraband in the house, so there's no way you can get a midnight snack to keep your blood sugar level. You have to wait till the next morning before you get your next bite to eat.

Edward Ryan, 22, Waynesboro, Pennsylvania

They have me on a special diet for weight control, so I usually don't eat the regular food. I stay with salads and fruit and stuff like that. This is the first time in my whole life that I ever ate healthy and I'm going to stick with it when I leave here.

When asked what Navy chow appealed to them, several recruits mentioned meatloaf, perhaps because, with mashed potatoes and gravy, it's the favorite comfort food, and at this point, the recruits needed all the comfort they could find. In the event that a hundred starving Navy recruits might wander by some evening, here's the official recipe, provided by a helpful Navy mess specialist:

Meatloaf for 100 Recruits

Ingredients

Beef patty mix, bulk, or beef, ground, thawed	30 lbs
Bread crumbs, dry, ground (coarse)	4 lbs (1 gal)
Salt	4 oz (6 tbsp)
Pepper, black	1/4 oz (1 tbsp)
Garlic powder	1.2 oz (1 tbsp)
Milk, nonfat, dry	4 oz (1 cup)
Water	2 lb 12 oz (5 1/2 cups)
Celery, fresh, copped	1 lb (3 cups)
Onions, dry, chopped	1 lb (3 cups)
Peppers, sweet, fresh, chopped (optional)	1 lb (3 cups)
Eggs, whole, slightly beaten	2 lb 8 oz (4 1/2 cups)
Juice, tomato, canned	3 lb 1 oz (5 cups)

Directions

1. Combine the beef with breadcrumbs, salt, pepper, and garlic powder, and mix till well blended.
2. Reconstitute the dry milk with water.

3. Add milk, celery, onions, sweet peppers, eggs, and tomato juice. Mix lightly but thoroughly.
4. Form into loaves.
5. Bake for two hours or until meat thermometer registers 165 degrees. Skim off excess fat.
6. Let stand for 20 minutes before serving. Cut 13 slices per loaf.
7. Serve 100 recruits.

Jared Ward, 20, Taylorville, Illinois
They say the Navy has the best food of all the services. God help the Army and Air Force.

5
Raise High the Guidon

"Attention on deck!" Standing at GQ at the foot of their racks, the recruits snapped to attention as the procession of officers and petty officers entered Compartment D-01. The buff and white walls had been brushed down, the deck shined to perfection, and each three-person locker had been checked and rechecked to ensure that all clothing was properly arranged and stowed. Friday, 13 October, would be a *lucky* day for Division 005.

"On behalf of Captain Gantt, our commanding officer, it's a real pleasure to congratulate all of you on your decision to join the world's greatest Navy, and I am proud to formally welcome you to Recruit Training Command." Lt. Erin McAvoy (USNA '93), Ship Eight's officer, was about to commission Division 01-005. From now until graduation, each recruit would know exactly where the division stood in the training cycle. Today was their 1-1 day (first week, first day). Their goal was to reach 8-5 day, when they would depart RTC.

"When a ship is ready to begin its life at sea, the birth of the ship is marked by a commissioning ceremony. The area commander receives orders to place the ship into commission. The commanding officer gives the order to 'set the watch,' and the officers and crew take their stations.

"I am now giving the order for you and your RDCs to 'set the watch' and to unfurl and display your guidon proudly, just as a newly commissioned ship displays a commissioning pennant. These orders also direct you to begin your training here at RTC, and I challenge you to begin your path by *honoring* your decision to join the naval service, by remaining *committed* to the Navy, and by having the *courage* to reach the goal you set before coming here.

"Today marks a major milestone in your own personal naval history. Today, you are here to participate in the official commissioning of your division. This is more than just a ceremony, it's a time-honored naval tradition. It's performed for every new ship, squadron, and shore installation. It was on this very date, 13 October 1775, that the U.S. Navy itself was established. In 1911 Seaman Recruit Joseph W. Grigg entered the gates of this base as the first recruit on board. Since then, over three million others have completed their training at this facility. Many have gone on to distinguished naval careers. Today you stand where they stood before, as recruits, ready to chart your course into naval history."

Much of that naval history is rooted at Great Lakes. By the turn of the twentieth century, it became clear that the Navy's training facility at Coasters Island, Rhode Island, was inadequate. By 1902 the Navy decided that a training center on the Great Lakes would be useful, and considered eight sites in seven states. In a decision greatly influenced by local citizens who ceded land to the government at reduced cost, the Navy chose Lake County, Illinois. As would happen many times over the next century, the influence of a major training establishment upon the local economy was quickly appreciated. Congressman George Foss, who had spearheaded the campaign, became known as the "Father of the Great Lakes Naval Station." On 28 October 1911, three hundred newly minted sailors passed in review before President Taft and ten thousand invited guests. Joseph Grigg of Indiana was the first sailor in line, and even today, recruits are held accountable for identifying him as the first "boot" to graduate from their training center.

The base grew rapidly during World War I. A total of 125,000 men were trained during the war, with a peak one-day census of 47,741. The base grew to over twelve hundred acres and for the first time expanded west of the Chicago and Milwaukee Electric Railroad, to the space now occupied by Recruit Training Command. Much of the credit for developing the current recruit training areas belongs to Capt. William A. Moffett. The Navy later recognized Moffett by naming the in-processing area north of Buckley Rd. in his honor. Although the name is less frequently used today, the area "through the tunnel" is still the first port of call for the Navy's newest recruits.

At war's end the base reverted to caretaker status, with but a handful of graduates each year. The base remained quiescent until 1 July 1935, when it reenergized and prepared for the expected war in Europe.

Within two hours of learning of the Japanese attack at Pearl Harbor on 7 December 1941, Capt. Ralph Spalding, CEC, USN, sprang into action. On his own authority, the public works director quickly authorized the construction of thirty-two new barracks, two galleys, and a host of support buildings on base. It is a tribute to his engineering expertise that several of those temporary buildings, including four huge drill halls, are still in use today. On 19 March 1944 the base reached its peak one-day census of 100,156 sailors. In all, 965,259 recruits graduated from boot camp at Great Lakes during the wartime years.

In the drawdown following World War II, the future of the Great Lakes Training Center was often questioned. After GLTC had served as an out-processing and separation center for nearly a half-million sailors at the end of hostilities, the Navy gave serious consideration to the possibility of consolidating recruit training at Norfolk and San Diego. The Navy decided to keep Great Lakes, however, and, along with centers at Bainbridge, Maryland, and San Diego, the base played a critical role during the Korean War. Nearly seventy thousand new recruits passed through the training center in 1951. The majority of their instructors and company commanders were battle-hardened World War II veterans who brought a wealth of experience to the training of recruits.

The third great wartime contribution began in the mid-1960s, as Great Lakes supported the Navy in Southeast Asia. Working from plans developed in 1957, the Navy brought twelve new thousand-man barracks into service by 1966. For the first time, all recruit training was consolidated at Camps Moffett and Porter, west of Sheridan Rd. In 1965 alone, 86,445 men graduated from Recruit Training Command. Then, in perhaps the most sweeping change of the last century, Great Lakes instituted full gender integration of all recruit training, accepting its first female recruits in 1993.

When Lieutenant McAvoy had completed her prepared comments, Senior Chief Tucker handed the furled guidon to Chief Zeller, as Petty Officers Russell and Kent stood at his side. Chief Zeller untied the half-hitches that had bound the wrapped pennant to its stick. Over the next weeks, the unfurled guidon would precede the recruits wherever they went: to class, to drill, and finally to graduation. They would be taught to guard the guidon with all their resources: scorn and unimaginable shame would fall upon any recruit who allowed others to purloin the simple blue cloth bearing their division number. Recruit folklore was replete with tales of "Ricky Ninjas" who had managed to sneak into a rival division's compartment, and capture their "battle flags." No one wanted 005's honor to be so besmirched.

Both Senior Chief Tucker and Lieutenant McAvoy nodded approvingly as Collins, Caldeira, and the other recruit petty officers posted the colors at the front of the compartment. The division's elongated P-day period had given them a chance to learn basic marching and facing movements, and their military bearing was noticeably better than other divisions at a similar stage of development. Still, marching with furled guidon and ship's flag had advertised their newness and rookie status to everyone they encountered. The recruits were happy to shed the stigma of furled banners.

Mark Walls, 19, Aikoi, West Virginia
I hated it when we were still caterpillars. That's what they call a division that can't fly their flags. We look just like a caterpillar— two sticks up front for antennas, and a couple hundred legs, going down the road. I was glad we at least could show our number.

The recruits remained at attention until the commissioning party left, and spent the remainder of the day stenciling, folding uniforms, and practicing stowing and unstowing their belongings in the very small lockers provided for them. Much of the first week of training would be consumed by these simple, repetitive tasks. Petty Officer Dan Kent explains: "Well, the need to stencil everything is pretty obvious. There are eighty male and eighty female recruits in two brother divisions. With six pairs of socks, six sets of skivvies and tee shirts each—well, you figure out the odds of finding your own stuff on laundry day. As for folding and stowing, we tell them there are two reasons for our insistence on doing things exactly. First, the amount of space here or aboard ship is limited. But, much more importantly, this is the first lesson in following orders to the letter. I tell them nobody is going to care how you fold your skivvies when you're in the fleet, but they *are* going to care if you can't follow a work order, or tech manual, or instructions from the bridge. This is where they begin to develop the mindset of 'there's only one way—the Navy way'—to do something."

Dan Kent had been a parachute rigger for nearly twenty years. (Although the rating was broadened to include other aspects of aviation survival equipment maintenance, the incumbents fought for, and kept, the prized PR designation, as well as the winged parachute for their specialty mark.) The recruits could have no better role model for achieving perfection, each time, every time.

The remainder of the first week of training concentrated on basic military values, naval history, the Uniform Code of Military Justice, and regulations that guided the relationships between male and female recruits, as well as between officers and enlisted members. While most mornings were spent in close-order drill, or logistic tasks like fitting uniforms, afternoons were spent in classrooms at either the main schoolhouse, Building 1127, or the training annex at Building 927. Not every moment of class was enjoyable.

Parker *Classes here are deadly. It's always warm in the classroom building. The instructor usually talks in a monotone. Most people have a real hard time keeping awake. Occasionally, though, you'll get a hip one that can keep you awake for a while. The good thing is, though, if you can stay awake and take good notes, your notebook will get you through the academic tests real easy. The EPO [education petty officer] keeps good notes, and during night study, you can check someone else's notebook and see what you missed if you fell asleep.*

Professionals in adult education would agree with Seaman Recruit Parker's assessment. Classes were usually conducted in enormous rooms with a minimum of 175 tablet armchairs; indeed, some had over 200. Many rooms were dingy and poorly lighted. Training aids consisted of charts, overhead projectors, or, if the recruits were exceptionally fortunate, computer-generated PowerPoint presentations. It was necessary to dim the classroom lights in order for the recruits to see the overhead projections. Instructors quickly learned that the combination of darkness, warmth, and recruit fatigue did not facilitate learning. Recruits were encouraged to walk to the back of the class if they felt drowsy, and within the first ten minutes of any class there was no standing room left along the rear walls. The constant movement of students from desk to rear, as well as those making head calls or refilling canteens, made for a challenging learning environment.

One instructor, who asked to remain unnamed, teaches classroom units dealing with sexual harassment, fraternization, and discrimination: "The things we teach are very important, but it's difficult to keep the recruits' attention. Even though I use a wireless microphone, and have a good, clean PowerPoint presentation, it's difficult to keep their focus—hey, it's difficult for me to keep *my* focus, what with recruits getting up and down; standing, moving, knocking books off these tiny desks, and so forth. Our rules require us to allow hydration at any time, so there's always someone going out to fill canteens. And although we only allow two recruits of each gender to go to the head at once, there's usually a line formed up by each door.

"While this stuff is important, it's certainly not much fun. Today, for example, we used a videotape 'Brown Eyes, Blue Eyes' about attitudes toward people who are different from us. It was made for grade-school students—in the late 1970s. You can imagine how that plays to the MTV generation, right?"

Fortunately, there were other, more active diversions. On Tuesday, 17 October, the recruits had their first exposure to the Olympic-sized swimming pool at Building 1425. The temperature outside was 66 degrees by noon; the morning's haze had burned off, and the twenty-five-minute march from the galley to the pool was pleasant. After showering, the recruits were led to the water's edge, and briefed by a water-safety instructor. Those who claimed to be unable to swim left the main group, and assembled on benches near a smaller, 3-foot-deep pool. The remainder climbed the 10-foot-high tower, stepped off the platform in groups of three, swam and practiced treading water for five minutes, and mustered beside the pool. Nonswimmers entered the smaller pool, where a cadre of instructors individually tested their aquatic abilities. Some were judged fit to attempt the swim test immediately, others after some remediation and practice, and still others were enrolled in a full course of swimming lessons, which they would complete over the next four weeks.

GMC(SW/CC)* Dave Gardner was chief of the deck for Division 005's swimming qualifications. "We're really proud of the new pool here, and our swimming instruction program. Recruits must qualify as third-class swimmers before graduation. That means they must swim at least 50 yards, tread water for at least five minutes, and understand survival procedures if immersed.

*Chief Gardner is a chief gunner's mate (E7), with both surface and close combat warfare qualifications.

The new pool cost the Navy over $9 million—which is a pretty good sign of how important the command feels water safety to be. All of the instructors here are first-class swimmers. Most are SEALs, Special Boats qualified, or air-sea rescue swimmers. And one other thing—the day of throwing recruits off the tower to watch them learn to swim on the way down is a thing of the past. We work with recruits who have a fear of heights or a fear of water, and, if necessary, their RDCs will refer them to the psychologists at the Recruit Evaluation Unit to try to get to the root of the problem. The shrinks even suggested that we change our command from "jump" to "step" to make it less threatening. But jump or step, these recruits will learn to swim, at least well enough to abandon ship if necessary, before they leave here."

Most of the recruits thoroughly enjoyed the dip in the pool, particularly after some time in the muggy and humid atmosphere of the pool house.

Freeman *That was the best moment so far in boot camp. I love swimming, and want to be a rescue swimmer. I went in, and the only problem I had was that there were so many people swimming around that I got kicked while I was treading water. But other than that it was fun.*

Pankratz *Well, promise you won't tell? Some of us thought it was so much fun that we got out early, so that the instructors would yell at us and make us go back up. I went off the platform twice, and got twice as long in the pool.*

Gildersleeve *I never swam when I was coming up in Birmingham, so I just went over to the "kiddie pool," and sat down on the bench. I thought they'd be yelling and screaming, but I had this lady instructor, and she said, "You ever swim?" And I said no, so she didn't hassle me. She just told me to go see the guy at the table and get times to come to class.*

Petty Officer Russell, who had accompanied the division to the swimming pool, explains: "There is some percentage of recruits who never learned to swim, and a smaller portion who are plain scared of the water. Why someone who is afraid of the water would join the Navy is something I never understood, but they do. So, rather than yell and scream and make things worse and slow down the swimming qualifications, we just have instructors with long poles every ten feet around the pool, and about ten more instructors in the water. You couldn't drown during swim test if you wanted to."

After completing their swim qualifications, and marching to Galley 928 for evening chow, the recruits returned to their compartment for more folding and stowing practice and routine evening duties. And, as was the case every night during those first weeks away from home, the recruits had a chance to reflect on things after taps at 2200.

Rasco *I was starting to make friends, and that made things a lot easier. I wish that I could say that I became a friend with everyone in my division, but that just wasn't the case. But there were several females in my division who were wonderful people and I started to think of them as family. There were times when it feels like I had forty moms, forty sisters, forty friends, and forty enemies! I guess I was pretty lucky when it came to shipmates. One night, when we first got here, I received a letter from my mom, and I was reading it after taps, and I began to cry uncontrollably. Several of my shipmates came over to my rack and patted me on the back and reminded me that we would all be okay, and that they were there for me if I needed to talk. I'll never forget that night. I believe it was the first night that I had finally felt somewhat at ease. I lay there and cried for awhile, and my shipmates knelt by my rack and tried to be good shipmates and friends. And when I heard Volk, Adams, and Starks crying one night, I tiptoed to their racks, and I spoke to them briefly about what was bugging them. After each one told me their problems, I told them that I would say a prayer for them and that if they needed to talk any more I was there for them. I was glad to do for them what my other shipmates had done for me.*

Many were a bit cautious about making friends too quickly, but by the end of the first full week of training, relationships had begun to form.

Gildersleeve *When I first got to boot camp I was kind of skeptical about hanging with the crowd, you know? Because I wanted to focus solely on myself and get out of boot camp fast. So at first I sort of stayed to myself. I sat back and checked out the guys to see who I can associate myself with. At first, I met this guy named Watkins. He was cool, and I began to realize we had a lot in common. He was easy to relate to. He was from Georgia and I'm from*

Alabama. We had the same taste in music and down-south women. But he got ASMOed on our 1-2 day. I have seen him since, but things aren't the same, because we aren't in the same house. Then, as time began to pass and I started getting familiar with everything, I started to chill with the crew. I hung with all the guys, getting to know their ways, and I got closer to picking my boys. We're the "nasty nine," and most of us clean the heads during field day. I hooked up with Caldeira, and he's a cool and funny recruit. We can laugh and enjoy this boot camp and make time fly. Caldeira is from New York. I have cousins from New York so I can relate to his ways a lot. He has big dreams about being in the Navy and I hope that God blesses him and he can accomplish everything he set out to do. That is all he talks about: being an officer and flying planes for the Navy. He knows all his stuff and is very enthusiastic about going through with it. He caught my attention one day by being so jittery, moving all the time. And one day I said, "Yo, man, you can't be still for nothing!" And we've been cool ever since.

My other buddy is Betton. Now, Betton and me are from opposite sides of the world. He is from L.A. and I am from Alabama. Betton is kind of brash and cocky. That's one of the reasons why I think I click with him. He reminds me of myself when I was his age. Betton, Caldeira, and I are all going to the same school in Florida. So we will be together for a while longer but after that, who knows?

The recruits continued their heavy schedule of morning drill and afternoon classes. By the middle of the first week, the RDCs began to accelerate the pace of physical conditioning, to prepare the recruits for the intermediate PT test (PT-1) and final test (PT-2). Recruits had specific goals to meet for pushups, curls (a form of sit-ups), and the mile-and-a-half run. Failure to meet these goals by the seventh week of boot camp would disqualify a recruit from running battle stations, and without battle stations, one could not graduate from boot camp. Recruit folklore was full of stories of recruits who had failed their physical training tests repeatedly, and had spent six months or more at RTC before finally graduating. Attitudes varied regarding PT, which was usually performed well before dawn, either at a drill hall or on the grinder behind Ship Eight. It was fairly clear that it was almost no one's favorite part of the day.

Leitner *I've heard some recruits call PT "puppy training " or "pet training": roll over, sit, stand, and so on. When I think of PT, I think of a healthy lifestyle. Since I'm a nutrition and food science graduate, eating right and exercising was a big part of my life. My husband I and lived a very active lifestyle. Once your body becomes adjusted to exercise, you can't go long without it. Before boot camp, I did step aerobics three times a week. And my husband and I enjoyed bike riding and roller-skating.*

PT in Navy boot camp is challenging, though. I never did PT with "crackers" in my eyes at 0400 before. Therefore, this was definitely an adjustment. PT in the training process is not made to be fun for recruits; it's like a punishment, "puppy training"—on your stomach, on your feet, and so on.

I do think that more emphasis needs to be placed on nutrition, and the value and long-term effects of physical training on Navy recruits. The younger recruits feel threatened and don't enjoy it at all, which makes it difficult for everyone as a team. Moreover, everyone is "beaten" by the RDCs if someone is not motivated, and I don't feel that's right. For me, physical training is a stress reliever, relaxation, and cleansing of my body. However, being "ITEd" and "cycled" should not be part of the regular training for good exercise. The RDCs yell and threaten, which is not encouraging and motivating.*

More emphasis needs to be placed on running, which is the most important goal to complete before battle stations. Yet I feel that, whatever you put into it, that's what you get out of it. Everyone knows his or her goal and the time to achieve it. I feel you can do anything you've put your mind to.

Recruit Leitner had identified one of the chief contradictions of Navy boot camp. Over the last several years the Navy has deliberately tried to change its culture from one of indulgence to one that prizes physical fitness. Gone are the "two for one" happy hours at most service clubs. Smoking is banned at most facilities; indeed, at Great Lakes, smoking is prohibited even inside a private vehicle on base. And markedly increased

---

*"Being beaten" and "cycling" are recruit jargon for what is properly called ITE (instructional training exercises). ITE is one motivational tool permitted to RDCs. It consists of a very energetic series of exercises, and must be conducted under strict guidelines, with specific cycles of exercise, hydration, rest, headcalls, and so forth.

Table 1. *Minimum Physical Training Standards for Navy Recruits*

	Sit-ups (number)	Push-ups (number)	1.5-Mile Run (time)
PT-1 (Male)			
17–19	62	51	11:00
20–29	58	47	12:00
30–39	51	41	13:45
PT-1 (Female)			
17–19	62	24	13:30
20–29	58	21	14:15
30–39	51	17	15:30
PT-2 (Male)			
17–19	71	60	10:30
20–29	66	55	11:30
30–39	59	48	13:00
PT-2 (Female)			
17–19	71	30	13:00
20–29	66	36	13:45
30–39	59	24	15:15

emphasis has been placed on physical conditioning to build stamina, agility, and overall well-being. Unfortunately, one of the few forms of chastisement or correction available to RDCs is to require additional physical fitness training for even the slightest misdemeanor. Recruit Leitner—at age thirty-five, both the oldest and best-educated member of the division—quickly recognized the contrarian effect that this has on recruits. Who can develop a positive attitude toward exercise, when avoiding additional punitive exercises is the goal of every sensible recruit?

Others felt the same way, even if they articulated it less eloquently.

Caldeira *I dread PT the most. It usually happens at about four-thirty to five every morning. It is pretty stressful to have to run and do pushups and situps and the large numbers of stretches we are required to do.*

But then again, you have to look at PT as a motivational type of workout. When we do PT, we sing and have some fun. I just wish that it was a little bit later in the day.

The main reason that we run PT every day is to prepare for the PT tests. Of those two tests, PT-2 is the big cheese. If you fail PT-2 you won't be able to run battle stations, therefore keeping you from your goal, which is passing in review and graduating.

So you have no other choice but to love PT, and to try your hardest to give 110 percent all the time. If you do, you'll be fine when it comes to PT-2. Our division has a pretty good overall score at PT-0 [the preliminary baseline screening test], and we want to earn the "A" flag, which is the athletic flag. But I felt as if we just barely scratched the surface, because PT-2 is nothing to mess with. A pretty good number of recruits get ASMOed during this time. You just have to give your all and try to enjoy PT as best you can.

For one recruit, Physical Training was also an introduction to the loneliness of command.

Daniel Smith, 22, Vancouver, Washington

I'm the recruit athletic petty officer (APO). Nobody loves the APO. We jump out of our racks at four in the morning, and everyone knows that we are going to PT, so they are already mad at the APO. We get in our PT gear and head over to the drill hall.

When PT begins, it consists of a five-minute run as a division, and then we start the stretching and aerobics, which consist of 25 jumping jacks, 25 half-jumping jacks, 10 windmills, and 10 rotations. After stretch and aerobics, we run for ten minutes at my pace.

And again, everyone is cursing the APO. "Slow down, slow down, my legs are killing me," and stuff like that. After the run we do a cool-down, stretch, and aerobics, with 25 more jumping jacks, rotations, windmills, hamstring, and deep bends.

Every other day we do in-house or courtyard exercises that consist of the same stretches and aerobics. But instead of running we do push-ups and sit-ups.

Now, when we are running in the drill hall some people drop out and go into the head. When I catch them I give them an UNSAT in their hard card, and I show that to Chief or one of the Petty Officers and they give them ITE [Instructional Training Exercises—more PT]. It seems to me that they should just finish the run and they would not have to work out more.

I personally like PT, although I wish we could work with free weights. The RDCs give me a lot of freedom as the APO, but nobody ever likes the athletic petty officer, anyway. I don't mind, though.

Nevertheless, as the week ended, there was a noticeable improvement in physical conditioning among the recruits. Those who had been able to manage only a few push-ups or curls now were well into double digits, and the RDCs were able to increase the pace slightly for each morning's run. Chief Zeller comments: "One of the big differences between when I came into the Navy and now is the level of physical activity that these young men and women are used to. It might be video games, or MTV, or what—and I've noticed it with my own kids, too—but they just aren't as ready for physical challenges as we were fifteen or twenty years ago, I think. The problem is, though, that a hawser weighs just as much now as it did then, and loading munitions on a flight line hasn't gotten any easier. They must pass PT-2 or risk a setback, and we use that to motivate them when we have them in the drill hall for morning PT."

6

The Early Weeks of Training

During the second week of training, the recruits were introduced to formal military inspections. Augmenting the RDC's daily checks, the Fleet Quality Assurance Organization (FQA) conducts bimonthly inspections "for the record." FQA inspects and grades four training elements: personal appearance, bunk and locker readiness, general compartment cleanliness, and drill. These first inspections, called the Command Assessment of Readiness for Training (CART), would not be counted as part of the division's overall grade at graduation, but subsequent inspections (the Total Ship Training Assessment, or TSTA) would be graded and averaged into a final score. Although division scoring had little impact on the individual recruit, it weighed heavily in the personal assessments of the RDCs themselves. And in the time-honored tradition of military service, pressure placed at the top would cause unpleasantness to flow—downhill.

Jon Hebert, 21, Leland, Mississippi

Inspections are scary, and you are always rushed. Personnel inspections are the scariest. You are worried about how you will do; will you answer the questions correctly, or will he find something wrong with your uniform? And you don't want to let down your division because the flags that we win are based on division scores. You stand there, with stuff running through your head, like "is my gig line straight, is my shave close enough and my boots shined enough?" It's a really tense time when you are standing there, and you see the inspector coming down the line.

Seaman Recruit Hebert's apprehension was shared by many. The division had spent the evening of Thursday, 19 October, preparing for Friday's inspection. Recruits used "Ricky lawn-mowers" (fingernail clippers) to remove stray threads from their still-new uniforms. PR1 Kent worked with the male recruits to ensure they had the best possible shine on their Navy boondock-ers, and DC1 Russell worked with the female recruits to see that both their uniforms and lockers were presentable. "Some male RDCs get nervous about female uniforms and clothing," DC1 Russell remarked. "So they prefer to have a woman around to be sure that everything is squared away. Some of these salty old sailors stammer and turn red if they have to say, 'Fix your bra straps' to a female recruit. I wonder how they act when they hit a good liberty port," she added with a chuckle.

The division stood at attention at 0800 Friday, awaiting the triple knock that heralded the FQA inspectors. All inspectors were chief petty officers or above, and all had completed at least six "pushes" as RDCs. They work from specific guidelines, and the recruit yeoman would follow the inspector to record demer-its, comments, and suggestions for improvement.

Division 005 was in luck. GMC(SW)* Timothy Youell was the morning's senior inspector, assisted by ETC(SS)** Mike Wagner. Kent and Russell breathed a sigh of relief as Chief Zeller led Chief Youell into the compartment.

"He's one of the better ones," Kent said. "He'll be tough, but fair. He doesn't have any axe to grind. And I knew Wagner when he was an RDC. He's a good guy."

Chief Youell began the personnel inspection with the recruit petty officers. He found few major discrepancies, although he had a penchant for checking the polish on usually overlooked areas of the recruit's boots. DC1 Russell made a note to herself to purchase spare toothbrushes so that the recruits could get polish down along the welt line between the uppers and soles of the heavy leather boondockers. "Each inspector looks for differ-ent things," she commented later. "You try to get the recruits to be 5.0, but there's always something that gets overlooked."

Both Chief Youell and Chief Wagner questioned the recruits. During CART inspection, questions were limited to the general orders of a sentry, rank insignia, and the chain of command. The RDCs chuckled quietly when Chief Youell asked several recruits

*Chief Youell is a chief gunner's mate (E7), with surface warfare qualifica-tions.
**Chief Wagner is a chief electronics technician (E7), with submarine war-fare qualifications.

what collar device the commander-in-chief wore. Most recruits were thrown off balance by the unexpected question. Answers ranged from oak leaves to silver stars. Finally, Seaman Recruit Hooton-Hetrick made the connection, and sounded off firmly that the president of the United States wore no uniform, and so therefore had no need of collar devices. Personnel inspection was followed by bunk, locker, and compartment inspections, and the inspectors departed shortly before noon. The recruits breathed a collective sigh of relief.

Gildersleeve *I don't mind the inspections that much, it's the standing there at attention for three hours that gets bad. That, and tearing our lockers apart every night before the inspection, and practicing, practicing getting it right. I wish they'd just let us get the locker set right, and then leave it be, you know? It's the tearing it up and down that messes it up, and you're never sure you have it back exact, when the inspector comes.*

Betton *Well, I was so proud to get my uniform, and getting out of the sweat suits. It made me feel like I was really part of the Navy. I had begun to have some military pride, and I felt good. Getting looked over by the chief and getting asked questions didn't really bother me. The material inspection went okay, too, although I got a hit for my rack. The worst part of it was that I was working with my bunkmate, and the part I got the hit for was something he was supposed to take care of. Which just goes to show, if you want something done right, you had better do it yourself. My locker, though, was in really good shape, so I came out of it with two out of three things perfect. Lots of others did worse.*

One recruit expressed a concern felt by many of the female members of the division.

Bruce *Inspections are the pits. Imagine having some loud-mouthed [guy] come to your house to inspect the clothes you are wearing, then inspect the bed you sleep in to be sure that you made it right, and then go through your clothes and underwear to make sure you folded them right. It's kind of embarrassing to have some strange guy looking at your underwear and then yelling at you because you forgot to put an adjustment fold in your skivvies. And what is really fun is to have to stand there during personnel inspection while he fingers your uniform and asks a question* *about the chain of command or your general orders. It's also a test of military bearing, so you can't look directly at the inspector. You can't look, but somehow you are supposed to figure out his rank. You don't ever want to call a senior chief just "Chief," right? So how am I supposed to see this tiny little silver star on his anchor, if I can't look at him, right? Finally, after about three hours, watching all your stuff get touched and tossed around, the inspector leaves, and your RDC comes around and yells and screams at you for having a messy locker. I mean, what's the point?*

Nevertheless, the division had done relatively well on their CART inspections. With 5.0 indicating perfection, they had scored 4.29 for the personnel inspection, 4.88 for the locker inspection, and 4.95 for the previous day's drill inspection. Only the maintenance inspection, in which they scored 3.44 was a matter of serious concern.

"Well, we were marching pretty well by that point," commented Chief Zeller later. "But it's a shame about the barracks. We talk about boot camp being the Quarterdeck of the Navy, yet we really have to work to keep the place from collapsing around our ears. I don't think it makes a good impression on recruits when three out of eight sinks in the head are out of service, or if we have to post a sign by the scuttlebutt [drinking fountain] to warn everybody that it's not bolted to the deck. It's just not what I'd want the first impression to be. We try, but still . . ."

Petty Officer Russell understands. "About three minutes before the inspectors arrived, I'm standing there on a chair, next to a locker, trying to hammer a coat hook into place so that the recruit doesn't get a hit for having gear adrift. What's the recruit supposed to do?—the hole for the hook is so worn that the bolt and nut slip right out. So I'm standing there, and the only tools I have are a pair of vise grips, and I'm hammering away trying to get the hole in the sheet metal to close up enough so that the weight of his peacoat doesn't pull the coat hook out in the middle of inspection. Hammering with a pair of vise grips—and I'm in an engineering rating. That looks good to the recruits, right?"

Lt. Erin McAvoy ruefully agrees. "This is a middle-aged building, built about 1964 or thereabouts, and some of the others were built as early as 1959. They've been in use, all day, every day, since they were built. This building is undermined; we had a sewer flood in March 1999, and when they investigated, they found that everything washed away underneath us. Now, that doesn't mean that it's unsafe—they gave it a clean bill of health—but just as an example, the back wall of this building leaks water six months of the year. There's a roof leak, going down into the wall, and they can't seem to find and fix it. We get assistance when we need it; we're in line with everyone else, but when everyone's pipes are clogging up—not just yours, but every single barracks building on base—you can't just move to the top of the list. So Public Works wants us to fix things ourselves when we can, and that's good, except my RDCs are all out pushing recruits, so I have to assign one to fix the pipes, but she's not a plumber, so she assigns a recruit to fix the pipes, and he may or may not be a plumber—but what I really need is a plumber to fix the pipes. We inefficiently take care of ourselves. The plumber is just an example. Have you heard alarms going off at odd hours around here? We have a ground in the alarm system: we find it, fix it, and it pops up someplace else. We haven't had a chance to stand-down in this building for two years, and it's not slated to be taken off-line for routine maintenance for awhile again. We're going to see fifty-four thousand recruits next year: where else are we going to put them?"

Even though the division as a whole had scored well, some recruits were having individual problems. For example, one young suburban recruit was having difficulty relating to his African American shipmates. Several had problems with reading and comprehending their training material, and one young female recruit, who had had a very difficult childhood, had significant issues with male authority that needed to be sorted out. After a lengthy discussion among the RDCs, these recruits and some others were referred to special units where they could receive individualized attention.

CMDMC Mike McCalip is the command master chief petty officer for Recruit Training Command. A twenty-two-year veteran, he occupies one of the key billets in the development of the Navy's enlisted force. He has counseled thousands of sailors at sea and ashore. He says, "It's unrealistic to expect every recruit is to be an honor graduate. It just doesn't happen. And if it did happen, it would mean that we've made the entrance standards so tight that we'd never man the fleet. What we do, though, is to give every single recruit an opportunity to succeed here. I tell them that nobody knows, or much cares, who you were, or how well you did, before you got here. You're all dressed alike, you are treated alike, and, so far as we're concerned, you are alike until you prove us wrong. If you need special attention, for academic or physical or emotional reasons, we'll make sure that you get it. But we're not giving up on you, and we don't want you to give up on us."

Special programs have been instituted over the past few years to help recruits who have problems adapting to military life:

1. The Fundamental Applied Skills Training (FAST) program assists recruits whose literacy level precludes successful completion of recruit training. FAST provides basic training in vocabulary strategies, reading comprehension, graphic interpretation, and study skills. Listening skills and English grammatical structures are also taught to recruits with limited English proficiency. Any RDC who finds a recruit not performing well academically and who feels that the recruit may benefit from the program may make a referral. Recruits with competency in languages other than English will be assigned to an ESL (English as a second language) stream. A recruit may complete one or both streams before returning to a line division for further military training. The fifteen-day reading skills program covers four topic areas: vocabulary, graphic interpretation, reading comprehension, and study skills. The verbal course, also fifteen days, assists the recruit with naval vocabulary, grammatical structure, and language fluency. These programs are designed to help recruits, and in no way are considered disciplinary tools.

2. Academic Capacity Enhancement (ACE) is a program for non–high school graduates. Unlike the FAST track, this program emphasizes self-worth, the value of completion vs. fear of failure, personal choice vs. victimization, self-control and self-discipline, and goal setting. Recruits are placed in a one-week orientation program, immediately after in-processing, and remain together for the duration of their military training. Their RDCs are carefully screened, and trained to work with these "higher risk" recruits. The Navy has reduced the risk of repeated failure by insisting on much higher AFVAB (Armed Forces Vocational Aptitude Battery) cut-off scores (50-plus, rather than 31-plus for high-school graduates) to further reduce attrition among the five thousand non–high school graduates accepted annually. Each recruit is afforded study time and opportu-

nity to take the GED test before graduation; nearly 80 percent of recruits who have taken the test while in the program have passed.

3. The Personal Applied Skills (PASS) program trains and mentors recruits having difficulty with racial, cultural, or gender diversity; dealing with authority; stress management; low self-esteem; conflict resolution; goal setting or achieving; and problem solving. Many of these recruits come from backgrounds that did not allow them to develop the social skills and maturity required to make the transition to military life. They may refuse to train; express suicidal notions, gestures, or attempts; engage in disruptive behavior; exhibit low self-esteem; or lack motivation. These recruits have a low probability of successful completion of military training without intervention. The PASS training group helps these recruits develop social skills and provides them with a foundation for success both in the Navy and in their personal lives. Through an intense, five-day interactive educational program, these recruits are led on a journey of self-awareness and empowerment, which lets them take responsibility for their own actions and release their "past" to establish a methodical system of goal setting and achievement.

4. Physical Fitness Training Unit. Designed for those who either fail to meet minimum standards of their physical fitness screening test or repeatedly fail PT-1 and PT-2. This unit emphasizes healthy lifestyles, including nutrition, weight loss, athletic techniques, and aerobic conditioning. Recruits will remain in this unit until they have successfully completed the necessary physical fitness tests or, in exceptional cases, until the tests are waived by a board of examiners.

5. Recruit Holding Unit. Those recruits are experiencing a "time out" from routine training because of their physical condition. Recruits with injuries or medical conditions more serious that those permitting light limited duty (LLD) status are assigned to this unit until the condition is resolved. This division also includes Recruit Special Quarters, a secure berthing area designed to eliminate risk of injury to the recruit. Recruits are generally kept under close observation during the limited time during which they may be assigned to special quarters. Recruits who have expressed suicidal thoughts, or who have made suicidal gestures or attempts,

and those who either are a threat to, or are threatened by, others may temporarily be assigned to special quarters.

Those recruits whose problems exceed the capacity of the special units at Ship Fifteen are referred to the naval hospital's Recruit Evaluation Unit. This group is staffed by commissioned clinical psychologists, psychiatric nurses, and enlisted neuropsychiatric technicians. The unit is located, along with the medical dispensary, at Building 1007. Any recruit may ask for a referral to REU, and that request must be honored by the command. The RDC or a member of the medical staff may also refer the recruit for preliminary psychiatric evaluation. RDCs are instructed to immediately refer recruits who exhibit worrisome behaviors signaling mental or emotional difficulties, including the following:

Suicidal thoughts, statements, or gestures. In the event of an actual suicide attempt, the recruit receives emergency medical treatment, followed by referral to the clinical psychologists or psychiatrists.

Persistent depression, including sleep or eating disturbance, frequent crying, prolonged sadness, and so forth.

Persistent anxiety, including panic attacks, shortness of breath, chest pain, racing heart, or trembling.

Social isolation, avoidance of others or high need to be alone.

Overly aggressive behavior, including threat of harm to others, punching people or things.

Strange, odd, or bizarre behaviors, mannerisms, speech, or verbalization; evidence of illogical thought process; confusion.

Severe stress reaction, including acute onset of anxiety, depression, psychosis, inability to function, multiple physical complaints.

Significant behavioral change, including appearance, hygiene, sleeping, eating, energy level, interaction with others, or performance.

Group living problems, including bedwetting, sleepwalking, or night terrors.

Any "new" history that is revealed to the RDC, including prior substance abuse or mental illness and treatment or hospitalization.

The role of the clinical staff is limited to determining whether or not an identifiable mental illness or deficiency is present. The providers adhere closely to the provisions of the *Diagnostic and Statistical Manual*, fourth edition (known as *DSM-IV*) of the American Psychiatric Association. By law, referral to the unit can not be used as a threat, punishment, or a vehicle to dispose of an "unwelcome" recruit. Additionally, the staff encourages RDCs not to make referrals in the following types of situations:

When the recruit wants to go home or separate from the service. Missing family members and friends is a normal human reaction and not a sign of mental illness. Most REU clinicians remark privately that any recruit *not* wanting to escape boot camp would be of much greater concern to them than those who do.

When there are concerns about sexual orientation and related behaviors. The Navy views this not as a psychiatric problem, but as one that should be referred to the legal department for resolution. If, however, sexual acting out between recruits results in emotional distress, the staff will provide the required counseling.

When the recruit is overemotional. Elevated emotional levels are common in high-stress situations such as boot camp. If, however, the heightened emotional level consistently interrupts daily progress for a week or more, the unit will facilitate evaluation and counseling.

Master Chief McCalip says, "I really hate to ASMO anyone out of a division. In a way, it makes me feel like we've failed as leaders. But if they are going over to Ship Fifteen, to special programs, I know they'll get the help that they need. It's unfortunate, but with eighty to ninety-four recruits in a line division—especially in an integrated one—we just really don't have the time to work with special recruits the way we'd like to."

The remainder of the recruits in Division 005 were relieved that inspection had gone so well and that they'd remain with their new friends in the division. As a reward for the division's performance, the RDCs allowed each recruit a ten-minute telephone call home. For most, this was the first meaningful conversation with loved ones since they had arrived. Many had reached answering machines when making their safe-arrival call from Building 1405, and even the fortunate had had less than thirty seconds to speak to family or friends. The calls were a godsend to many.

Maria (Tess) Alcazar, 21, Los Angeles, California
That call saved me. I was getting so down on things, and when I had a chance to talk to my family, it really cheered me up. They asked about what was going on, and who my friends were, and it was nice to talk to someone who really cared about me, finally.

Lisa Orlando, 20, Selden, Long Island, New York
My dad wanted to know about life in the barracks, how things were going, and what it was like to be in an integrated division. When he was in the Navy, it was all guys in boot camp.

The "fun part" of boot camp, during which the recruits begin to learn the sailor's craft of line handling, small arms, and damage control, wouldn't start for a few weeks. Thus, many of the recruits focused on interpersonal relationships when describing their experiences. For many, it was the first time away from home and in the company of strangers. For all, it was the first exposure to living in a privacy-deprived environment.

Mike Shelton, 19, Marlow, Oklahoma
It's not like what I expected at all. It's crowded all the time here, eighty guys trying to take a shower all at once, and there are arguments going on all the time and stuff.

Caldeira *It's not so bad, it's all right. Most of the fun is after dark, anyway, when the RDCs get out of here and we're alone, finally. After taps, it gets a little wild—we pray a little, when the RPOs [religious petty officers, one Catholic and one Protestant] say their prayers, but afterwards, we mess around a little. Ward, he's ridiculous—he's my bunkmate [laughing].*

Shelton *Well, I'll tell you one thing that happens—things turn up missing around here all the time. We call it the Ricky Ninja, and* *it's supposed to be somebody here in boot camp who gets up late at night, and crawls under the bunks, and swipes stuff, and messes up your skivvy stacks and stuff like that. I haven't had it done to me personally, yet. And then there were a couple guys in brother division—they went around putting shaving cream on people's faces during the night—they got caught for it, didn't they?*

Caldeira   *Yeah, I think so. It's wild after taps, sometimes. Especially with brother division. We wouldn't do that kind of thing, would we? [Laughter.]*

Shelton   *See, the challenge of being a Ricky Ninja is, you have a forward compartment watch and an aft compartment watch, and you go from locker to locker, and the main thing that you do is try to get past the watches, and steal as many pairs of socks as you can, and then get back in your rack. The guys that are going into the SEALs and UDT, they seem to do that more.*

Ward   *That's where Ricky socks come from. Ricky socks are socks that nobody owns or claims.*

Nick Broders, 19, Tigard, Oregon
Because they're gross, man! Stinky!

Ward   *So we use 'em like our brooms and dustrags and stuff. I've lost a couple pairs already, but I know where they went, I think [looking suspiciously at Shelton, and laughing].*

Shelton   *I think we're beginning to come together as a team a little. At least, I think the males are coming together, I'm not sure about the females. There are still a few people who just don't want to listen, but they're coming around.*

Broders   *I really find it hard to get any time to myself. Just time to sit by myself, relax, and study for the tests. We have forward IG, where we all sit in the front half of the house, and the education petty officer leads 'study hall,' but it's hard for me, I like to study on my own, do things on my own, read the Bible and stuff, but it's hard to find time to do that. Everything is on a strict schedule and all. If we're not doing anything, then we're cleaning this house, and getting it on the spot. Everything has got to be perfect or we get dropped.*

Ward   *It's wild when we try to get all eighty guys from both divisions into the showers. You got guys sitting in there, putting on deodorant, fixing their uniforms, and you got guys yelling at the guys that are already in there to hurry up and get out, and it's stinky and smelly, and it's crazy.*

Caldeira   *Sometimes you have to break the rules to get things done without getting screamed at, you know? I ain't going to lie, if they don't know about it, we break the rules. We break a lot of the rules around here a lot of times.*

Ward   *Being a section leader and all—I can't say as I go breaking the rules—by the book, a straight shooter, that's me. [Wild laughter, and three people punching, choking, and generally attacking Ward.] Hey, everybody thinks section leaders go around yelling and being big dogs, but we keep getting dropped for stuff the other guys do. It's not that great a job, trying to keep this crowd in line. [More laughter.]*

Broders   *I think it must be hard for the ASMOs who came in. I mean, we've got a lifestyle that we've started in this division. If I hear one more guy say, "That ain't what we did in my last division," I'll choke him. But it must be hard for them to adjust to us, because we've got little teams together, and we know everybody and stuff.*

Caldeira   *Yeah, and when they come in, they have an attitude, because they all were ahead of us, so they down us.*

Broders   *They throw us off our beat. We've got a pattern going, and they throw us off rhythm, and they disrupt it and all. We've got, like, what, six or seven ASMOs since we got here. We had, like, what, Ward, four of 'em arrive the night before last, right?*

Shelton   *Yeah. And another thing is brother division. It's different with them because they aren't here all the time, and they have different RDCs, and their RDCs are more strict than ours. They don't have to pitch in and clean up our house, they clean the house upstairs where our girls are.*

Ward   *Well, you will see them on head crew with Gildersleeve, every once in a while. And I do see them down on my section, because I'm near the back of our end of the house, and . . .*

Caldeira *And we get in trouble because of them too, sometimes. We get dropped for stuff that they do. We got in trouble for them about our bunks, one time, too; we were done, and they were still doing theirs. And we all got dropped for it. We get dropped for stuff that they do, but I don't think they get dropped as much as we do, you know?*

Shelton *Like, the other night, we usually wait till the lights go out, but those guys didn't know that we still had Chief Zeller up in the office, and they started cutting up, so we all had to get back out of our racks, put our tennis shoes on, and we all got dropped.*

Broders *Reveille around here is crazy, too. It all depends on who wakes you up. Chief Zeller, I don't mind waking up to him, but Petty Officer Russell [laughter and imitations of DC1(SW) Lela Russell]: "Reveille! Reveille! Get out of those racks, Recruits, before I come down there and beat you! You gonna get me a captain's mast yet, Recruits!" [More laughter.]*

Caldeira *I remember the first day, I was the last person left in the rack! You guys remember—I was sleeping, with my head down, and I opened my eyes, and she was, like two inches from my face! "Recruit! You think you're special or something?" And I see her, and she's screaming at the top of her lungs. I forgot where I was, and then I realized, and I got out of that bunk, quick.*

7
A Sailor's Life for Me

So far, the recruits had spent most of their training day in the classroom or drill hall. Most of the classroom training had concerned academic or life-skill topics: the history of the Navy, customs and courtesies, rank and rate, or personal finance. Now, finally, they would get a chance to learn the sailor's trade.

Petty Officer Russell had strong opinions on the subject. "I've been in the Navy for eleven years, and, except for some shore duty in Italy, most of that time has been spent at sea. I can't think of anything worse than a sailor who can't pitch in when necessary. It doesn't matter if you're a boatswain, a yeoman, or a storekeeper; there are basic things that every sailor ought to know. Basic knots and splices, what to do and not to do on deck, even real simple things like how to navigate around their ship. Not navigate the ship—that's the quartermaster's job—but how to find where things are stowed, and how to get from one place to another in a hurry. Big ships like the carriers—they have thousands of small compartments. You can imagine how lost you could be if you didn't know the basics of port and starboard, fore and aft, and how decks and compartments are numbered."

The recruits welcomed the change.

Rasco *I was afraid I'd get caught sleeping in class every time we went into the schoolhouse building. I'm twenty-four—do they really think I need classes on things like writing checks, and setting up a personal budget? Hey—at least in this job, the paycheck is steady. They ought to try budgeting a waitress's tips sometime, huh?*

It was likely that few recruits would fall asleep during hands-on training. They'd spend most of their time at the seamanship training division, a series of small buildings on the southeast corner of the base that housed, among other things, the USS *Marlinespike*. *Marlinespike*, a quarter-sized replica of a fleet auxiliary, could easily accommodate a complete division of recruits, manning various action stations on pier, deck, or bridge.

AOC(AW)* Mike Lucas is a nine-push RDC, who led the most recent division to win the coveted chief of naval operations (CNO) award for merit. He related, "I got to talking to an old sailor here, one day. This guy had gone through here in the mid-1960s, and I showed him around the *Marlinespike*. Back when he was here as a recruit, seamanship training mainly meant standing around an old World War II drill hall over where Building 1405 is now. An instructor would stand in front of a hundred recruits and demonstrate how to tie simple knots and bends, using "small stuff"—pieces of cotton line that looked a lot like your grandma's clothesline.

The recruits would practice all day, tying knots around one-inch pipe rails that extended out from the bulkheads of the drill hall. There was also a painted outline of a ship in the middle of the floor, and the instructor would stride up and down the silhouette, saying things like, "This is the fantail" or "This is the port side of the forecastle." There were large, cardboard-mounted pictures on the bulkheads, showing bits, chocks, cleats, and other deck fittings. Every now and then, a couple signalmen would wander out, coffee cups in hand, and demonstrate flag signals, using a rusty hoist fastened to the overhead. They'd do a quick demonstration of semaphore, using hand flags, and pull a couple likely recruits from the sidelines and teach them a few elementary signals. If you could make heads or tails out of what they were trying to teach you, you'd probably wind up in signalman's school on mainside after you graduated.

"Surprisingly, things weren't much different until the early 1990s. I know when I went through boot camp down in Orlando, we didn't have any kind of shipboard trainer, although by then the cardboard-mounted pictures had been replaced by real hardware. Things weren't much better over at San Diego. Guys would

---

*Chief Lucas is a chief aviation ordinanceman (E7), with air warfare qualifications.

go to sea right after boot camp, and be of no use to anyone for a couple weeks till they got their bearings.

"Along about 1990, though, operating commanders finally convinced Recruit Training Command that we had to do a better job. Something had to change, and *Marlinespike* became part of the solution.

"As usual, though, training dollars were in short supply. So the company commanders [RDCs of their day] and instructors pitched in and did much of the design and construction work. There were a lot of ships being decommissioned around that time; guys would wrangle TAD orders to the decommissioning sites and come back with all kinds of equipment for the mockup. If you look closely, you'll see little black tags at the base of the binnacle, on the sound-powered phones, and on the watertight doors and hatches. Each one lists the name of the ship from which it was cumshawed. There are a couple dozen tags up there, I bet.

"There are a few other things you might not notice at first glance. Down below, inside the trainer, there's a sample berthing space, copied exactly from a *Burke*-class destroyer. Seeing that is often the first time that recruits realize exactly how cramped things are aboard ship. The *Marlinespike* is designed as a generic ship—everything on board is common to every ship from a yard tug to a cruiser. Recruits really enjoy the *Marlinespike;* it's the first thing they do that is really 'Navy.'"

There was a palpable sense of excitement after noon chow on 1 November, when the recruits crossed Indiana Street from Galley 928, and turned south to the *Marlinespike*. Taking their place on bleachers in an adjacent classroom, they listened while SM2 Fines Stevenson explained the various types of natural and artificial line and steel cable they might encounter aboard ship. They learned the safety precautions necessary to avoid being injured by a line that could part under strain. The recruits learned the standard shipboard precautions: never stand in the bight of a line, never kneel or sit on the deck, and never handle fiber lines without heavy protective work gloves. They learned basic knots and bends, just like the sailors of the 1960s, and practiced for several hours, using lengths of "small stuff" provided in the classroom/laboratory. Finally, it was time to "go to sea." Petty Officer Stevenson opened a set of double doors, and the recruits of Division 005 got their first glimpse of the stationary trainer.

Wirsch   *I thought that was just awesome! I mean, it's so big, and it really looks like a ship. They have it painted gray, just like a real Navy ship, and they even painted the decks under the brow to look like sea water. I've never seen a real Navy ship. But I bet this one looks just like a real one.*

Ward   *I thought, well, we're going to sea at last. It's going to be hard to sink a fake ship, but I bet this division can do it . . .*

Stevenson and his assisting boatswain mates divided the division into teams, which would rotate tasks during the exercise. While some remained pierside as line captains or line handlers, others would work the main deck area, as signalmen, talkers, or deck hands. Still others would man the bridge and act as watch officers, messengers, and talkers. Each station was connected via sound-power telephones, and one of the first lessons the recruits learned was proper shipboard communication. Chief Zeller, as a fire controlman, understands that clear, concise shipboard communication is vital. He explains, "You have sailors from all over the U.S., and some were even born in other countries. Accents become a real problem, especially on sound-powered telephones. So the recruits learn standardized pronunciation of letters and numbers, as well as the phonetic alphabet. They really get a kick out of practicing that, saying 'niner' for the number nine, and 'Kay-bec' for the phonetic word for the letter 'Q.' You'll hear them joking around with it when they get back to the compartment after class. But it's important, and it's something that a sailor has to know when he straps on a pair of sound-power phones and becomes a telephone talker at sea."

The seamanship instructors also used the *Marlinespike* to reinforce traditions and courtesies taught in the classroom. As sailors have done since the founding of the republic, the recruits would climb the brow, display their ID cards, face aft, salute the national ensign, turn and salute the junior officer of the deck (JOOD), and formally request permission to come aboard. "There's no sense turning a recruit loose in the fleet, if the first thing he does when he reports on board is screw up," Stevenson noted with a chuckle.

Petty Officer Dan Kent stood just aft of the quarterdeck, as the recruits prepared to board. "There's a story here," he remarked, "and it tells you a lot about the Navy and about the people who care about these recruits. As you probably know, in the fleet, you'd normally be met by both the officer of the deck [OOD] and the JOOD. Did you wonder why the *Marlinspike's* watch is manned by a JOOD only? Watch what Stevenson is doing now."

Very quietly, as the recruits were being organized on the pier, Petty Officer Stevenson stepped behind the superstructure and retrieved a framed, glass-covered corkboard. Silently, he placed it on an easel between the U.S. and Navy flags, just behind the JOOD's station. Dan Kent continued with his story.

"As Chief Lucas said, a lot of sailors pitched in to bring the *Marlinespike* on line. One old boatswain's mate, in particular, was a real sparkplug in making all of this happen. He'd been scheduled to retire before *Marlinespike* was commissioned, but he extended to see the job through, and the command honored him by asking him to stand here on the quarterdeck to welcome the commissioning party aboard. After the ship was up and running to his satisfaction, he put in his papers, and the skipper allowed him to have his retirement ceremony on board. With his family and friends gathered around him, he was piped over the side, and the guys from the seamanship training division acted as his sideboys, just as they would have done had this been a real ship.

"There's more to the story, though. A very short time later, he suffered a massive heart attack, and died before he reached the hospital. His shipmates were devastated. And so . . . ." Kent pointed to the corkboard in its polished frame. On it hung the red rope and "cookie" of an RDC, an instructor's nametag, a photograph, and a plank owner's certificate for the USS *Marlinespike*. Below them all, a gold plaque read simply:

To the memory of BMC Calvin Herring
Eternal Officer of the Deck
USS *Marlinespike*
28 March 1991

"The recruits don't seem to notice it," Kent continued. "And to be honest with you, we really don't bother to tell them. But you see, since that day, well, the first time these kids climb aboard a Navy ship, about a half-million new sailors have saluted Chief Herring's memory. Kind of special, don't you think?" And it is, indeed.

After reporting aboard, the recruits simulated getting the ship under way, using the skills they had already learned. Various commands were relayed from bridge to crew, heaving lines tossed from deck to pier, hawsers recovered and faked down on deck, and colors shifted, just as if the *Marlinespike* were ready to pull out of Norfolk and head out to the North Atlantic. Recruits traded position, and bells sounded as the *Marlinespike* "came alongside" and moored yet again. By the end of the training period, most recruits had had exposure to several positions, and all had practiced the sailor's trade. Tired from the physical effort of manhandling hawsers and lines, the recruits requested permission of the JOOD and, when it was granted, happily left the ship for "liberty"—or, at the very least, a well-deserved head call.

Chief Zeller comments, "I always think that the day aboard *Marlinespike* is the day that you can see them stop being 'civilians in utilities' and start seeing something that looks as though it might be a sailor, someday. I'm not alone in thinking that; lots of RDCs will tell you that it's in their third or fourth week that recruits begin to 'get it.'"

After returning to the compartment, several of the female recruits gathered to discuss their impressions of their training thus far.

Mary Smith   *That was really fun. That's what I thought the Navy would be like. It was fun watching the males react to females as line captains and JOODs! I think most of them sort of wish we'd just go away, and they hate it when an instructor puts one of us in charge.*

Demitrus (Mimi) Starks, 18, Chicago, Illinois
Yeah, but we have just as much trouble when we're alone up here in the female compartment, too. All the backbiting and bickering and everything.

Wirsch   *The biggest problem is attitude! [Agreement from the others.] If people could just drop all their little remarks and comments and suck it up! Start folding and stowing something, and don't talk! That would solve so many issues, I can't even begin to explain.*

Starks   *It's like in the showers. When I got made the female MAA [master-at-arms], I had to force people to take showers two at a time, one to wash up, and the other one to soap up. It's hard with* *forty-two females, with six showerheads, in fifteen minutes; it's always crowded. But they just have to get used to it.*

Jennifer Hattrich, 19, Fort Mill, South Carolina
It's really hard to share with the other division, too, because it's their house, and they get to do things first. And then they tell us that we're taking too long, but it's their fault, because they take more than half of the time, and we have to hurry and rush so fast.

Starks *The males don't understand it, but we have it harder than they do, because we have six RDCs jumping on us, because we have our own, and then we have Division 006's, because we're really living in their house. That's the worst thing about being an integrated division—the unfairness of the other RDCs.*

Cari Williams, 19, Lake Charles, Louisiana
There are good things, though. We get to bond more with each other than we do with the males. I mean, we argue a lot, but we bond with each other a little bit, and it helps a lot. Look how good the forward team did today.*

Hattrich *Except those big ropes were heavy!*

Starks *It made me feel happy on the* Marlinespike, *when I saw the girls coming together. It was like that time, on our best morning, when we wanted to make DC1 Russell proud of us, and we all got up thirty minutes ahead of time. We went to the head, five girls at a time, and we had to be very, very quiet, because we didn't want to wake brother division. We wanted to be the only division doing it, and we wanted it to be a surprise. And we got our bunks made, we stripped our bunks and brushed our teeth and made head calls, and then everyone woke someone else up to do the same thing. There was so much teamwork, because we wanted to do something right. And as soon as "Reveille, reveille" came on, we were all standing at GQ, and it was so cool.*

Wirsch *Of course, we got in trouble, because we found out that we weren't allowed to do that, but it was so empowering.*

---

*By chance, the forward line-handling party on the *Marlinespike* was all female.

Williams   *That's a good word. We're like all seventeen or older, up to twenty-five or more, and sometimes it's like kindergarten, we're treated like little kids, told what to do and when to do it and how to do it—we're even told how to write, just like in kindergarten. I'm a married women with a baby, and it's, like, weird, you know?*

Wirsch   *I actually came here for some of that, though. I have, like, a real problem making decisions, so I'm learning by people telling me what to do and when and how, and it's all laid out for me, and I don't have to figure anything out, although I'm gaining those skills with the division yeoman job and all.*

Williams   *I know I've changed since I've been here. Back home you can do whatever you want, but here you have to follow the routine. I think that's why we did so good today, the guys were all figuring out ways to beat the system, and we just did what we were told.*

Hattrich   *I was getting used to being away from my family, but once we were able to make that first phone call home, I realized that I was missing it all over again. You get used to it, but it comes back.*

Wirsch   *You know what I miss? I miss music! We haven't heard any music since we've been here. [Others agreeing.] I sing in the shower when I can. I had all of these tunes going through my head when we were standing waiting to go aboard the ship. When we're in the compartment, I'll have all these oldies going through my mind, or I'll be really, really tired, and I'll just have to sit there and start singing some cheesy song, some Britney Spears song, or some Madonna song, and everybody will all start dancing and fooling around, and it wakes us up and all.*

Williams   *I think music helps out the division everywhere. On Ricky Sunday, when the RDCs leave us alone, we'll just get together in the corner, and sing songs, and dance to 'em and stuff. That's a group thing that we all do, we sing. And we sing anything and everything! We sing Disney songs. We were singing "The Little Mermaid" the other day.*

Hattrich   *It's great. On Ricky Sunday we get a chance to take long showers, alone, and write letters, and we sing and talk and just enjoy ourselves for the morning.*

Wirsch   *I was just thinking about that last time. After church I was ironing my clothes and shining my boots, and I thought, what a relief. But I mean—who at home would believe that doing laundry and shining shoes would be a great way to spend your Sunday morning, huh?*

That evening, Petty Officer Dan Kent sat in the RDC's office. Wirsch, Adams, and Smith-Comma-Mary were busily working on division correspondence. "Has anyone ever told you recruits the difference between a fairy tale and a sea story?" he asked. All shook their heads no. "It's easy. Fairy tales usually begin 'Once upon a time . . .'; sea stories always begin 'No kiddin', this really happened . . .'"

RDCs, especially those with a few pushes behind them, have a wealth of "sea stories" about recruit training. Some are hilarious, some bizarre, and some are tragic. But no kiddin', these really happened . . .

Petty Officer Dan Kent   *The oddest thing I have seen since I got here was one day after we had just finished battle stations. The division was beat; most had been awake for at least thirty-five hours. Some of them had been up for over forty-eight. We were marching back from Galley 1128, and we go to make the turn into our ship, and one recruit keeps marching straight ahead. I think to myself, what is with this knucklehead? So I catch up to him, and I scream at him, and he keeps going. So I grab him by the shoulder, and give him a shake. He had been fast asleep. Fast asleep, and marching down Illinois St. That's how tired he was. Can you believe it?*

Chief Mike Lucas   *I was coming into work; it was daylight, so it must have been in the fall. But it was cold outside, maybe, oh, right around freezing. Chief Hennessy catches me on the grinder, so I roll down the window, and he's talking to me in my car. And along comes this recruit, dressed in running shorts and a tee shirt. Now, remember, it's freezing outside. So Jim sort of does a double take and says, "Did you see that?" So I get out of the car, and we catch up with this sucker. And Jim asks what does he think he's doing out on the grinder, dressed like that. "I'm sick of all this place, and I'm leaving." He even had his ditty-sock tucked into the waistband of his shorts. So Jim says, "Well, where do you think you're going?" And the kid says to the bus stop. "Do you know where the bus stop* *is? You'll freeze to death before you get half way."* So Jim took the guy back to his compartment, and both of us saw him at pass-in-review a couple months later. *[Shaking his head.]* Recruits . . .

Senior Chief Atkinson   *I was LCPO at Ship Ten when we got one of those "All available RDCs, muster on the quarterdeck, ASAP!" alerts over the 1MC. So you know right away something is going down. And there's an incident going on over at the drill hall. I take off at a run, and I see this crowd over there. And there on the roof, naked as a jaybird, is SR So-and-So. Throwing rocks, and cussing out everybody around him. It took about an hour to get him down and over to 5E [the naval hospital psychiatric ward]. Guys were ragging me for months: "Can't control the recruits in your ship, eh, Senior Chief?"*

Chief Lucas   *Oh, I've got thousands of 'em. I'm outside one day, standing on Illinois St., right by the gate, and this car with two civilians and a kid in Navy sweats pulls in. The woman driver stops right by me, saying, "We just gave this young man a ride back to the base." So this guy gets out—he has bright red hair and glasses—and I start to ream him, because no way is a recruit ever supposed to go outside those gates. "Just what, exactly, do you think you're doing, knucklehead?" "Oh, I just went out to Burger King. We just got here, and I didn't know if you guys were going to feed us. The nice lady gave me a ride back to the base." I lost it—for the only time since I've been here, I actually lost my military bearing. I was laughing so hard, I just took him over through the tunnel and deposited him at 1405. Now, I knew the RDC that picked him up, so, a while later I asked about him. "Oh, yeah, that kid, B.K.—that's what we call him, B.K., for Burger King. He wound up over at REU. That kid had more problems that anybody around here was ready to deal with."*

Petty Officer Russell   *The best one recently has got to be the recruit who got fed up with the place, and snuck out of his ship one afternoon. Now, there was a civilian contractor outside, up in a bucket truck, working on the phone lines. And this recruit hops in the truck, with the guy still up in the bucket, screaming and waving his arms, and heads off base. They caught up with him over in a civilian housing area, down in some guy's basement, holding off the cops with a trashcan lid and a toilet plunger.*

Not every story that RDCs tell is quite so humorous, unfortunately.

Chief Zeller *I've had recruits who really work hard, and get all the way through boot camp, but just can't pass battle stations, regardless of what they do. They try and retry, and yet they can't graduate with their division. And it happens so late in the training schedule—we give them every chance to pass that we can—that their parents get up here to see them graduate, and their kid isn't there because he or she got set back. The RDC is usually the one who has to explain to mom and dad why their child isn't out there on the drill deck. It's not fun.*

Petty Officer Kent *We have, oh, maybe five deaths per year here. I had a recruit die in my very first division. We were running PT-2, and this guy just collapses right there in Drill Hall 1400. They started CPR immediately, and the duty corpsman was right there, but the recruit's heart just gave out, and he died on the way to the hospital. The hardest part was taking the division back to the compartment. They kept asking what had happened, was he all right, and stuff. Now, we got a call right when we came back, but they told us not to tell the recruits till the chaplains could get over and break the news. That was a tough hour or so, waiting for the chaplains to come. The recruits wound up putting his name on their division flag, and dedicating battle stations and their cruise book to him. But it was awful.*

Every RDC takes inspiration from those recruits who overcome tremendous odds and keep on fighting till they reach their goal.

Chief Zeller *We had one recruit in the last division—man, this kid was lost. Just a soup-sandwich when we got him. We figured he'd be gone in a week, but he worked hard, and his section leader took him under his wing, and—what do you know?—he graduated on time. We had another one in my first division, a guy that weighed probably 240 pounds, and by the time he left here, I think he had lost 50 or 60 pounds, he became a real lean, mean fighting machine. We had to call the ambulance for him the first time we did PT, though. I thought we were going to lose that kid. And he wasn't faking it, either. His eyes rolled back and he was huffin' and puffin'. But he kept trying, and he was a real outstanding example* *of a guy who really wanted to make it. His mom came up to me at graduation and said that she was worried because she didn't see him in the division when we marched in. Well, he was there, it's just that he looked so good his own mother didn't recognize him.*

Petty Officer Kent *The best thing is seeing a guy who, when he walks in, looks like he won't make it past his first week, but then something happens, and he changes, and he comes up to you and shakes your hand at graduation, and tells you that you were the motivation to do it. I had a female with a broken foot, who ran battle stations with it, and who had a cast on her foot the next day. She didn't want to let her shipmates down. And I had one who was shining his boondockers and crying—because these were the first pair of shoes that he had ever had for his very own. All his others were hand-me-downs from his brothers or whatever.*

Petty Officer Russell *There is one kid here who must have weighed 230 when he got here. I know he was 28 percent body fat, because I stood right next to him when they did the measurements. He's not going to make it out of here with this division, but then, he knew that back on day one. But he's lost a ton already, and he'll make it out, I know he will. The others used to laugh at him when he first got here, but now they look up to him and treat him with a lot of respect. Their boot camp is hard; his is horrible. But he wants to be a sailor, and a guy with that much heart—you just know he's going to make it.**

Petty Officer Kent *The payoff in this job—even with the long hours and the frustration from the recruits—is when one of the parents comes up to you at graduation, and shakes your hand, and says, "What have you done to my Johnny? I was never able to get him to do anything I asked—he had a terrible attitude, was on his way to prison or whatever, and now he's yes sir, no ma'am, and standing up straight and all. I just want to thank you for what you've done." That's the payoff.*

*And he did.

8
The Right Way, the Wrong Way, the Navy Way

The end of the recruits' fourth week of training brought heavy rains and squally winds to Great Lakes. On Thursday, 9 November, they crossed through the tunnel for their second boot camp haircut. By the time they returned that afternoon, the slow, steady rain had turned into a freezing downpour.

Ricky Davis, 19, Chicago, Illinois

Man, I live here, and it gets cold around this time, you know? When it rains like today, it's like an ice-cold shower. And when we got back through the tunnel, we had to wait for, like, twenty minutes so the civilians could get across the street for graduation. I was soaked. We all were.

Senior Chief Atkinson looked out the window of MCPON Hall. Named in honor of the Master Chief Petty Officers of the Navy, it houses the base Visitor Center. "I feel bad for those recruits out there in this weather," he said. "They got caught in the traffic. It's coming up on time for Thursday graduation. This time of year, we run two separate ceremonies: Thursday afternoon and Friday morning. It's not unusual to have three thousand guests each day. And there's no way we can fit three thousand people into this building. Usually, they wind up out on the grinder, waiting to get in here, but in this driving rain we're moving them as fast as we can to Drill Hall 1200 for the ceremony. When it's in Drill Hall 1200, we have to time it perfectly, because when we release the people to go over there, it stops all southbound traffic. And recruit divisions coming from the other side of the tunnel get stacked up.

"Visitors will come up to the desk, and they're really agitated. How can the Navy let things be so messed up? I just point them to the large posters on the wall, and tell them that we're in the process of redesigning the base from the ground up. It won't help their recruit, and it's not going to do anything for those kids out in that downpour, but it will make things easier down the road."

The recapitalization plan for the base is extensive. By fiscal year 2008, the command will replace inadequate, outdated buildings, including existing barracks, drill halls, and support facilities. Base layout will be reversed, with separate areas for in-processing, berthing, training, and public access. Problems that the Navy has endured for decades will finally be corrected. Known deficiencies in the barracks include the following:

Inadequate space (50 square feet per recruit rather than DOD standard of 72 square feet)

Inadequate ventilation and no air conditioning

No fire sprinklers

Asbestos and lead-based paint throughout the buildings

Inadequate temperature controls for existing heating system

Structure not designed for existing live load (100 pounds per square foot)

Inadequate wastewater capacity

Inadequate water pressure

Exterior windows and walls not energy efficient

Low ceilings inadequate for fire sprinklers, heating, and air conditioning

Inadequate number of water closets (male/female)

Inadequate number of shower heads (male/female)

Lack of space to expand mechanical rooms

Inadequate electrical outlets in berthing compartments and bathrooms

Stairs and veneer mortar joists deteriorated

Existing lighting inadequate, not energy efficient

Lighting replacement parts not available for repairs

The situation at the four drill halls is even worse than this list would indicate. Built in 1942 as temporary buildings with an intended useful life of five years, they have been under continuous repair since 1943. Wooden arches are delaminating and decomposing. A near catastrophic failure of several arches occurred in 1982, causing one drill hall to collapse. While major renovations in 1984 extended their useful life for fifteen years, by 1998 accelerated wood rot, delamination of the arches, and deterioration of roof decking and beams were obvious. New drill halls are a priority of the recapitalization plan.

Because of weather, most physical training is conducted at one of the deficient drill halls or in the barracks. A new gym will provide a single, purpose-built platform for PT. And because of the large number of visitors at MCPON, the Navy is planning a new visitor facility, adequately sized for its mission.

Battle stations, the Navy's crucible, now consists of twelve separate events conducted over a twelve-hour period. These events are currently conducted at different venues, requiring recruits to double-time from event to event. The existing facilities do not provide full naval replication, nor does the weather often cooperate. The command plans a single, high-tech simulator, designed to replicate a realistic shipboard environment.

Finally, the existing galleys are based on outdated and labor-intensive technology. New systems produce better food with less labor. A new food service system will use bulk cooking and chilling processes, with food produced in a central facility and delivered to receiving kitchens in the new barracks.

These plans might be of interest to Division 005, but the recruits had more immediate concerns. "We were drowning out there. I was beginning to worry about the NQSs [nonqualified swimmers]," Petty Officer Russell joked later.

Sensing a break in the pedestrian traffic between MCPON and Drill Hall 1200, Petty Officer Russell hustled her division down First Ave., and, by cutting through the grinders separating Ships One and Two, outflanked most of the guests scurrying from the visitor center to the drill hall. "We have strict traffic rules as to where we can lead the division," she said later. "Some streets are one-way for marching, on some you have to stick to a certain sidewalk, there are places where you can sing, and places where you can't. It takes a lot of study in RDC school just to figure how to get around this place. But on a rainy day, and with us late for Service Week briefing, I figured getting out of the rain was more important than catching an SI [street infraction]."

The Service Week assignments were critical to the division's morale over the next week or so. Explaining Service Week, Senior Chief Atkinson noted that during their fifth week of training recruits assist with simple logistics. Typical of naval usage, the term "Service Week" applies both to the process and to the recruits participating. "With these outdated galleys, the food service people need nearly four hundred recruits each day just to serve the divisions," he said, "and two to three hundred are needed in other service areas, such as routine cleanup and base maintenance. But that's not the most important reason to maintain the Service Week tradition. For their first four weeks, recruits have everything done for them. Someone gives them a haircut, or gives them their shots, or serves them food. But that's not the way it is in the fleet. It's the same on every ship, from a yard tug to a carrier—everybody pitches in, all the time. If you're doing an underway replenishment at sea, it doesn't matter what your rating is; the deck crew gets augmented by yeomen, dental technicians, musicians, whatever. Recruits need to appreciate that before they go to sea. This is the first opportunity for these recruits to learn the discipline of doing a job the Navy's way."

Division 005's first surprise came when they found that Service Week might extend from four to thirteen days, depending on the number of divisions aboard and the dates of formation and graduation. Division 005 was lucky. Although their Service Week period began Friday, 10 November, and continued through Sunday, 18 November, having two full weekends during the period meant a more relaxed and laid-back atmosphere on many jobs. That could be critical to a recruit's happiness during this hiatus in training.

Chief Zeller explained, "There are really four different types of assignments. Recruits can be assigned to one of the galleys, and most usually are. But others get assigned to ship's crew, or house crew, and are responsible for building and compartment maintenance. Those that really luck out are assigned as 'general billets,' and these can be interesting assignments as messengers, assisting in various departments, working in the chapel, or whatever." He went on to explain that manning requirements were sent to each division during the fourth week of training, and that the RDCs had significant discretion as to who went where. "I usually keep the recruit petty officers out of the galley if I can," he continued. "While I can't be sure what job the general billet people will get, it's a safe bet that it beats scrubbing pots and pans, or cleaning the grease trap at Galley 928. And it gives them a good idea of what kind of Navy jobs are out there. I've had recruits who were scheduled for, say, fireman apprenticeship, who, after working at the photo lab or garage, came back and wanted to become photographer's mates or construction mechanics. So it's good exposure, at least for some of them."

There was a palpable sense of expectation, then, as the dripping recruits filed in out of the rain and took seats in Drill Hall 800 to hear their assignments. Since all divisions in a graduation group work together, they were joined by recruits from Divisions 003 through 006.

James Sison, 20, San Diego, California

It was cool talking to other divisions that were going on service week with us. We never had much chance before service week, except maybe in the line at the NEX or something. We found out that some divisions had it harder than we did—they'd get cycled almost every other day and stuff.

Sean Herring, 18, Chino Valley, Arizona

I had gotten separated from the guys that came up from Phoenix with me, but I ran into some of them there. They're in 003 and 004, all males, and they say it's harder than being in an integrated division. But how would they know, if they never did it?

Coordinators explained the various procedures that would apply during the period. Reveille would slide forward to 0330 to accommodate opening the galley for breakfast at 0430. Physical training, which normally followed reveille, would be moved to staggered times in the afternoon and early evening, so that more recruits could participate. Recruits were specifically reminded of the rules that guided their relationships with civilians with whom the recruits might come into contact. Recruits were prohibited from asking for or accepting money, gedunk, or rides in civilian vehicles. Violations, the coordinators warned, would result in the opportunity to experience Service Week again, and again, and again. "About four weeks' worth would be about right," one coordinator remarked, as the others laughed. The recruits laughed, too, but only to be polite.

General billets, the smallest group of assignments, were announced first. Eighteen recruits from Division 005 stood, relieved, as their names were called. Division 005 had a greater percentage of recruits assigned to general billets than the other divisions present. "Dan [Petty Officer Kent] hand-carried the lists over to the office," Petty Officer Russell remarked later. "He's been here longer than Moses—he knows everybody, and everybody likes him. That's how things get done."

Alcazar   *When they said I'd be the DMT's yeoman, that was the scariest time in boot camp for me. Everybody said he was so mean, and that he'd ASMO you for anything wrong with your uniform. I was terrified. I didn't want to even go over to his office, I was so scared.* When I first went in there, the yeoman and all were harassing me, asking me my general orders and stuff. I thought the commander was on leave or something, and here I was helping him, and I didn't even know who he was. But one of the chiefs there told me to go help him at the copying machine. I thought he was just a normal commander—and when I first met him, he's like a grandpa! He's not a mean man—you have to be squared away, and keep your military bearing, but he's really nice to his Service Weeks.*

Steven Leonard, 19, Morenno Valley, California
Well, I pretty well got screwed. They sent me to the schoolhouse, Building 1127. And they were supposed to have, like, six Service Weeks over there in the schoolhouse, but I was the only one there. I got stuck cleaning all the heads and the classrooms, and then, when I got back to the ship, I had to stand watches.

Guiterrez   *I was working on the grounds crew. I was doing mechanical things, like changing the oil on the tractors. I would go around and empty trash containers and stuff. It was a pretty good job. We'd sneak off and sleep whenever we could.*

Arcia   *They told me I'd go to Safety and Supply. I just answered phones and ran errands. The RDCs can be so humble when they*

*The director of military training, or DMT, is third in command, and is the base disciplinarian.

want something! Like, they didn't pick on you when they needed supplies for their compartment or something.

Twelve other members of the division—six for house crew and six for ship's crew—would not leave Ship Eight during Service Week. The recruit masters-at-arms, Gildersleeve and Starks, would lead six-person teams in the male and female compartments, respectively. Their major focus would be on the deck. The previous occupants had been a ninety-four-recruit division, during summer surge, and wear and tear resulting from extra racks along the centerline of the room was obvious. "Sure, they had cleaned the decks," commented DC1 Russell, "but see, they didn't have a chance to really field-day it because they were so crowded. It was time for us to really get that deck squared away."

Kayne McClellan, 18, Phoenix, Arizona
Me and Ward were on the house crew. Man, getting that place cleaned up was [a real problem]. There were, like, rust spots where the bunks had been down the middle. And all the window ledges, up above where the inspectors could get to them, were pretty dirty. We really had a lot to do.

Ward *We worked house crew during the day, but we had the night off. We folded and stowed everyone's gear, and we stripped and waxed the deck. We put, like, thirty coats of wax on there, till it really looked good. Some old sailor came by and told us that if we used a blanket under the buffer, it would take the swirls out of the wax job. We did, and it really started to look good.*

McClellan *For the first time since we got here, we were allowed to have the radio on, and that was really cool—except we used to get into these hassles about what we were going to listen to.*

Ward *No hassle when Petty Officer Kent was here. It was country music, or the radio went off.*

Starks *Well, 006 took care of our deck in the female compartment, but I was taking care of all the yeoman stuff—the medical yeoman, dental yeoman, and the regular yeoman's stuff. And I had to keep up the house crew too, washing and folding everyone's gear when they were at the galley. But I felt that my job was important,* *and that made me feel good. There were things that I had to do, like pick up records and set up dental appointments, that made me feel good. And picking up my yeoman's bag and just going out on the street by myself, that was great. It felt really good to go out there and be responsible, and to feel free, and not marching in the middle of eighty other people, you know?*

Alcazar *I'm like Starks. I was the DMT yeoman, and being away from the office, going from one building to another with messages, and the schedules, and so on. When people saw the DMT bag— well, that was like my magic carpet to cross the quarterdecks and all. And when I'd see an officer in a car, I'd salute, and they'd salute back, and it was really cool.*

Starks *The worst day was when I got stuck with three watches on one day. I didn't get a whole lot of sleep like some people did, but I tried to sleep in the head. Then I went and sat at the table with the other girls, and didn't brother division's senior chief walk up behind me when I'm dozing there. He got me good! I was so afraid! He's like, "Recruit, come in my office!" He made me feel like the worst person in the world—that if I went out there to the fleet and fell asleep I could kill someone. He started talking about my sister—he knows her from before, and what a good sailor she is—and I felt like the worst person in the world, you know?*

The majority of the division, however, were introduced to Galley 928, the Navy's largest dining facility. MMCM(SW)* David Wisch, master chief for food services, explains: "There are two galleys here at RTC. Last year we served 10.3 million full meals on this base. Of that number, we served about 6 million at this building alone. We have eight serving lines here at Galley 928, and six at the smaller galley (Building 1128) which serves the ships at the north end. Usually, we serve more here than those proportions would indicate. During the winter, or slow periods, we shift more recruits to this building to take advantage of economies of scale."

Galley 928 is mammoth, covering a complete city block. Two hundred civilians prepare food under the supervision of nearly seventy Navy mess specialists. Four hundred Service

*Chief Wisch is a master chief mess management specialist (E9), with surface warfare qualifications.

Week recruits provide unskilled assistance. Nearly fifty masters-at-arms maintain order and discipline among the twelve thousand recruits who pass though the turnstiles for each meal.

Master Chief Wisch continued, "We can move a division of eighty recruits through the line in slightly less than nine minutes. That's from the time the first recruit hits the first food station till the last recruit sits down at a table and begins to eat. The MAAs are instructed to allow a reasonable time for the recruits to eat—not dawdle or converse, but not be rushed either—and we generally can get the division up and moving again about twelve minutes after the last recruit sits down. We've pretty much eliminated the old 'Eat up and get out!' commands, but we do have to keep it moving, or we'll never get everyone fed in time."

The task is, indeed, herculean. While the average hotel kitchen might have one floor-mounted mixing bowl, this galley has several, each positioned to serve a particular food preparation line. Service Weeks pop frozen chicken strips into one end of a 30-foot-long convection oven, and they pop off the conveyer at the other end, ready to eat. The minutes before the serving lines open are controlled chaos. "Because we rotate Service Weeks in and out of here constantly, we've broken down every job to the smallest task possible. It generally takes us less than thirty minutes to have a new Service Week recruit productive in our system. I doubt McDonald's has it down that fast," Chief Wisch remarked.

Edgar Lee, 25, Mazee, Mississippi

I was working nights. I worked in the bakery. It was great, actually. We got lots of free doughnuts out of that job.

Christopher Crist, 18, Westland, Michigan

Well, working at night was a pretty good deal. Working at night, I actually got more sleep than I would usually. I got, like, nine hours of sleep a night. We'd go in at 1630 and eat, and then sort of phantom-cleaned, just to look busy. We'd muster at 1800 and work till midnight, when we'd get a break. Then we worked till 0400 and ate, and got off at 0500.

Sixteen thousand meals means sixteen thousand sets of dirty dishes. GI cans full of soapy water, familiar to generations of veterans, are no more. Huge dish-washing machines, full of soapy, near-boiling water, kept pace with the meal service. Still, the familiar steel pads and scrub brushes are in evidence. And each is in the hands of a Service Week recruit.

Crist *I was the night crew scullery captain. During the day they just do dishes all day, but at night you have to clean up the mess they leave. I had to clean up the Dragon—the big machine they use to clean the dishes. It uses, like, 190-degree water to clean all the dishes and pans and stuff.*

Herring *I was the captain of the deep sink. That's where all the disciplinary cases go. But I was the captain, see, so I got to order them around and have them do all the gross jobs. They had to scrub the floor with Brillo pads.*

Sison *Sometimes they had to "man the torpedoes." That's when they take all the leftover food and put it in this big machine that mashes it all together. Sometimes we had to clean out the garbage disposals with gloves and buckets and stuff. Working around the deep sinks, well, they stank real bad. There were filthy each night, it was pretty bad.*

Crist *I used to work in a steakhouse, and I worked in a Wendy's, too. I think the galley wasn't as clean as the steakhouse where I used to work. When people got tired, they just pretended to clean.*

Sison *Well, I knew the galley was clean before we left every night, because I was the guy that got stuck cleaning it.*

There's an old Navy saying: "There are only two good ships in the Navy: the one you used to be on, and the one you're going to next." Griping is a sailor's long-cherished right, and the recruits of Division 005 were no exception.

Sison *Well, I worked days, and you got no sleep, ever. They woke you up at 0330, and you stayed till 1900, and you still had to stay awake till taps at 2200. So we got no more than five hours of sleep a night.*

Crist *I had as much trouble over here in the house as I did in the galley. See, nobody cares about the night crew, anyway. The house crew is there, cleaning and stripping the decks and stuff, and we're trying to sleep.*

Leonard *Well, the galley guys were yelling at us, like they were the only ones working. We worked all day, too, and we stood night watches, and they didn't. So I don't see what they were complaining about, really.*

McClellan *What those guys didn't realize is that this is a big house, and there were only, like, six of us working over here. So we were really hustling when we had to get stuff done during the day.*

Arcia *The worst part was missing my shipmates! Towards the middle of Service Week, it was, like, house crew and general billets against the galley crew, and that was sad, because we lost the shipmate thing. It was, like, "well, you get to sleep all the time, and we have to work all the time."*

Kristin Dizon, 20, Hayward, California
For me it was the hours. There was one day doing courtesy watches, and I didn't get to eat breakfast or dinner, nothing. I was on watch all day, till I finally got supper.

Ward *It was terrible. Until you snuck off and took a nap. [Laughter.]*

9
The Warrior Weeks

Following Service Week, on Monday, 20 November, the division started its 6-1 day, marking the beginning of the home stretch toward their graduation and departure for the fleet.

Shawn Jackson, 18, New Brunswick, New Jersey
Time had really started to fly by. As soon as we got done Service Week, we only had three weeks left, and one of them really didn't scare anybody, because it was after battle stations, you know? If we could make the next two weeks, we'd be okay.

Chief Zeller explains, "These are the warrior weeks. They learn small arms, damage control, and fire fighting, and prepare for the battle stations exercises at the end of week seven. It's about the easiest time to be an RDC. They've finally figured out what we want, they are getting closer to their goal, yet they aren't so salty that they think that they run the place. I always like having a division in weeks six and seven."

The week's activities began at the weapons simulator. For many years recruits at Great Lakes carried 1903 Springfield rifles, with firing pins removed, wherever they marched. For live firing exercises, the Navy substituted commercial .22-caliber rifles. Many of the recruits were embarrassed to return home with stories of firing the .22 in boot camp. The country boys had fired more powerful weapons when hunting with fathers and friends; the city boys, often enough, had access to firepower more deadly than anything they were likely to see in the Navy.

During the Vietnam War, the Navy chose the M16-A1 as its combat weapon. When the Springfields were retired, recruits marched, drilled, and fired using the M16, just as did recruits of the other services.

As time went on, two problems came to light. One was ecological: decades of use by millions of recruits had left the weapons range contaminated with lead dust and particles. The second problem was social: there were growing concerns that ready access to assault weapons and the stress of boot camp were not an ideal mix. A gunner's mate, who asked not to be identified in this context, commented: "It's easy, real easy, to restore the M16 to live fire. You wouldn't even need the real parts, you could jury-rig it fairly easily. The guys in the armory knew that; everybody knew that. Everybody was hoping the Chuckies didn't know that."

By 1998 the command had determined that the problems of storage, maintenance, and security of fifteen thousand weapons exceeded any possible benefit from their use. The weapons were collected and shipped to the Navy weapons facility at Crane, Indiana, and recruits were spared the drudgery of marching and drilling with shoulder weapons.

This begged the issue of weapons training, however. Everyone agreed that recruits should be familiar with individual weapons, even if the likelihood of their use by sailors in the fleet was small. Laser-light simulators, mounted to simulate small arms, were chosen as the temporary expedient. Meanwhile, a new, state-of-the-art facility, optimized for the 12-gauge shotgun and 9-millimeter handgun used in the fleet would be built on the far western perimeter of the base. This facility was scheduled to open during Division 005's time at Great Lakes, but construction difficulties delayed completion. As a result, Division 005 was be among the last to use the simulator.

"I was hoping they'd get the new range up and running before I pushed my last division," said Petty Officer Kent. "I'm an outdoors person, and I would have enjoyed teaching these recruits about firearms. It wasn't destined to happen, however, so we spend our weapons time at the simulator."

Hopkins *Basically, it was dumb. Can't think of another word for it. I'm from the country—I've been around guns since I was little. It was stupid, is what it was.*

Daniel Callahan, 22, Fort Worth, Texas
Well, I lived in Texas before I joined the Navy. I've seen laser target pointers on 9-millimeter handguns, so I knew what they were try-

ing to do. But it was like little kids playing laser tag or paint ball as far as I was concerned.

Disappointed, the recruits returned to their compartment, with hopes that the remainder of their "warrior training" would be more energizing. Tuesday and Wednesday were devoted to basic damage control. Because of the impending Thanksgiving holiday, this training was limited to classroom work. The recruits spent the mornings in drill and completed their second set of TSTA (Total Ship Training Assessment) inspections. They did well on their personnel inspection (4.8 on the 5.0 scale), but poorly on the bunk, locker, and compartment inspections (4.2 and 3.5) Their RDCs were not amused. In the words of Petty Officer Kent, "It was all dumb stuff, all stupid stuff. Gear left adrift, the forward hold not squared away, crummy faucets in the head, stuff like that. The compartment looked like a P-week division lived there."

Discouraged, perhaps, by the poor showing, the recruits had difficulty getting motivated for the remaining classes. Although vital, these were hardly entertaining. The recruits learned the fire triangle and the importance of determining the proper extinguishing agents for Class A (general combustible), Class B (petroleum-based), or Class C (electrical) fires. They learned how to don and wear personal protective equipment, such as oxygen breathing apparatus and Scott air packs. They learned the basic organization of a ship's damage control party, and how to identify the common tools found in most damage control lockers. But mostly they just waited for their first "day off" since before Service Week.

Stephanie Prosper, 18, Vista, California
I was dead. This was getting so old. I told Jonesie, my bunkmate, that we'd been on the go every day forever, it seemed. We all needed a day off, bad!

After class on Wednesday, the RDCs mustered with Senior Chief Tucker in the LCPO's office. They discussed the TSTA results and the division's overall progress. Feeling that a shakeup was in order, they decided that Seaman Recruit Hopkins should replace Seaman Recruit Collins as RPOC, and that Seaman Recruit Rasco would replace Seaman Recruit Jones as his assistant. Collins and Jones would take other leadership positions, and an additional shakeup of section leaders might get the division back on track. While all agreed that Collins and Jones were outstanding recruits, the realignment gave the Red Ropes a chance to discuss the motivation of recruits in general:

Chief Zeller *You know, I think a lot of these recruits are spoiled. It seems to me that they arrive here with worse attitudes than recruits had in the past. It's like the world or the Navy owes them something, just because they volunteered. I think of them as the Nintendo generation, because very few of them are in good physical shape when they arrive here.*

DC1 Russell *I see a lot of spoiled kids. Some kid gets into an argument with his parents, and mom and dad have finally had it up to here, so they tell them, "Hey, if you're so smart, go off on your own," and the kid says to themselves, "I'll show them—I'll run off and join the Navy." The recruiter takes them, of course—family arguments don't disqualify you from the Navy—and they get here, and they get a rude awakening. Because we're ten times worse than mom or dad ever tried to be. [Laughing.]*

PR1 Kent *I do think we have smarter kids than when I came in, in 1980. Those that come in now have more independence than those when I came in. Maybe that's due to working moms, or whatever. But, in a way, that can be a disadvantage. They are so used to being on their own, and they have to get used to doing things as a group here.*

Senior Chief Tucker *Yeah, but we had a better work ethic back then, I think. And that's just over the fifteen years I've been in; it probably was even more certain, say, twenty-five years ago. Kids would grow up working with their fathers and with part-time jobs. Maybe half these kids didn't have a father or any male to look up to. Today's kids are better educated, most of them are computer savvy, but their work ethic is way lower. Their values have slacked off a little, and that's a part of the culture these days, I guess. I know that you won't find the level of patriotism that you found during wartime, either, but then, the threat to the United States isn't as visible as it was, say, forty or fifty years ago.*

Chief Zeller *I think people came in then with an attitude that they wanted to serve. They weren't so cry-babyish. Today's kids can tell you how much they'll get for college, and where they are going* overseas, and all that stuff that the recruiters feed them. Nobody told them boot camp would be tough, so now you have people crying and quitting. And the kinder, gentler Navy seems ready to let them out if their mom yelled at them too much as kids, or whatever. We're shorthanded, yet you see people leaving here every single day. Makes no sense to me.

Petty Officer Russell Still, I'd be comfortable with the average recruit I've seen here. Not the knuckleheads, but the average ones. Our recruit petty officers—hey, I'd take 'em into my repair locker at sea, any day. But then, for a damage controlman, things are a little different than if I was, say, a yeoman. If you're a DC1 in a repair locker, you might have a hundred sailors in the repair party. You become a people leader as well as a repair specialist. So I talk to these kids like they were going to be on my next repair party, you know. Because they might.

Chief Zeller Well, don't get me wrong. I'm fairly comfortable with the recruits we are putting out. What bother me are the attitudes. They have this attitude, this disrespectful style that the civilian world seems ready to tolerate. They wind up getting away with a lot more than I think they should.

Petty Officer Kent They want everything to happen so fast. They have difficulty in waiting for things to happen. They come up to you in the first week here, and say things like, "We can't seem to get any teamwork going." And you just have to say to them, "Well, these things take time, and trust us, it will happen for you."

But even with the deficiencies that these senior enlisted identified, there's a lot of good visible in the current crop of recruits.

Chief Zeller I wouldn't say they were more intelligent, maybe, than we were, but they seem to be wittier. They have a lot of street smarts, and really good ingenuity. When they come in, if they get on board with the program, you can really turn them into good sailors.

PR1 Kent Sure, these recruits are lots smarter than we were. You'll always hear RDCs complaining about how "some dumb recruit did this" or "that knucklehead did that," but they really are smarter. I'll tell you one thing—they see right through stuff that's set up to trip *them up. They can see the man behind the curtain with the smoke and mirrors, and that makes our job that much harder, because you can't B.S. them. It's like over at 1405 at the "moment of truth": we used to threaten them with jail and fines and so on if they concealed anything. Hey, every one of those kids knew we were bluffing. These kids have been lied to all their lives; they can spot it a mile away. So we cut out the B.S. and just say to them, "Hey, if you did something we need to know about, now's the time, my man."*

DC1 Russell *And even the ones that ain't so smart, at least some of them are really willing to try. They might be a little slow, but they want to move from the rut that they are in to somewhere else. It might take a little work on our part to help them, but they want to give it a try. We normally see it right about now, and you can see it in the recruit petty officers, and a lot of the others. They're good recruits. Maybe the holiday will give them a little break.*

As the RDCs were discussing Division 005's progress, at MCPON Hall Senior Chief Atkinson consulted the stack of index cards on his desk. "Every year we get more and more," he remarked. "I've got over two thousand families willing to take in a recruit or two for Thanksgiving dinner, and they're still coming in. We'll have requests even on Thursday morning, I bet." The affable quartermaster explained that it had long been the tradition for local families to share dinner and hospitality with the recruits at RTC.

"I'm not sure when it began, to tell you the truth, but it has certainly been going on for a very long time. We encourage civic groups, churches, and fraternal organizations to organize things from their end, and we'll provide the recruits. It's the same spirit that motivates people to send letters to 'Any Sailor, Anywhere' through the Dear Abby or Red Cross programs, I guess. It sure makes you feel good when you're away from home, knowing that somebody cares."

Julie Boesel is the family program volunteer coordinator for the Family Service Center at Great Lakes. "People in this community are fabulous," she remarked. "We've got a really good working relationship with groups in the surrounding towns. It works both ways—they pitch in to host recruits on major holidays and brighten up what could really be a pretty depressing day for them, and students from Service School Command and base personnel volunteer thousands of hours for school and community projects in the area. We participate with groups all the way north to the Wisconsin state line, and sometimes even beyond. I know that there are families right at the fifty-mile limit for recruit liberty that sign up every single year to take a young sailor or two for a day."

Thanksgiving dawned, cloudy and cold. Although the division observed holiday routine, and slept till 0500, it was still only 22 degrees as they made their way to Galley 928. There was a treat in store. Perhaps realizing that there would be few recruits available for dinner or evening meal, the galley crew had gone out of their way to provide a hearty breakfast. Pancakes, sausage, bacon, eggs in any of several varieties, as well as the standard cold and hot cereals, met the recruits as they worked their way along serving line 3.

Cari Williams   *It was starting out as a really good day. Sleep-in, no PT, Megan [Wirsch] finally got us a door where we didn't have to walk all around the galley to get in, and when we get there, there's all these paper turkeys and decorations, and a special breakfast. I had to catch myself. I was starting to like boot camp.*

The festive air extended to the usually dour masters-at-arms. Demerits for talking or dawdling were few and far between. The recruits ate in a leisurely way and returned to their compartment to prepare for liberty.

Ward   *Once we got topside, Chief Zeller told us to get squared away and get into our winter working blue uniforms. Except for trying them on, and getting them fixed at the tailor's, this was the first time I ever got to wear the Johnny Cash suit. Cool, man.*

At 0730, when the division integrated in Compartment D-01, the male members of the division, for the first time ever, saw their female shipmates wearing makeup, discreetly applied under the stern eye of ITC(SW)* Tabitha Brown, the female RDC from Division 006.

Shannon Nance, 17, Southlake, Texas
She was turning 'em back at the door. I'll say this much about her, though, she was yelling as much at her own people as she was at us, for a change. I guess she wanted everybody to look good when we went off base.

*Chief Brown is a chief information systems technologist (E7), with surface warfare qualifications.

Under Chief Zeller's direction, Hopkins and Rasco mustered the division outside, and proceeded down Indiana St. to Drill Hall 1200. Arriving at 0800, they took positions in the bleachers, and awaited Captain Gantt's opening remarks. After a few words explaining procedure, the recruits were mustered and allocated to the families and groups waiting for them at MCPON Hall.

Keith Brunney, 19, Foxworth, Mississippi

We left the drill hall at 0900. We had been in the drill hall for about an hour before we actually left. They told us the rules about no drinking, staying within fifty miles of the base, and how to act. We had to be back on board about 1945 hours that night.

After the usual awkwardness, the recruits began to warm up to their host families.

Mary Smith *Freeman and I were adopted by the Elk Grove Baptist Church. We went there and had breakfast with about sixty other recruits. We went off with a twenty-two-year-old girl and her mom and spent the day with them.*

Leonard *I went with the church people, down to the Baptist church. They were very nice, they gave us doughnuts and coffee. We played basketball in their gym for awhile. Then they introduced us to our families. I went to this house—we watched football— they had three little kids. We threw a football around with the little kids awhile. Then we all sat down and ate. It was great.*

Teresa Volk, 19, Manayunk, Pennsylvania

I went with the church group, and then with a family that had two grandchildren, the grandparents, and their son. There were four of us girls, and we hung out with the son, most of the time, and they took us to the store, and it was fun.

Taylor *Well, I went with my grandmother and aunt that live in Chicago, so for me it was family. I went to sleep like, forever, and woke up around two or something. I really enjoyed sleeping for a change!*

Paes *I went with the church group, too, and was introduced to a family, and we stayed the whole day and played video games, and watched movies.*

Some of the recruits in Division 005 had been at Great Lakes for nearly two months now. Many were surprised by their own reactions as they left the base for the first time.

Alcazar   *Going out the gate, I was sort of nervous. I was happy; I was seeing people and trees and little kids and old people. There aren't any of those around base. I just liked being myself, even maintaining my military bearing. That was the first time we got to wear our working blue uniforms, and it was great!*

Taylor   *I shouted hoorah out the window as I went through the gate. Well, I waited till after we made the turn, because I didn't want the gate guard to stop us. It was funny, seeing people wearing all kinds of different clothes, because, like, everyone you see around here is dressed exactly alike, you know? It was nice seeing people walking their dogs and stuff. It was fun.*

Richard Cumpson, 20, Inglewood, California
When we first got to the church I was looking around corners because I was afraid that FQA was going to pop up. We kept saying military things like "I respectfully request to sit down." [Laughter.] I think we even stayed in step when we went to the grocery store.

The recruits had heard their RDCs and others talking about the impact that the Navy uniform can have on civilians. "You'll never have to buy a drink at a VFW or Legion Hall" was a common refrain. While the recruits were forbidden to consume alcohol while on special liberty, they did get a taste of the reaction civilians often have to sailors.

Mary Smith   *When we got to the church, they looked at us like we somebody special, and that was nice, because around here you get treated like you're a little recruit peon or something. But they treated us great, in our new uniforms and stuff. It was special.*

Cumpson   *We went with that same group. It was nice to see how people treated us. More respect than we normally get. It makes it seem like, when we're here, we're doing something important. It was nice to be away and be with people not in boot camp. We had a traditional Thanksgiving dinner with turkey and sweet potatoes. There were lots more vegetables there than I'm used to seeing. They had mashed potatoes and greens. I'm used to seeing more meat* and dairy products. *Seeing that they had other members of their family there, they put out their good silverware and dishes for us.*

Volk *I never had celebrated Thanksgiving before, so it was something new for me.**

In addition to the great food, the recruits also received other gifts from their host families.

Kahlil Dawson, 18, Mount Vernon, New York
They gave us a 300-minute phone card, and all of us used it and maxed it out. I called my fiancée and told her how we were doing. I didn't get to make any phone calls before, so that was the best part. But it's still hard to be away on the holidays, you know?

Paes *My family was surprised to hear from me. It was great, I got to talk to everybody that day.*

Mary Smith *[Laughing.] Me and Freeman fought over the phones and e-mail and everything, trying every way we could think of to get hold of our families and friends. I didn't reach my mom, but I talked to my sister for awhile, and we made some digital pictures and e-mailed them to everyone we knew.*

Alcazar *They took us shopping for candy and potato chips, all the stuff we couldn't get here. And the male recruits—the people wouldn't let us pay for anything—the males were buying everything they could see and we're saying to them, "Hey, chill out already, guys, don't be such pigs."*

Cumpson *We watched an Illinois State game that they have on videotape. The lady's son was the quarterback on the team. He had played in the game and got knocked out. We watch the tape over and over again. He still has a problem with tunnel vision since he got knocked out.*

Mary Smith *We were crying when we had to leave. The people were so nice to us. I'm going to be staying at Great Lakes for service school for a few months, and they gave us their telephone number,*

*Seaman Recruit Teresa Volk was born in Calcutta and retained her Muslim faith when she was adopted by an American family at the age of seven.

and told us to call and to think of them as our families when we're here. And they had just met us that morning, you know?

Ward   *Well, if I ever did it again, me and Mac [McClellan] would stand around MCPON Hall and wait till some real babes came in to pick us out. Maybe a couple with a trailer house, you know?*

10
Confronting Fear

The euphoria of the holiday and special liberty quickly wore off, and by Friday morning there was a palpable sense of dread and expectation in the air. The weather had continued cloudy, and it was 26 degrees at reveille. A cold, damp wind blew from the west as the recruits returned from PT and prepared for morning chow. Today the recruits would face the "Chemical, Biological and Radioactive Confidence Area"—in other words, the "gas chamber."

Hooton-Hetrick *I was scared, terrified. In fact, every time I thought about it the day before, I got scared again. I'm not going to lie, I had been dreading that since I got here.*

Freeman *I woke up scared to death. I didn't know what to expect, and I heard so many stories from before, how people throw up all over themselves, and snot everywhere. But I knew there was no way out, and I had to do it.*

Not every recruit was apprehensive, though. For some, it was just another training day.

Jason Burger, 19, Holmesville, Pennsylvania
My stepfather had gone through it, and he told me all about it.

Andre Grayer, 19, Orange Park, Florida
I never thought anything about it. It was like any other day. Just another day in RTC.

Jackson *I was looking forward to it, actually. I wanted to see all the people spitting and throwing up and stuff.*

Jones   *I thought most of us females woke up pretty motivated to do it. I sort of took it as, well, it's going to suck, but there wasn't anything I could do about it.*

Recruit folklore was full of suggestions for how best to handle the experience. Some recommended puppy-breaths (shallow rapid breathing), others had foolproof schemes for where to stand, how to conduct themselves with the instructors, and how to minimize the irritation caused by the CS gas. One constant theme ran through the folklore, though—it was the height of folly to eat anything you didn't want to see again later that day.

Bruce   *Well, I didn't eat any ice cream or dairy products at lunch. I figured I might see 'em again later that afternoon, and I didn't want to do that.*

Freeman   *Heck, I ate everything they had for lunch. I was hungry after the morning!*

Kelly   *I didn't change the way I ate at all. I figured, if I was going to throw up, it's better to have something, than to have the dry heaves and all.*

Fortunately, there was much to distract the recruits during the morning. After a short forward IG conducted by Chief Zeller and Petty Officer Kent, the division adjourned to Drill Hall 1000 for the drill portion of their second TSTA inspection. The ninety-minute drill period passed quickly, and the recruits cheered when they learned that they had scored a perfect 5.0 on the important event. In addition to winning the coveted drill flag, they were particularly pleased to learn that they had beaten their archrival, Division 006, by 0.3 points. Chief Zeller was ecstatic.

"Gas chamber is a 'danger day' for a division," Chief Zeller recounted later. "Generally, we bring all three RDCs on line that morning, and stay with them until they have completed the course. Recruits are under a lot of pressure, anyway, and the additional stress of facing the gas chamber—and all the rumors and stories that surround it—makes it tougher. Recruits have been known to freak out, or attempt to go UA, or refuse to train on that day. So, winning the drill flag, and beating brother division—well, that got their minds off it a little, I guess."

Hopkins *Well, to be honest, I didn't think much about it all morning. Like, I knew we were going, because Scorsone had marked it on the chalkboard, but I was concentrating on the drill test, and getting all my commands right. We were on our way to chow when I remembered what we were going to do that afternoon.*

Stamp *I wasn't sure what the heck was going on. I had seen "Confidence Chamber" on the board, and I thought, cool, we're going to run the confidence course again. I always enjoyed the obstacles, and it wasn't till we were at chow that I heard someone whispering in the line about the gas chamber. Then it hit me.*

After chow at Galley 928, the recruits started the long march to the Confidence Chamber, located at the far northern end of the base. They had time to ponder their fate during the mile-long march northward. One recruit, who asked not to be identified in this context, said: "I really didn't want to do this. I had dreaded this all along. The closer I got, the less I wanted to go. When we got right by the gate, before we went down the tunnel, I looked around to see if the gate guard was paying attention. If I ever wanted to go UA, that was about it."

Freeman *When we were going through the tunnel to go over there, I had butterflies in my stomach and my hands were sweating and stuff, but when we got into the classroom I was okay.*

The recruits arrived, and filed into the classroom. DCC(SW)* Pam Besaw, who had been with them earlier in the week, was their instructor.

Grayer *We got in the classroom, and I started getting this nervous feeling—not scared or nothing but, like, I'm somewhere where I don't want to be.*

Much of what Chief Besaw had to say to the recruits was neatly summarized in their *Bluejacket's Manual* and the course notes that accompany it. "These days, it's likely that our enemies might resort to what we now call unconventional weapons," she began. "In the Navy, we call these CBR weapons, which means chemical, biological, or radiation devices. While these are all different in many ways, the ways that we defend against them, particularly chemical and biological weapons, are similar. Even

*Chief Besaw is a chief damage controlman (E7), with surface warfare qualifications.

if you are standing at ground zero—right next to the device that lets the biological or chemical agents loose—you can still protect yourself from danger if you have the right equipment, know how to use it, and keep your head. But you have to believe in it—believe that it will work and will protect you—or you are liable to panic at a time when you need to remain clear-headed. That's what today is all about."

Chief Besaw demonstrated the MCU-2P gas mask, the micro-filters of which will protect the wearer against almost any airborne pathogen or chemical agent. In combination with the chemical protective outer garment (the CPO suit) a sailor can work in close proximity to deadly gases for up to six hours. The recruits witnessed a demonstration of the proper way to don the CPO suit, and Chief Besaw showed them how to function in the uncomfortable and unwieldy garment. "It's a real drag, no doubt about it" came the muffled comment from within the protective covering. "But so is getting KIA [killed in action]."

A team of instructors assisted each recruit individually, to ensure a clean and snug fit for the demonstration masks. Chief Besaw continued: "When you get to the chamber area, there will be masks hanging on hooks on the port-side wall. They are graded as small, medium and large. I don't want any recruit to leave this classroom till he or she is sure—absolutely sure— what size they need to wear. A loose, floppy mask won't do you any good, and one that is too small will hinder your vision and may cut off your breathing. Get this right, people!"

Ward *At this point, I looked around, and noticed everyone was getting nervous, like. Even the dudes who were saying "no big deal" all day. Me, I just wanted to get it over with.*

There were a few instances of comic relief. EN2(SW)* Jack Linsey was the duty emergency medical technician for the day. Relieving Chief Besaw at the podium, he began a long litany of ailments that would disqualify a recruit from participating in the event. Delivered with sardonic good humor, and an increasing air of wonderment, the list mainly included disabilities that would not only disqualify a recruit from the gas chamber, but would likely have the person in the intensive care ward.

"Okay, anyone missing a lung? No? Okay, anyone here have a glass eye? If so, take it out. Anyone allergic to eggs or milk?" Sev-

*Petty Officer Linsey is an engineman, second class (E5), with surface warfare qualifications.

eral recruits happily raised their hands. "Too bad, no eggs or milk are used in the manufacture of this gas. Next!"

On a more serious note, Linsey warned the recruits that the CS agent used would fuse contact lenses to the surface of the eye, and while contact lenses were not permitted at recruit training, some recruits had been known to smuggle them in and use them to correct defective vision. "If you can't see too good now, just imagine how you're going to see if the lens gets welded to your eyeballs, eh? If you've got them in, don't be afraid to be seen taking them out. Otherwise, we'll be glad to take them out for you, over in the eye surgery unit of the naval hospital."

Jones *Well, you won't believe this: I was so tired that I fell asleep during the class. I figured, we're going to have to do it anyway, so what the heck. I know that's hard to believe, but I wasn't the only one. So I'm like, dozing, and after I woke up that EMT had me rolling on the floor, he was so hilarious. He said all these diseases you could have, and I'm like, why would you be here if you had those? It was so funny!*

Grayer *I missed the whole thing, too. When I woke up, and the instructor said that this was the only time he was going tell us this, it was, like, oh man! What did I miss?*

Bruce *I had been in the hospital with pneumonia, so I went up to him when he asked if there was anyone with any diseases he needed to know about, but he said it had been three weeks since I got out, and I'd be okay. I told him my lungs still hurt, and my nose was running and he said, well, look around you. Do you see anyone whose nose isn't running and who doesn't feel lousy? So I had to go.*

Quietly, while Petty Officer Linsey distracted the recruits, a cadre of senior petty officers took up station in the passageway linking the classroom and the confidence chamber itself. "There's always somebody who thinks he's the first one to think about hiding in the head," said GM1 Christopher Black, safety officer for the event. "Like we haven't seen that before, right?"

Hooton-Hetrick *My thought then was if you freaked out, this was going to be a terrible experience. But if you just chill out and stay calm, you'll get right out of there, and you'll be all right.*

The recruits, led by their recruit petty officers, filed out of the room and turned right, down a short ladder to the ground floor of the building. They entered an anteroom, equipped with stainless steel sinks down the center and with gas masks arranged on the walls. Petty Officer Linsey continued: "We call this the 'spit and git' room, recruits. When you are inside the chamber, and you have anything coming out of your head—anything—you will cup your left hand below your chin, like this, understand?" Demonstrating to the recruits, he continued. "If you have lots of things coming out of your face, then you will pull your shirt open, and let them all run down your chest inside your shirt, is that clear? Do not let anything fall to the deck; we don't want a trip hazard in there, and if you do, we'll just keep you there till you clean it up. So, when you come out, and you want to get rid of anything, do it in the 'spit and git' sinks. Keep moving—the people behind you don't want to spend any more time in the room than you do, understand?"

The recruits selected their gas masks and waited. Chief Besaw entered the anteroom and addressed the recruits. "Now, here's what I want you to do, recruits. When I tell you, you are going to put on your masks and go into the gas chamber. You'll stand in ranks of fifteen, five or six deep. When you are all in there, I'm going to place two capsules of CS gas on a hot plate in the front of the room. CS is an irritant, but it's not deadly. I want you to be confident that the mask will protect you if you ever need it. After the gas gets going good, I will walk along the line. When I come to you, you will take off your mask, and sound off with your name and division number. When I tell you, and only when I tell you, you will exit the chamber through the door by which you entered, and do what Petty Officer Linsey has told you to do. Is that clear, recruits?"

The resulting "Yes, Chief" was hardly enthusiastic. Division 005 filed into the room, led by Chief Zeller who—in the honorable tradition of "leading from the front"—would inhale the CS gas alongside his division.

Freeman   *When we went in, I was in the middle row, and the middle of that row. So I got to see about half the division take off their masks before me. When I first put the mask on, it was burning, because there was still gas on it from the last time, but when I wiped it off, it wasn't too bad.*

Chief Besaw deposited the CS capsules on the hot plate, and the room quickly filled with the pungent, irritating fumes of the harassing agent. Starting down the line, she elicited the required responses as the recruits removed their masks, coughed, or occasionally vomited, and quickly exited the room.

Jackson   *My mask worked 100 percent, I was breathing normal. I thought, hey, this isn't so bad. Till she told me to take off the mask. Once I took mine off, I held my breath till I left the door. My eyes and nose were running, I was catching it in my hand.*

Freeman   *I took my mask off, and for two or three or seconds, I was okay. Then I was crying, and snotting, and when the chief got to me, I couldn't sound off or anything. But it was okay.*

Hooton-Hetrick   *I didn't tear bad, or have snot, but I couldn't breathe. I felt like my chest was closing on me. I was fine, except I felt like there was a fist on my heart or something.*

Jones   *My eyes were just watering really bad, but it wasn't as bad as a time I got gasoline splashed in my eyes. The short people are lucky! The gas cloud rose up, and Volk and Zaragoza [the two shortest recruits in the division] are going, like, "Okay, so where's the gas?" and stuff! [Laughter.]*

The more fortunate recruits quickly sounded off and left the room. Some were not so lucky.

Grayer   *They put me as a guard at the door, and that meant I was, like, the last person to leave. And when I saw all those people, playing the fool, I thought, No, I don't want to be here no more. I wanted to get out of there, right out the door I was guarding.*

Burger   *I was right in front of the hot plate, and the fan that was moving the gas. Bad spot. It was about ten or fifteen minutes after I got out till I started feeling better.*

Nance   *It was like smoking a really, really bad cigarette. I didn't feel good for the rest of the day.*

Grayer   *After I got out of the gas chamber, my stomach was burning, and it did even till we went to eat supper.*

The discomforts of the gas chamber would later be offset by the euphoria of a run to the Navy Exchange, as well as a telephone call home. Those who were expecting family and friends for graduation began to stockpile small gifts and souvenirs for their visitors. "It's funny," Petty Officer Kent remarked. "You could take two sticks, a hunk of old rope, and put a 'Go Navy' sticker on it, and some recruit would give you five bucks for it, if you sold it in the exchange. Of course, I remember getting liberty cuffs sewn in my dress jumper when I got out of boot camp, and I recall lots of guys buying pillowcases that said 'Mother' on 'em, back then. Some things never change, I guess."

On Saturday, the recruits participated in athletic competition with other divisions in their graduation group. Mustering at Drill Hall 1400, the northernmost drill hall on base, the recruits engaged in three-on-three basketball games, softball pitches, rope climbing, relay races, and a tug of war. The atmosphere was relaxed, and although Division 005 didn't win (okay, they finished dead last), the recruits and RDCs thoroughly enjoyed themselves.

"We had fun, and that's what Captain's Cup is all about," remarked Petty Officer Russell. "Some of these divisions take this way too seriously. Did you see [that RDC] over there, moaning and complaining about how her people did? She kept wanting Chief Zeller to change the rules to give them a break on the scoring. That attitude looks good to her people, right?"

Freeman   *Well, I played competitive softball in college. Tossing a softball through a hole in the canvas was a piece of cake. We beat brother division at that, anyway.*

The Captain's Cup competition traditionally ends with a group run back to barracks. Usually taken at a fairly easy pace, this run is one of the few times that the graduation group, often numbering eight hundred recruits or more, will have a chance to run together. Since the competition is held on Saturday morning, many base visitors use it as a photo opportunity to capture the recruits in action. Today's visitors would have a special treat. Capt. Ed Gantt, commanding officer of Recruit Training Command, would lead his recruits during the 1.5-mile jog back to quarters.

Mary Smith   *I was so happy when Captain Gantt showed up. That man is so inspiring, he's the kind of officer that you'd follow anywhere. It was great having him there for our run.*

Chief Zeller agrees. "He's a mustang [former enlisted man], and it really shows. He's not putting on an act for visitors, he really wants to be out here with his recruits. Some guys call him a 'chuck hugger,' and that's about the worst thing an RDC can say about anybody, but I think of him as a real leader. The Navy can use a lot more guys like him."

The massed divisions took off across base, with Captain Gantt in the lead. A large number of visitors had assembled at the south end of the tunnel to see the divisions, flags and guidons massed in front, pass by. When they came, they were surprised to see Captain Gantt trailing, not leading, his command. But their surprise turned to cheers when they realized that Captain Gantt was supporting two recruits who had become winded on the run back to barracks.

"He'd have picked 'em up and carried them if he had to," Chief Zeller concluded. "He's that kind of guy."

11
Body and Soul

"Attention in the ship, attention in the ship! Now all recruits for Roman Catholic divine services—muster at the after brow." Seaman Recruit Trindade was surprised. Usually the 1MC sounded Catholic church call at 0650; this morning's call was nearly five minutes early. Quickly, the recruit religious petty officer (RPO) shouted out to the Roman Catholic recruits to hurry below, lest they miss muster.

Marcia Trindade, 19, Edison, New Jersey
I volunteered to be the Catholic RPO because church is important to me. My family is from Portugal, and it has always been part of our life. And besides, it gives us a chance to get out of the compartment for an hour or so, and be a little more relaxed. I know that a lot of the Protestants feel the same way.

The Roman Catholic males met the females as they descended the aft ladder. Because of the relatively small number of recruits attending religious services, an integrated group from all divisions would march to Mass together. Today's escort was ET1(SS)* Russ Redekop of Division 006. "We do things a little differently for church call. It doesn't seem right to be calling recruits knuckleheads, or grousing about how they march on the way over there. You might have some recruits who have already passed battle stations and are waiting to graduate, and others that are on their 1-1 day, so it would be difficult to look good, anyway. And, besides, there's a lot of automobile traffic around the chapel on Sunday morning. I'm happy if I can just get them there and back in one piece."

*Petty Officer Redekop is an electronics technician, first class (E6), with submarine warfare qualifications.

Trindade and the others joined the formation, which marched west on the pathway behind Ship Eight. After waiting for a seemingly endless stream of traffic, Redekop spotted a break, and posted road guards to protect the recruits as they crossed to the chapel plaza. A following detachment, seeing the break, sped up, and replaced Ship Eight's road guards with their own and further held traffic till all were safely across the road.

"Traffic on Sunday is a circus, and we may or may not have an RPOC in the detachment," mused Redekop later. "And since we don't carry flags or cutlasses into chapel, it would be difficult to identify who it might be, anyway. So it's just 'head 'em up and move 'em out' at that point. We hate to look drifty in front of parents and visitors, but . . ."

Drifty or not, the recruits arrived at the chapel a few minutes before Mass at 0700. With recruit RPOs acting as ushers, the main sanctuary quickly filled. A volunteer choir began the entrance hymn, and the congregation rose to greet the morning's celebrant, Father Milton Gianulis, a Navy chaplain and priest of the Archdiocese of New York. Dressed in green liturgical vestments, Chaplain Gianulis greeted the assembled recruits, led them in the penitential prayer, and presided as recruits read the scripture passages appointed for the date. After each reading, the choir led the assembly in the responses.

Father Gianulis rose, approached the lectern, and read from the thirteenth chapter of St. Mark's gospel, in which Jesus commands his disciples to be ever watchful. Chaplain Gianulis expanded on the concept during his short homily, providing relevant examples from the recruits' own experiences. "A watchstander has to be a person of trust," he said. "You know yourselves how important it is that the watch keeps a good vigil at all times. Your gear, your uniforms, all your possessions depend on how alert the watchstander is. Well, it's the same with your soul. The devil can sneak in if you don't take care." The congregation reflected on the possibility of someone—perhaps the dreaded FQA inspectors—arriving in their compartments unannounced. No doubt, in the minds of the recruits, the comparison between FQA and the Prince of Darkness was particularly apt.

The choir sang "Bread of Life" as an offertory hymn, and the recruits knelt silently as Father Gianulis repeated the age-old words of consecration that, in the Roman Catholic tradition, made the risen Savior physically present at the altar table. The recruits rose, and received communion from Chaplain Gianulis, assisted by a cadre of lay members of the congregation. After a few brief concluding prayers, and general remarks by Father Gianulis, the entire congregation stood and sang, with vigor and feeling, the Navy Hymn.

> **Pankratz** *Well, I had a little trouble hearing the sermon or the gospel reading. I was in the back, and there were a lot of recruits with the Ricky Crud, and they were coughing a lot. But I could understand the point about keeping alert. But the hymn got to me. You never know what's going to happen—I suppose bad things could happen to me back home in Montana as easily as out in the fleet—but you know the dangers are greater out there.*

The recruits mustered on the only empty area of the drill field/parking lot, and, after dodging the hazards of base traffic yet again, were shortly back at Ship Eight. From 0800 until noon chow, their time was their own.

As they returned, several recruits were chatting in the head, the scene of most philosophical discussions in boot camp. When a visitor wandered in, one asked, "Do you think it's better to be Catholic or Protestant?" Startled by theological debate at this unlikely spot, the visitor asked what precisely had triggered the unexpected question. Were there concerns about predestination? Transubstantiation? Or was it simply a disagreement among budding scholastics about the relative merits of grace freely given versus good works?

"Naw," said the irrepressible Recruit Ward. "The Catholics go to church at 0700. The Protestants don't go till 0930, and their service is longer. Is it better to go early and have a long, uninterrupted Ricky Sunday, or is it better to loaf around from chow till 0930 before you have to get up and go outside?"

The visitor sighed, and moved on.

"Well, at least they were thinking of going to services," chuckled Lt. Diana Lantz, when told the story. "Unfortunately, only about a quarter of the recruits avail themselves of religious services when they are in boot camp. There was a time when the Navy coerced recruits to go. I've been told you even had to get a 'heathen chit' to be excused! But now, it's a matter of personal choice to go or not to go."

Lieutenant Lantz is not the only female chaplain on active military service, but it's a fair chance she's the only active Kiwi female chaplain in the U.S. Navy. A native of Invercargill, at the southern tip of New Zealand's South Island ("The Mainland," she proudly points out), Chaplain Lantz is the most recently assigned chaplain at Recruit Training Command. Ordained for the Presbyterian church, she served as pastor in rural Ohio before heeding her denomination's call for more chaplains to minister to the military. Married to a former USAF chaplain, she has been in the Navy for less than a year, and RTC is her first duty station. She freely admits to being overwhelmed with the incongruity of the situation at times.

"My family emigrated to New Zealand from the Netherlands, mostly to avoid military conscription. While we didn't have anyone at Galipoli with the ANZACs, we did have others who served in the New Zealand forces during the war. But I can't help wondering what my schoolmates back in Invercargill must think when they hear that I'm a serving officer in the Yank Navy. I'm where God wants me to be, though."

Chaplain Lantz, in addition to her duties at the recruit chapel, is also the visiting chaplain for Ship Eight and chaplain for Division 005. "I try to visit them once a week or so, particularly when they are in high-stress times, like their P-days, Service Week, or the night they run battle stations. I just try to let them know that there is someone who cares about them, someone who won't yell or scream if they make a mistake, and that we're here to help them as best we can. Sometimes recruits come to us and tell us that they regret joining. We tell every recruit we meet, 'We can't get you out of here,' but we also tell them that they're not the first recruit to feel that way, and that the vast majority go on to productive and happy careers in the Navy."

Chaplain Lantz is one of several Protestant chaplains at RTC. "Each of us comes from a different tradition," she noted. "The chaplain whom I relieved was an Episcopalian, and his services were more liturgical than mine. I made just a few changes so that I would feel more comfortable, and most chaplains do that. We're not so much nondenominational as multidenominational. At last Sunday's service, I issued an altar call—something that I don't usually do—because it felt right at the time to do it. Our goal is to make everyone feel welcome, and to give them just a little bit of 'home' here while they are undergoing basic training. And every chaplain provides an opportunity for appropriate religious instruction, for those who wish to commit to a particular faith or be confirmed in it. So with that, plus our duties as liaison to the Red Cross and Navy relief societies for sailors dealing with personal tragedies or financial crisis, we stay pretty busy."

Services other than Protestant and Roman Catholic are available to the recruits. "There are actually several smaller chapels inside this building, in addition to the main worship space," Chaplain Lantz noted. "We can have concurrent services for smaller communities, and, in fact, we host Orthodox Christian, Lutheran, and LDS (Mormon) services each Sunday. At the appropriate times, the chapel hosts Muslim, Buddhist, Jewish, and Seventh Day Adventist services, conducted by lay leaders— often members of the command—who have been certified by their faith communities to minister to their members. In many ways, the recruits have more access to religious expression here than they would in the civilian community," she concluded.

Leitner *When I was preparing to come to the Navy, I was told that we would have church services. This definitely is an advantage. I was raised in a Christian home, and my family attended church every Sunday. I was reborn at an early age. I love to praise and give thanks to the Lord—it's a part of me. The first Sunday we were allowed to attend church services was a happy moment. Everyone got up at reveille and it seemed like everyone was helping each other. It was like the calm after the storm. Everyone was craving spiritual well-being, serenity, and peacefulness—a time without RDCs, without the yelling, fighting, and swearing—it really filled me with joy.*

I was happy to see my husband* I was happy to meet all the others from his division and have fellowship with them. Everyone was singing and rejoicing, there was not a dry eye in the chapel.

What's nice about the service is that recruits from different parts of Christianity are made welcome and don't feel left out. The staff is there to make you feel comfortable and safe from "RDC terror." You even get invited to sing a solo or testify, if you want to.

The chapel has been a great link for my husband and me. We get to use a counseling room to converse and catch up on what's happening in each of our divisions. We feel particularly blessed to be able to do this, because most recruits' loved ones are out of reach, and we have each other, right here at Great Lakes. But when

*Seaman Recruit Leitner and her husband enlisted together, but, following RTC policy, were assigned to separate divisions.

services are over, and you walk out those doors, reality strikes again. Spiritual time is over for awhile, and it's back to boot camp again!

Seaman Recruit Wirsch is a member of the Church of Jesus Christ of Latter Day Saints (Mormon). Her parents, Mike and Pam Wirsch, have graciously shared a letter she wrote shortly after arriving at Great Lakes:

Dear Mama,

Hi, it's me again. I'm just writing to tell you about my first experience going to church here.

The reason why I thought you'd want to know is because I know you're worried about me, and with good reason, I guess. Especially when you consider that one experience here, they say, is being put through a gas chamber. Having your baby girl put into a room filled with teargas could make any parent uneasy. However, there is a reason I bring this up. I'm not trying to make you any more nervous, what I am trying to get across is that the church is a safe environment in a very volatile, confusing place.

During the most stressful time in boot camp—during the first week or so when we were still in our P-days—we couldn't get to church. Finally, though, we were able to go. But something always comes up to stop you from going to church, just like at home, sometimes. In my case, we had come back late from chow, so it was already nearly 0700, which is when all of us going to the meetings leave from our ship. We don't get called separately, we leave with the Catholics, because their service is at the same time as ours. I ran up and down and found out that they had already left. I was frantic, and went to Senior Chief Nelson of brother division and asked what to do. I was crying and all, but he was real nice and told me to go to the quarterdeck and ask for Petty Officer Russell who was there in the lounge. I ran down praying that she wouldn't yell at me, or that the other RDCs in the lounge wouldn't yell either. I had only a few minutes to get over to the chapel, and I was really crying hard, I was so upset. I was really scared to knock on the door of the lounge—the other recruits call that "swimming with the sharks." But just as I was ready to knock, the quarterdeck watch said she wasn't there—she had gone off duty. I was bawling as I went back to our compartment.

Now, Mama, you know how hard brother division's female chief has been on us sometimes. But Chief Brown saw me crying, and asked why, and I could hardly get the words out. I had been wanting to go to our meetings since I got here, and I had missed my chance. But, Mama, she was so nice! She left her division alone and walked me over to the chapel, and talked to me on the way over, she was so really nice! I was crying all the way over, and when I went inside I was crying from the opening hymn "The Spirit of God" to the last amen two hours later. I could almost feel Heavenly Father walking, sitting, standing, and praying right next to me the whole time. So close that when I was looking forward marching his hand could have been brushing mine. It was a miracle that there was any way I could have made it to church that day. But it's more than that, Mom. They will take us to Thanksgiving dinner, they send us mail to lift our spirits, call our parents for us, and pass out blessings and hugs for us when we're there. I'm always excited about Sundays, and love to see the other church members going with me to the chapel. Mommy—Heavenly Father is taking care of me, as well as his ever-supportive servants. He is everything to me, and all I can do is try to be a good example.

And she was, indeed.

For the recruits, Monday, 27 November, was the beginning of the end. Although they were still on their 6-5 day of training because of the Thanksgiving holiday, this would be the last full week of training before battle stations. But first, they must past the dreaded physical training test (PT-2). Failure here would mean a panic attempt to pass later in the week, and unless a passing score could be posted by Thursday morning, disqualification from battle stations, and probable setback to another division.

Stacey Williams, 19, Brooklyn, New York
I knew we were going to firefighting in the afternoons, so I tried to concentrate on that. I didn't want to think about PT-2 any more than I had to. I knew I had to get through that or get set back. And I most definitely didn't want to get ASMOed, that's for sure.

Shelton *I just figured, well, we ran on Saturday, and that's about a mile and a half, and I wasn't winded or anything, so I'll just get over there, run, and do my best. What else can you do?*

The final PT test was held at Drill Hall 1400, the site of Saturday's Captain's Cup games. Attitudes were strikingly different, however. While Saturday was fun and games, this was serious business. They'd be measured on push-ups, curls, and the 1.5-mile run. Because of the importance of the day's measurements, a full cadre of PT instructors would observe, grade, and monitor their performance.

"This one is the big cheese," said Petty Officer Kent. "Make this one, and the front gate opens up for you. Blow PT-2, and unless you get lucky and get a chance to try again before battle stations, you're hanging around Great Lakes a lot longer than your shipmates."

Once again, passing scores were pegged to gender and age. The division did well in the push-up and curl portions of the event. The run—which was timed electronically using small anklets that triggered an electronic clock—was another story. "We had nine PT-2 failures," remarked Chief Zeller. "That's way out of line even for an integrated division. What's worse, we had some really dumb failures. We had a couple recruits who couldn't keep track of their laps—they needed to do nine around the track, and they stopped after eight. That's just plain stupid."

The RDCs negotiated for the opportunity for failing recruits to retake the test later. The division was fortunate—summer surge was over, and there was time on the schedule for retests. The PT instructors decided that, if one RDC from the brother divisions (005 and 006) would accompany the test takers, they would be permitted to retest very early each morning. Senior Chief Nelson, who had recently been reassigned as a ship's LCPO, agreed to escort and motivate recruits from both divisions. His offer was greatly appreciated.

Petty Officer Russell *That was really decent of Senior Chief to do that. He had his own ship to worry about, and, honestly, most of the retest people were from 005 and not 006. But he volunteered to come in early and go with them. I thought that was pretty classy.*

Alcazar *I was really broken up about flunking the run. I just missed my time by a couple seconds. I was crying, and Senior Chief Nelson took me aside and got me back on track. I really appreciate what he did, he didn't have to do that.*

Scorsone *I was one of the ones that missed a lap. I don't know how I did that, but I did. I was keeping score on my fingers every* *time I passed the clock, but somehow I just missed one lap. I was on a pretty good pace, too, I thought.*

The recruits had little time to commiserate with their shipmates. For the next three days they'd be involved with hands-on firefighting training, putting into practice those skills and techniques they had learned in the classroom over the past week.

James Troeger, Mountlake Terrace, Washington
I figured that was going to be fun. We'd seen other divisions on the fire deck when we were in the classroom, and they looked like they were enjoying it. I like getting up and being active, and it had to be better than being in class.

The division spent Monday through Wednesday afternoons on the fire deck of the Fire Fighting Training Unit. Formally designated as the 19F5 simulator, the twin red-framed buildings, linked by a grinder, were located at the far northeastern corner of the base.

Dedicated in December 1990, the facility gives recruits an opportunity to fight any of three classes of fire: Class A (ordinary combustibles); Class B (petroleum-based); and Class C (electrical). Additional lab space is dedicated to teaching the proper way to control a "wild hose" (a fire hose that has slipped from the hands of the linesmen). One exposure to the wild hose was enough to make all the recruits extremely careful when handling charged fire hoses.

Volk *That part was scary. That nozzle was whipping around, like, a hundred miles an hour. I didn't ever want to see that happen for real.*

Instructors divided the division into fire parties, and taught them to find, identify, contain, and extinguish fires at sea. The recruits practiced the proper procedures for opening watertight doors, and how to advance, carrying the charged 1.5-inch lines. They learned how to escape from smoke-filled compartments, as well as how to activate and care for their oxygen breathing apparatus.

Chief Zeller *It's good that firefighting training is right before battle stations. The instructors will be the first to tell you—this is the* *only area where there is real risk to the recruits. When you're doing other things in battle stations, it's usually a simulation. But the flames are real, and they don't know you're just practicing.*

By Thursday, all but three of the recruits had passed the make-up sessions of PT-2. Those recruits would be prohibited from running battle stations that evening, and would eventually ASMO from the division. For the remainder, though, battle stations, the Navy's answer to the Marine Corps Crucible, was about to begin.

Division 005 recruits, photographed in the forward area of the male berthing space in Compartment D-01. The recruits worked together in this compartment when the division was gender integrated. *Standing:* Recruits Hebert, Treano,* Leitner, Parker, Buki, Miller, Guiterrez, Jackson, Castillo, McClellan, Carpenter, Troeger, Haight. *Front row:* Recruits Alcazar, Moonyhan,* Nance, Volk, Kyaw, Hattrich. (* Did not graduate with Division 005.)
W. Downey and D. Webster, Navy Exchange Photographic Services

Division 005 recruits photographed during their sixth week of training. Fighting exhaustion, they knew that the greatest challenges, including battle stations, were still ahead. *Standing:* Recruits Shelton, Callahan, Smith, J., Collins, Burger, Hooton-Hetrick, Gildersleeve, Betton. *Front row:* Recruits Starks, Gray, Pierce, Gamble.
W. Downey and D. Webster, Navy Exchange Photographic Services

Recruits standing just outside the RDC office in Compartment D-01.
Carrie William's comment "They even teach us how to write" is
echoed by the poster prescribing proper recruit handwriting, visible
in the upper right corner of this picture. *Rear:* Recruits Pasillas,
Tisdale, Lee, Mills, Stamp, Brunney, Arcia. *Middle:* Lopez, Ward,
Courtheyn, Williams, C., Fletcher. *Front:* Bruce, Orlando, Adams,
Prosper.   *W. Downey and D. Webster, Navy Exchange Photographic Services*

The heavy peacoats lining the back wall of the barracks were
lifesavers, as the division completed training in mid-December.
Rear: Recruits Miller, Atitsogbuie, Jones, Jackson, Broders, Schau,
Treano.* *Front:* Paes, Zaragoza, Haight, Smith, D., Longacre.*
(*Did not graduate with Division 005.)
W. Downey and D. Webster, Navy Exchange Photographic Services

Chief Martin Zeller and a cadre of recruits, each wearing the despised RECRUIT ball cap. The caps would be exchanged for hats marked NAVY at the battle stations graduation ceremony. *Standing rear:* Recruits Taylor, Trindade, Kelly, Hopkins, Herring, Leonard, Freeman. *Standing front:* Rasco, Smith, M., Hardin, Abbott, Scorsone, Dizon, Cavillo.* *Kneeling:* Ryan, Caldeira, FCC Zeller, Pankratz, Wirsch. *Prone:* Burrell, Williams. (*Did not graduate with Division 005.)   *W. Downey and D. Webster, Navy Exchange Photographic Services*

Petty Officer Dan Kent and recruits. Kent retired from the Navy and began a successful civilian career as a corporate trainer shortly after Division 005 graduated from boot camp. *Standing:* Recruits Taylor, Smith, M., Abbott, Scorsone, Dizon, Williams, S. *Kneeling:* Cavillo,* Caldeira, PR1 Kent, Pankratz, Wirsch. *Prone:* Rasco, Hopkins. (*Did not graduate with Division 005.)
W. Downey and D. Webster, Navy Exchange Photographic Services

FCC (SW) Martin Zeller, leading RDC for Division 005. Shortly after Division 005 graduated, Chief Zeller was selected for direct meritorious commission to the rank of Navy ensign.
W. Downey and D. Webster, Navy Exchange Photographic Services

PR1(AW) Dan Kent, Division 005 RDC, wearing the "Johnny Cash" winter working uniform, which the recruits found both comfortable and attractive.
W. Downey and D. Webster, Navy Exchange Photographic Services

DC1 (SW) Lela Russell, Division 005 RDC. Petty officer Russell served as a role model for the female members of Division 005. The crossed axes and chevrons of a first class damage controlman are clearly visible on her winter working uniform.
W. Downey and D. Webster, Navy Exchange Photographic Services

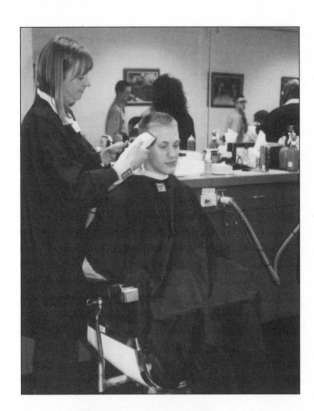

The moment of emotional transition from civilian to navy "boot." Recruits lined up facing a half-dozen barber chairs, and a typical recruit division was in and out of the barbershop in about twenty minutes. Here, Recruit Troeger is in the barber's chair. *U.S. Navy*

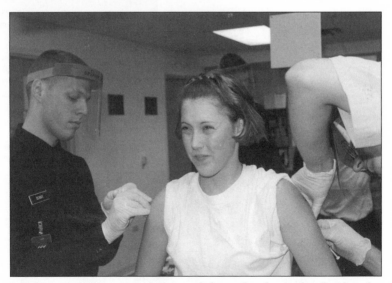

Initial immunizations were administered along a "production line," with each recruit receiving six injections in the space of three minutes or less. Here, Seaman Recruit Hattrich reacts to the first injections. *U.S. Navy*

The recruit confidence course played an important part in the physical training of the recruits. They would revisit the course, in the very early hours of 1 December 2000, as part of their battle stations exercises. Here, Seaman Recruit Mary Smith on the confidence course Jacob's ladder.
U.S. Navy

Both male and female recruits experience identical physical training challenges at Recruit Training Command. Here, Seaman Recruit Nance on the confidence course pole climb.
U.S. Navy

The recruits welcomed performance-based training in the seamanship training division. Here, Seaman Recruit Alcazar learns line-handling procedures in the seamanship training area.
U.S. Navy

Naval customs and traditions were reinforced aboard USS *Marlinespike*. Here, Seaman Recruit Broders reports aboard the fleet trainer.
U.S. Navy

USS *Marlinespike* has been designed as a generic fleet auxiliary, allowing recruits to practice the skills necessary in the fleet. Here, SR Hebert, Abbott, and Kyaw handle hawsers aboard the *Marlinespike*.   *U.S. Navy*

Recruit athletic competition—the Captain's Cup challenge—traditionally ends with a two-mile run from Drill Hall 1400 to Drill Hall 800, at the far southern end of Camp Porter. Recruits of Division 005 pass Ship One, shortly after exiting the tunnel linking Camps Moffett and Porter.   *U.S. Navy*

Fire-fighting training is one of the most important elements of recruit training. Here, Seaman Recruit Collins exits at the emergency egress simulation in the Fire-fighting Training Area. *U.S. Navy*

Many recruits considered the Investigate and Rescue exercise as one of the most difficult and frightening training exercises. Here, Seaman Recruit Wirsch's team is seen exiting the smoke-filled compartment during battle stations. *U.S. Navy*

The mass casualty drill during battle stations is designed to replicate the conditions following the attack on Khobar Towers in Saudi Arabia, during which scores of U.S. military personnel were killed or wounded. Here, Seaman Recruit Caldeira's team takes part in the mass casualty drill at battle stations. *U.S. Navy*

"Learn or Burn" is the motto of the Firefighting Training Unit. This unit is manned by experienced damage control professionals, and requires strict adherence to safety protocols by recruits and staff alike. Here, Seaman Recruit Davis charges the fire hose as the last element of battle stations begins. *U.S. Navy*

Recruits are drilled on the proper use of Oxygen Breathing Apparatus and other life-saving equipment during their time in the Firefighting Training Unit. Here, SR Starks and Abbott, wearing OBAs, advance the line.
U.S. Navy

Recruits of Division 005 attempt to extinguish a Class A fire during battle stations. Exhausted by their night's activities, SR Mills, Gamble, and other members of their fire party advance on the raging fire.   *U.S. Navy*

Most battle stations exercises are simulations, but while in the Firefighting Training Unit, the lives of his or her shipmates are in each recruit's hands. Here, Seaman Recruit Taylor acts as pump operator during battle stations.
U.S. Navy

Seaman Recruit Becky Freeman, lost and abandoned during the Investigate and Rescue exercise in the smoke-filled room, bounced back to motivate her shipmates during the long runs between events. Here, SR Freeman stands at attention as Capt. Ed Gantt calls the recruits of Division 005 "sailors" for the first time.
U.S. Navy

Seaman Recruit Rasco, having just received her NAVY ball cap, leads the Blue Team in singing the national anthem during battle stations graduation.
U.S. Navy

Seaman Recruit Hopkins, recruit chief petty officer of Division 005, leads the Gold Team in singing "God Bless the USA."
U.S. Navy

Capt. Edward Gantt, commanding officer, Recruit Training Command. A former Army enlisted man, Captain Gantt exhibited the best qualities of a military leader, and was both loved and respected by the recruits and staff of Division 005.

W. Downey and D. Webster, Navy Exchange Photographic Services

CMDMC Mike McCalip, command master chief petty officer, Recruit Training Command. As the senior enlisted member assigned to RTC, Master Chief McCalip led a cadre of over seven hundred RDCs as they converted civilians into physically fit, basically trained sailors, ready for assignment to the fleet.

W. Downey and D. Webster, Navy Exchange Photographic Services

Recruit Eric Hopkins, recruit chief petty officer, Division 01-005. The Indiana native was also honored as the outstanding recruit petty officer in his graduation group, 8 December 2000. *W. Downey and D. Webster, Navy Exchange Photographic Services*

Recruit Schelly Rasco, assistant recruit chief petty officer, Division 01-005. Her leadership abilities were evident even at the Military Entrance Processing Station, when she was selected to lead a draft of recruits from Kansas City to Great Lakes. *W. Downey and D. Webster, Navy Exchange Photographic Services*

Recruit Robert Gildersleeve, recruit master-at-arms, Division 005. The Birmingham, Alabama, native ensured that good order and discipline prevailed when the division was in quarters.
W. Downey and D. Webster, Navy Exchange Photographic Services

Recruit Megan Anne Wirsch, recruit yeoman, Division 005. Her ability to keep track of myriad forms, chits, letters, and other artifacts of naval bureaucracy was considered amazing by her RDCs, and her constantly cheerful approach to boot camp was a delight to both the staff and her shipmates.
W. Downey and D. Webster, Navy Exchange Photographic Services

12
Battle Stations!
Fighting the Good Fight

2030, 30 November 2000, Ship Eight, RTC Great Lakes

Dan Kent and Lela Russell mustered with the Division 006 RDCs in the first deck lounge. Senior Chief Nelson rose and searched for a weather report on television. "Too early for the news, Senior," remarked Russell. "I know, but I heard we might get snow this evening," Nelson replied. "That's what the radio said, anyway."

Kent, Russell, Nelson, Brown, and Redekop were dressed in coveralls—standard issue, except for Kent's. Kent, as a former battle stations facilitator, wore dress coveralls, identical to those worn by the staff at Building 1312. Royal blue, with gold accents, the dress coveralls identified "the best of the best." Each battle stations facilitator had pushed at least six divisions as an RDC before winning the coveted assignment.

On the second deck, compartment D-01 was quiet. Taps had sounded at 2000. The only sounds were a few muffled coughs, and the footsteps of the compartment watch, provided tonight as a courtesy by Division 032. Battle stations was considered an all-hands evolution, even if several members of the division— those who had failed PT-2 or were sick in quarters—would not participate.

Gildersleeve lay in his bunk, exhausted. Earlier, there had been much debate among the Nasty Nine, as they conducted field day in the head. Was it better to get one hour's sleep, or stay awake and let adrenaline carry you through the night? In the end, it was a moot argument, for the master-at-arms, like most of his shipmates, was too keyed up to sleep.

Topside, Stephanie Prosper tossed and turned. At reveille that morning, she had banged into Jenny Jones, her bunkmate, as they both jumped out of their racks. Her left knee throbbed from the collision. Let me keep going tonight, Lord, she prayed. She promised herself that in the morning she'd go straight to sickbay if it continued to hurt.

Below, on the quarterdeck, the outer door opened. The JOOD snapped to attention. A team of six battle stations facilitators, led by SM1(SW)* Scott Bowser, reported, turned, and entered the lounge. Bowser greeted Senior Chief Nelson and the assembled RDCs. "005 and 006 tonight?" Nelson nodded. Bowser checked his clipboard. "All eleven events are operating tonight. We'll double-time between locations—the temperature is still about 35, and the wind chill is holding at about 24 or 25. If we get ice or snow later, we may slow 'em down, but right now it looks like we'll run all evening. So, if you guys are ready . . ."

Senior Chief Nelson nodded again. Three divisions would run this evening. In addition to 005 and 006, Division 902, the band, choir, and drill division, would also participate. Dan Kent smiled. During summer surge, it was not unusual for six divisions to run, in two groups. With a single group, battle stations should finish not much later than 0800. That should help avoid total fatigue, he thought.

The facilitators reviewed the rules for tonight's event. Any of three major infractions would cause a recruit to immediately fail, and be returned to the barracks. Cheating, gundecking, or attempting to "beat the system" was an automatic failure and, indeed, would no doubt result in a two- to three-week setback to a junior division. Balking at any of the exercises—the formal term was "refusing to train"—would also result in failure. Stopping during any run, or falling so far back as to exceed permitted transit times, was also grounds for immediate failure. Bowser explained that a recruit incurring three "strikes"—minor infractions or safety violations—would fail, and be required to repeat battle stations during the following week.

Because of the threat of snow and ice later that evening, the facilitators agreed to some leniency regarding transit times between events. They agreed that, so long as a recruit neither passed the facilitator leading the run, nor fell behind the RDC running as the aft safety observer, actual times would not be recorded.

Bowser also reviewed roles and responsibilities for the

*Petty Officer Bowser is a signalman, first class (E6), with surface warfare qualifications.

evening. Facilitators would conduct the events; two RDCs would accompany the division at all times to motivate and maintain discipline among the recruits. Unspoken, but understood, was the requirement to lead by example. While the RDCs were not permitted to assist the recruits in any way, they were expected to participate in the runs between venues, as well as to act as casualties, safety observers, and general cheerleaders for their divisions. Kent would lead two twenty-member sections of the division (the Blue Team); Russell would lead the remaining two, designated as the Gold Team. Chief Zeller, who had drawn duty as the ship's OOD this evening, would remain behind as the "catcher," responsible for any recruit who failed battle stations and returned early.

"No problems? Let's go, then!"

2100, Compartment D-1

The 1MC squawked into action. A recorded announcement, with sound effects, filled the berthing spaces. "General quarters, general quarters! All hands man your battle stations. General quarters, general quarters. All hands man your battle stations. Incoming missiles, port side! Incoming!"

Bowser, accompanied by facilitators PN1(SW)* Robinson and AD1(SW)** Velasco, burst through the door of D-01. "RPOC! You have seven minutes to get your division into full battle dress and integrated! Move!"

Katie Abbott, 19, Pensacola, Florida
I was ready, because they were prepping us up earlier in the evening. I didn't even sleep because I was nervous and excited, so I was ready when they came in.

Hattrich *I slept good because I knew we were going to be up all night. But then, when I woke I up I was, like, where am I? What's going on?*

Quickly, recruits jumped from their racks, dressed, and grabbed their prepositioned seabags. The male members of

---

*Petty Officer Robinson is a personnelman, first class (E6), with surface warfare qualifications.

**Petty Officer Velasco is an aviation machinist's mate, first class (E6), with air warfare qualifications.

Division 006 raced out the back door and up the aft ladder toward their space. As 006's males entered the topside compartment from the aft ladder, 005's female members left by the forward door. The first female members arrived in D-01 within four minutes; but it was nearly seven minutes before the division was completely integrated.

Bruce *I think we were slow getting downstairs because most of us were tired, even those who slept. We couldn't move that fast. And another thing. I don't think we were listening to what they were saying. We weren't following instructions.*

Veronica Burrell, 18, Painesville, Ohio
I think it was because we were scared. This was our first battle station and we didn't want to get any strikes or anything, so we were scared of getting failed or something.

There was additional delay, as it became apparent that there were not enough road guard vests to safely move the division between venues. Kent called Chief Zeller at the quarterdeck, and extra vests were quickly appropriated from other divisions in the building.

Bowser positioned the teams. The Blue Team mustered forward, the Gold Team headed aft. Confusion continued among the recruits: during "dress rehearsals" they had stood at their GQ positions, in front of the racks, facing inboard.

Andrew Krofta, 22, Cleveland, Ohio
There were some people, males and females, who were sleepy . . . I think the time was pretty good, at least in getting integrated.

Xavier Pasillas, 26, San Bernardino, California
We were anticipating things. I don't think very many people went to sleep. We were just expecting them to come in there and start tearing the place up.

Katie Adams, 18, Hillsborough, North Carolina
We practiced different than what they wanted us to do. Like, we practiced getting to GQ, but they wanted us all forward. And we got mixed up with the 006 females, and it was a mess for a couple minutes.

Because of the confusion, it was eleven minutes before Hopkins reported the group ready and accounted for. Bowser noted the discrepancy on his tally sheet. The slow start would count against the division's total score, but would not be counted against individual recruits. He began the formal introduction to battle stations.

"For the last eight weeks your RDCs have taught you everything they could about the Navy. Your classes have been focused on the technical knowledge you must possess and the discipline and teamwork has been steadily increasing as you went along. Tonight is your call to arms! You have drilled on getting into battle dress and handled some of the tools of a sailor's trade. In a few short weeks you will be on station. Tonight you must put yourself in the place of sailors already on station and fight the enemy, just as you will when you 'relieve the watch' in the weeks ahead. Remember that tonight you are on a mission, just as surely as if you were at Valley Forge with George Washington, on the USS *Yorktown* at the Battle of Midway or in the submarine USS *Louisville* launching the first Tomahawk missile at Iraq."

The facilitators inspected the teams, and except for a few minor discrepancies, all was well. After a final discussion with the facilitators, Petty Officer Russell led the Gold Team out the aft door and down the ladder, while PR1 Kent and the Blue Team exited through the front doors. Battle stations had begun.

2130, Indiana St., Just East of Ship Eight

The teams assembled in the roadway. It was cold outside, a few degrees above freezing. A northeast wind blew steadily off the lake at about ten miles per hour. The recruits were clad in battle dress—utility shirts and pants, with collars and sleeves buttoned, and trousers bloused into their boots. All wore utility jackets, with guard belts and full canteens. Kevlar battle helmets, weighing 3.5 pounds, completed the battle stations uniform. Each group of four recruits was also responsible for a full seabag, containing spare clothing to be donned later. The loaded seabags, weighing 20 pounds each, would play an important role in subsequent events.

As a preliminary warm-up, it was standard procedure to march, rather than double-time, to the first event. After a nod from Petty Officer Kent, Hopkins gave the command, and accompanied by Rasco's familiar cadence "1, 2, 3, ahhh, 4," the team began the half-mile march to Building 1312.

Half of the night's events would occur at Building 1312, located at the extreme northeastern corner of Camp Porter, near the tunnel linking Camps Porter and Moffett. After each evolution at Building 1312, the team would double-time to another venue on the base. In total, the recruits would travel 4.7 miles, and, unless ice or snow prevailed, 4.2 miles of that distance would be completed at double-time. The longest segment of the run—about a mile—would be the section linking the Firefighting Training Center, along the far northern fence, and Building 1312. The recruits would gradually work up to that distance as the night progressed.

The recruits arrived at Building 1312. Facilitators quietly spirited away several larger recruits to act as casualties. As the recruits waited nervously, PN1(SW) Ed Robinson set the stage for the first event.

"Listen up. The story I'm about to tell you took place during the Vietnam War. But I don't have to remind you that we live and work in a dangerous—very dangerous—world. You know what happened aboard USS *Cole* a month ago. One of those young sailors was here, in battle stations, less than six months ago. Think about that. Think about how you'd feel if you were a casualty, depending on your shipmates to get you to safety.

"We've made this as realistic as we can, but there are no real bullets flying, no real explosions, and no real blood. The next time you do this, they might be very real. Naval history is full of examples of junior Navy personnel who have found themselves in harm's way and have risen to the occasion and performed heroic deeds. Two such examples are from the war in Vietnam.

"HM2 Alan C. James, stationed with the U.S. Marines in Quang Tri Province in 1968, took part in a three-day engagement with the enemy in which he personally organized company aid stations and casualty clearing points. He attended to each of the injured Marines and was almost constantly exposed to enemy fire. On several occasions he actually shielded the injured with his own body, and at one point he went outside the defensive perimeter to aid and evacuate a seriously injured Marine to a waiting helicopter. He refused rest and protective cover to assure the safety of these men.

"HM2 William L. Hickey, also stationed with the Marines in Vietnam, was along on a search-and-destroy mission when his unit came under heavy attack. He braved enemy fire and moved across an open field to aid and evacuate an injured Marine trapped in an amphibian vehicle. Although he was wounded he succeeded in removing the Marine to a safe area. Realizing that two other corpsmen needed assistance in treating the wounded, he again exposed himself to enemy fire to reach their position and was wounded a second time. He ignored his own injuries and continued to treat injured comrades and was wounded yet a third time by a grenade. Even with his multiple injuries he remained, refusing evacuation till the most serious of the wounded had been removed over a several-hour period.

"Here's the deal, recruits. Your team has been temporarily put in barracks in an overseas port while awaiting your ship to make a port call and pick you up. A group of terrorists has blown apart your barracks and four of your shipmates are badly injured. The terrorists are attempting to take control of the installation, and small-arms fire and shells continue to threaten your position. You are unarmed and have been directed to move your injured shipmates to a secure area where they can be evacuated. You must provide first aid to your wounded and move them as quickly as possible to the designated area. Remember that your ability to use your individual strength and your combined strength and ingenuity as a team will make the difference between life and death for you and your shipmates. In the case of Doc James and Doc Hickey, they lived to receive the Navy Cross for their efforts and sacrifice in helping the wounded under their care. Many of the men they went into battle with survived as a result of the Honor, Courage, and Commitment which they displayed. Now it's your turn, recruits."

The division again separated into Blue and Gold Teams. Several four-person stretcher parties would navigate a darkened wooden maze, painted flat black. The floor of the maze was carpeted with pea-sized gravel. Tunnels, barriers, low walls, barbed wire, and a realistic machine-gun emplacement at the halfway point would have to be negotiated before the teams reached safety. Recruits were assigned as scouts, stretcher-bearers, corpsmen, defenders, and other roles likely to be required by a rescue party. Two facilitators, designated as safety observers, mounted a catwalk from which all areas of the maze could be easily observed. Recruits detected in any unsafe act, or those who became separated from their teams or became mixed with the other team at the crossover point, would receive a strike.

Robinson, lead facilitator for the event, threw a switch on the bulkhead to begin the event.

The entire area was cast into total darkness, lit only by flashing strobe lights simulating weapons fire. Tape-recorded gunfire, explosion, screams, and other chaotic noises filled the area. The pre-identified "casualties," including Petty Officer Kent and three recruits, moaned and screamed in simulated anguish. All were sporting hideous, life-threatening moulage wounds.

Freeman *It was dark in there, and the sirens and the guns and the flashing lights and all, but the worst part was everyone screaming and stuff, and there was no way we could get organized. We couldn't even hear each other.*

For ten minutes, the teams labored to identify and treat the wounded and load them into Stokes baskets. As a siren sounded, the teams started through the maze, often spending precious minutes exploring dead ends before moving the casualties forward.

Gildersleeve *I was the team leader, see, and we got slowed down for a couple minutes on the first part of the course. I went and found this way through, but it gets smaller and smaller, and I figured there was no way to get the stretcher through, you know? So I went through, and from the other side, I could see the lights and saw the other way to bring him through. But we got hung up there for, like, three minutes or so till I got it figured out. It was a real rush, with the guns and the lights and all. It got me awake and going.*

The Gold Team had gotten a quicker start, and the two teams met somewhat beyond the midpoint. This provided a challenge, since they met in the narrowest part of the maze, and there was heated discussion between stretcher parties until the Gold Team retreated enough to let the Blue Team pass.

Bruce *I hated those little bitty passageways on the ground, with barbed wire and stuff, and you had to drag this, like, 200-pound person through there. Collins was in our stretcher, and he's, like, huge.*

Burger *I was a victim. The hardest part was screaming, and getting dropped on the ground twice, and someone kicked me in the gut when they were trying to get over me. Being a victim is hard, man!*

Stamp   *I was a victim, too, and someone stepped on me when we were in there. They put all the big people on the stretchers, and we got slid over these rocks and pebbles and stuff.*

The siren sounded again to end the exercise. Rising from his Stokes basket, Petty Officer Kent consulted with the facilitators, who agreed. "All in all, a pretty good run. Your south team leader got himself turned around as he tried to fit a 6-foot Stokes through a 5-foot hole, but, overall, they looked pretty good." Covered in dust from the gravel, and exhausted by their efforts, the recruits were unsure about their own performance.

Rasco   *I was dead beat, and I thought to myself, uh oh, this is only the first event. I ain't gonna make it through the night.*

Hattrich   *I liked it, but I wish we hadn't done that first, because we were all dusty and nasty all night, then. That dust and gravel gets all over your gear and in your hair and in your mouth.*

Josephine Castillo, 19, Gardena, California
I liked it, except for my knees being on those little rocks, and on my hands, and trying to drag that heavy victim across all those obstacles.

2300, The First Run

Division 005 had made it through the first event unscathed. After gathering their gear, they mustered outside and set off at a moderate jogging pace, southbound on Indiana St. toward the Weapons Simulator. The temperature was falling slightly. O'Hare Airport, twenty miles to the southwest, was reporting 34 degrees. The wind continued from the northeast, but the group was sheltered for much of the run by the bulk of Building 1127, the schoolhouse, as well as Drill Halls 1200 and 1000. Shortly after passing Drill Hall 1200, however, one recruit made a tactical error. Intending, perhaps, to show his "warrior attitude," he sped up and passed AE1(AW)* Richard Rotello, who was leading the run. Rotello picked up the pace, and what began as a jog quickly turned into a sprint.

"Facilitators run in the guidon position, outboard on the front row," remarked ATC(AW) Mike Witcher, battle stations

*Petty Officer Rotello is an aviation electrician's mate, first class (E6), with air warfare qualifications.

duty chief. "It's a safety issue. There's a lot of traffic at night, particularly trucks delivering to the galleys, and we don't want anyone hurt. The RDC runs in the aft-outboard position to provide coverage from the rear. I appreciate gung-ho attitudes among recruits, but that's not the time or place to get into a footrace."

Hopkins *I was up front, but I couldn't see much of what was going on because it was so dark. All I know is that when we were in front of Drill Hall 1200, we really started moving. I had a seabag, and it was awfully hard to keep up. People kept running up the backs of my legs all night, but that time was worse.*

Sison *I had a seabag, too. People kept taking the seabags, and then giving them up after just a minute or two. I wound up carrying one all night. And the run to the rifle range was terrible.*

The recruits—particularly those holding the seabags—were winded when they arrived at the Weapons Simulator. Shedding their utility jackets, they listened as the rangemaster described the scenario:

"Remember, as a sailor you may be called upon to perform extraordinary feats to accomplish any given mission. A good example of one sailor who rose to that challenge was BM1 James Williams. Being just eleven months from retirement in 1966, he believed he should do more and left his comfortable assignment on the East Coast and went to Vietnam as a boat commander for River Squadron 5 in My Tho, south of Saigon. He earned a Bronze Star in May 1966 for capturing enemy documents from a sampan his boat destroyed and just two weeks later earned a second Bronze Star for capturing another sampan with nine Viet Cong aboard. On 22 August of that year he was in charge of a two-boat patrol moving down the Mekong. Moving into what was an ambush, they encountered over one hundred enemy gun emplacements from both sides of the river. At the height of the battle, after knocking out several emplacements, he noticed a motorized sampan leaving the area. Suspecting that there might be high-ranking VC aboard, he ignored the enemy fire and pursued the fleeing vessel. Although wounded, he managed to kill the boat's occupants and retrieved over one hundred important documents. He earned his first Purple Heart and the Silver Star.

"On 31 October Petty Officer Williams was again in charge of a two-boat patrol on the Mekong. Without warning enemy fire erupted from two sampans, and he instantly returned fire, killing the crew of one sampan and causing the other to flee. He gave chase and followed it into an inlet where the VC had laid a trap.

"Now he found his boats under fire from four enemy vessels. At this point he attempted to pull back and called in choppers to finish the enemy because he was overwhelmingly outnumbered. Along his route he stumbled onto an even larger concentration of vessels and plowed his way through the enemy boats, destroying seven junks and fifty sampans. Minutes later the choppers arrived and, not content to let the choppers finish the job, he turned on his searchlights and went back into the fray to completely rout the enemy. He received the Medal of Honor on 14 May 1968. Petty Officer Williams would go on to earn many more medals, including the Navy and Marine Corps Medal for rescue of civilians from a vessel destroyed by a mine. He left Vietnam in March 1967, having earned two dozen medals in an eight-month tour. Clearly he was a go-getter! He also had undoubtedly good aim and a warrior spirit that allowed him and his crew to take deadly aim against the enemy even in overwhelming circumstances.

"You and your shipmates have used the M16 before, but this time you are tasked to shoot forty rounds at the target, using proper safety precautions. Your team is operating in low light, and because a gas cloud has been detected, you must wear your gas mask. Any time a sailor has to use an M16 it will probably be in less than ideal conditions. How effectively can you concentrate? Are you as accurate as you were before, now that the rules of the game are changed? Will you become part of the Navy's history or a statistic in the enemy's body count? Now you must show commitment to your shipmates by giving your best effort in targeting your prey. Now you must display courage in giving your best concentration despite the distractions of battle. Now you must display honor in either striking a blow to the enemy with accuracy or laying down your life for your country!"

Petty Officer Bowser explained the rules to the recruits. They would use the same laser-light weapons they had used in training. Even though no live ammunition was used at the range, any unsafe act (pointing a weapon toward another, failure to cease fire on command, and so forth) was a strike. Failure to don and properly fit the gas mask within fifteen seconds was a strike. Failure to take a proper defensive posture or to score on target, or a slow reaction to other, non-safety-related commands, would result in the recruit being declared "dead." Points would be deducted from the division score, depending on the number of deaths incurred during the exercise.

Petty Officer Kent spent three years at the Navy's SERE (Survival, Evasion, Resistance, and Escape) School at Rangely, Maine. He has a unique perspective on firearms training at Great Lakes. "The recruits may think it's rinky-dink, but the weapons range at RTC is designed only to give them a taste of what military firearms are like. In reality, except for the S guys [SEALs, Seabees, and Special Boats Divisions], most sailors never get near small arms. Those that do—gunner's mates, masters-at-arms, and so forth—will get specialized training once they leave here."

The recruits were issued gas masks, and the lights were lowered. On signal, each recruit began firing twenty rounds toward the targets fifty feet away. After the cease-fire command was issued, targets were scored, and additional groups moved to the firing line until all had had a chance to register with the M16-A1 laser-pointing simulator. At the command "Gas attack, gas attack," the recruits sprinted to the opposite end of the firing line, found their gas mask, donned it, and returned to their firing positions. They then fired an additional twenty rounds, before securing their weapons and leaving the firing line. The scoring criteria for pass-fail might seem comically low to members of another service—one hit out of twenty was sufficient to avoid a strike—but the evolution was designed more to remind the recruits of gun safety and the proper use of the MCU2P gas mask than to teach marksmanship.

McClellan *It was a cool event. I'm glad that we got to do that early, because if they tell you that you're dead, you just lie down. And there's a real danger of falling asleep. If you fall asleep, you're done for the night. So nobody fell asleep, and that's good. But if it was four o'clock in the morning, we'd have lost a lot of people.*

Dizon *Well, I died there. I didn't get my mask on in time, so right off, I got one strike.*

Bruce *I died because I was slow getting back to my booth, and when I got back there, Zaragoza was in my booth, and she should have been in the one next to me, and by the time we got it all sorted out, we were out of time.*

Alcazar   *I got a strike because I didn't hit the bull's-eye when we took off our face masks.*

Hattrich   *I got one because I didn't hear the "commence firing" command, when the lights went out, because I didn't really understand the instructions. They said you could pick your position, and I like standing up, but then you couldn't really hit the bottom target very well.*

Johnson   *We got a lot of strikes about the gas mask. Our team had one guy, Kyaw, who took his off too early.*

Adams   *I died too. I fired okay, but then they said the gas was cleared, so I took off my mask, and put it on the floor, and then they yelled "gas!" again, and I was fooling with the mask. But they didn't give me a strike. I just had to lie there for a couple minutes, and that was okay with me.*

Midnight: Investigate and Rescue

The teams gathered up their gear and mustered outside on Ohio St. Hopkins and Gildersleeve had nabbed those on the front row and issued death threats to anyone who tried to outpace the facilitators on the run back to Building 1312. "We meant it, too," said the 6-foot, 5-inch tall master-at-arms afterward. "No way these long legs were going to make it through the night if we kept movin' like we was." The division got the hint.

The group double-timed its way down Ohio St. The pace had slowed somewhat, partly because Petty Officer Russell had taken the lead, and neither she nor Petty Officer Kent had any desire to burn out the division early in the evening. The group did experience its first strikeout of the evening, however. A helmet had fallen from one of the recruits running near the front of the line, and Airman Recruit Cumpson stopped to pick it up. This was a serious safety violation, as it endangered those running behind him. The division had been drilled, time and again, that any loose gear was to remain on the road, and the road guards, running in the last rank, were the only ones authorized to stop and pick up gear. Russell escorted the crestfallen recruit to the barracks shortly after midnight.

Sison   *It was too bad about Cumpson. I think he was trying to help out. But they had told us to call out "Gear on the deck!" if* *something fell during the run, and to let it lie there for the road guards on the last row to pick up.*

Dispirited by the turn of events, the team reached the battle stations building behind schedule. They were met by PN1(SW) Robinson and AD1(AW) Velasco, who quickly ordered them to don oxygen breathing apparatus (OBAs) and divide into six-person stretcher teams for the investigate and rescue scenario—one of the most realistic and frightening exercises of the evening.

Petty Officer Robinson set the scene: "Your team has been assigned to investigate a smoke-filled compartment looking for, locating, and removing any victims to safety. You will have completed your mission when all of your team is accounted for, living or dead. Your assigned area is outside the primary fire boundaries, and because the ship's fire party is committed to the main casualty, your team has only OBAs, two Stokes baskets, and two battle lanterns available to complete the mission.

"During a shipyard overhaul in 1992, USS *Holland* (AS-32) experienced a spill of hazardous material when a 5-gallon container of Xylene (a thinnerlike, toxic cleaning solution) was crushed in a cargo elevator, spilling contents from the main deck to the seventh deck and into a storeroom. Toxic fumes contaminated the entire forward third of the ship within minutes of the casualty. Most of the areas affected were berthing areas that berthed up to five hundred personnel. The primary concern for the fire party was to locate and remove any crew members who may have still been in the berthing area and possibly overcome by the fumes. Electrical power had been isolated in that part of the ship, making location of personnel difficult. Due to the methodical and effective and quick search of the areas, several of the crewmen were located and removed to the weather deck where the corpsmen could attend them.

"This particular fire party was quick on their feet and, even though fire fighting was not the mission of the party, they adapted their skills, teamwork, and can-do spirit to ensure the safety of their shipmates.

"The need for quick and effective action in this type of casualty can occur in port or at sea at any time of day or night. You must be able to adapt to the situation. Now you must show commitment to your team by staying together and saving your shipmates. Are you ready, recruits?"

The division was sequestered in a closed anteroom, lined with shelves of damage-control equipment. Robinson explained the dangers of the standard OBA. Once activated, the canister becomes very hot and must be handled with fire-retardant gloves. The facilitators had three criteria for their inspection—OBA not properly activated, timer not set, and poor seal on the face mask—any one of which could lead to fatality in a real fire. The recruits donned their gloves, breastplates, and face masks, and assembled by the door.

The first stretcher parties exited into an adjacent passageway. At the far end was a standard watertight door, tightly dogged. Inside that door was a compartment, identical to a typical berthing space at sea. Rows of bunks, tables, chairs, and personal effects filled the room.

Each six-person team removed a Stokes basket from the port bulkhead, and lined up fore and aft facing the watertight compartment. Robinson inspected them again, paying close attention to the operation of the OBA. Although the smoke in the room was not toxic, once the door was closed behind the fire parties, the recruits would be unable to breathe without support. Several recruits received their first strike of the evening for improper use of their life-saving equipment.

Johnson *Well, I took one strike for not turning my timer back to 30. So that kind of disappointed me at that point.*

Several recruits had been quietly removed from the anteroom and had been positioned—wearing functioning OBAs—as victims within the watertight compartment. Unlike in the mass casualty exercise, these recruits would be rescued only once, and would return later as stretcher-party members. Dan Kent, properly equipped, remained inside the smoke chamber as a casualty/observer, assisting MM1 Mike Bandlow, the safety manager for the exercise.

A smoke generator filled the room with thick, black, greasy smoke, and the lights were extinguished. The casualties were positioned as one would expect in a sleeping compartment, although safety rules prohibited placement in the upper racks. Two teams of six would enter together and search the area thoroughly. Teams were to stay linked at all times. Only the team leader's hands were free to explore the deck, bulkheads, and equipment in the room. The others were required to keep one hand on the Stokes basket at all times, and the forward stretcher-bearer had the additional responsibility of holding the D-ring on the back of the leader's OBA.

With a nod from Petty Officer Robinson, the teams entered the smoke-filled compartment.

David Mills, 18, South Daytona, Florida
We went inside, and they closed the door behind us. It was pitch dark. You've heard people say, "I couldn't see my hand in front of my face"—well, I couldn't. The smoke was heavy, there were no windows, and no lights, and the mask of the OBA started to fog up. I had no idea where I was or what was around me.

McClellan *Our team leader took my team right to the very back of the room, and then proceeded to lead us around in a circle for the whole time, like a two-foot circle for the whole time. Meanwhile, Petty Officer Kent is up in the front, dying from the smoke.*

Alcazar *I was the search leader for that stretcher party. I was nervous, because they had us line up, because he kept yelling, "Person Number Six, get the battle lantern!" and I didn't realize right away that I was number six. You can't see real well with those OBAs on. When we went in there, it was difficult, because our victim was in a really hard place to find. When we found Petty Officer Kent, he was hiding between the corner of the bunks and the place where you came in. He was real close to the door, but we went all the way to the back, before we realized that the victim could have been behind us. And he was.*

Johnson *Well, we passed right by a body, because it was in the bunk right near the front door.*

Burger *My group only got one victim. That was Petty Officer Kent, and that's because he was big, and in blue. We never did find SR Burrell—they had her hidden under the bottom rack, right up against the wall. There was no way we could see her in the dark and smoke.*

Melissa Stamp, 21, Englewood, Colorado
I was the dead person for the first team. I was the first one they used as a victim, and that team never did find me, and I was in there for awhile. So, when I was holding the stretcher later, I was

trying to tell Freeman where to go and what to do, but she wouldn't listen.

Freeman *Man, I couldn't hear anything, with the noise and the masks and all, and it's a dark room and full of smoke, and I'm the search leader and I can't see nothing! I got a strike there because I got away from my team, tying to find the body. I went left and they went right, and I wound up back by the door, and that's where the body was, anyway. But I got a strike for getting away from my team.*

Gildersleeve *They had Atitsogbuie as our victim. That dude is heavy, and big—he's like six-six. I thought there was a dummy, he was so heavy, till I felt, and he was flexible and soft, like, and it was, Oh man! It's A.T.! We ain't never gonna get this guy outta here. But we did.*

Adams *I was the team leader on my stretcher, and all I could see was bunks and bunks and bunks. And I was so afraid that Wirsch was gonna let go of my D-ring, and I'd get a strike, because if she let go, we'd never get back together. The only thing was, the team that was in front of us found their victim before we did, and laid the stretcher right between the bunks, and I tripped over Atitsogbuie and nearly killed him.*

The teams cycled through the smoke-filled compartment. Some were successful in finding their casualties within the time permitted, others were not. The large number of strikes incurred by recruits who did not energize their OBAs properly concerned Petty Officer Russell. "That gets me right in the heart," she said. "I've spent my entire career as a damage controlman. These kids think it's a game. They get out into the fleet—somebody is gonna wind up dead from that kind of knuckleheaded mistake. They have got to learn that, and learn it now. We try to teach 'em but . . . ," she shook her head.

Still behind schedule, the team gathered outside Building 1312 for the transit to their next event.

Johnson *Here's the funny thing, see. I went back after we graduated, as part of field day, and man, that room is small! I thought it was, like, a gym or something, but it's not much bigger than this office [about 12 x 20 feet]. It just seemed big, in the dark with all that smoke and the OBAs on and all.*

13
Battle Stations!
Finishing the Course

The recruits left Building 1312 at 0050. A cold, light rain had begun to fall. The temperature hovered just above freezing as they double-timed south on Indiana St.

Not everyone was headed to the USS *Marlinespike*, however. SR Edgar Lee, who had picked up a safety violation strike at the weapons trainer, incurred two more at Investigate and Rescue, and was finished for the evening. He had forgotten to energize his OBA and to set the timer. Crestfallen, he walked slowly back to Ship Eight, accompanied by Petty Officer Russell.

Russell rejoined the division in time for the next casualty of the evening. SR Stephanie Prosper, whose knee had continued to swell during the evening, requested aid, and at 0100 the duty corpsman pronounced her unfit to continue. Fortunately, the *Marlinespike* trainer was just a few hundred feet from Ship Eight, and she was escorted to the compartment by the medical corpsman. By 0100 Division 005 had lost three participants, and had several more with two strikes. Things were not going well for the division at all.

Division 005's luck continued to deteriorate, along with the weather. The division had spent but a single afternoon aboard the *Marlinespike*, early in their fourth week of training. Unfortunately, seamanship training corresponded with the major outbreak of the Ricky Crud. Many had been sick in quarters and had missed those important hands-on exercises. For nearly a quarter of the division, this would be their first visit to the shipboard training simulator.

Stamp *I for one had had never been there before. I had ship's watch the day the division trained on the* Marlinespike.

Adams *I was on watch the day everyone else went. But I thought, hey, this is cool. I mean, it even looked like a ship, you know?*

Marlinespike, constructed in 1991, does indeed resemble a Navy ship. Nearly 50 feet long and 30 feet tall, it is an accurate, quarter-scale model of a Navy auxiliary and can easily accommodate a full recruit division.

As the recruits crowded the bleachers in an adjacent classroom, SM1(SW) Scott Bowser set the scene for the next event. "The USS *Marlinespike* has been ordered to sortie due to an approaching hurricane. This is an event often encountered by sailors on the East Coast, sometimes more than once a year. Often word comes when there is only the duty section on board. You, the crew of the *Marlinespike,* have just reported aboard and have very little experience. Still, the job must be done, and drawing on what your instructors before have taught you and using your ability to come together as a team, you must get this ship under way."

Bowser counted off various teams. About half the recruits would be assigned as line handlers; others would play various roles as telephone talkers, line captains, and port workers. A small group was randomly chosen to play ship's officers and was dispatched to the bridge. The team would have only seventeen minutes to get the ship unmoored and ready for sea.

The recruits filed out of the classroom, and climbed the brow to the *Marlinespike's* main deck. The lights dimmed, and eight stereo speakers surrounding the ship provided realistic sounds of a major storm overhead. Bowser started a large, visible timer and gave the order to get under way.

Nothing happened.

Few, if any, of the bridge crew had participated in the training sessions. Key telephone talkers had no idea of what to do, or when. Line captains awaited directions. Some recruits milled around on the main deck, others waited passively for orders. One line team took things into their own hands, and the members were soon declared dead from "line snapback," a natural consequence of attempting to disengage heavy hawsers still under strain. It quickly became a case of the living envying the dead: the dead at least were sequestered on the forecastle, and were spared further humiliation, which worsened as the clock ticked down.

Johnson *I was just confused. I was just totally lost. The last time I was on the pier, this time I was on the ship. Nobody knew what we were supposed to be doing.*

Hattrich *I don't think our team was very motivated; no one really wanted to take charge and get things going. We were, like, just hanging around waiting for something to happen. I was a telephone talker at the aft end, and I was trying to tell both teams things I had remembered, but they were just standing there.*

Shari Courtheyn, 19, Minerva, Ohio
Nobody knew what to do! No one knew how to bring in the line, and get it manned and ready.

Leitner *Well, they made me a telephone talker down on the deck, but the guy up on the bridge never did connect his phone, so I'm talking and talking, and there isn't anyone answering. I knew my phone was working, because I could hear the team on the aft end, but nothing from the bridge. Come to find out, they never plugged in their phone up there.*

Gildersleeve *Well, shoot, man. See, I didn't get a chance to do it before, because I was light limited duty when we were on it the last time. And didn't the man put me up in the house, and make me telephone talker. I didn't know what I was supposed to be doing, or anything. I'm just standing up there, like, I don't know, just standing up there.*

McClellan *When they had about four or five minutes left, and I had gotten a strike for allowing my knee to touch the nonskid surface of the deck, and everyone was standing there with their thumbs up their [butts], I knew it was gonna be a long evening.*

Tasheka Gamble, 19, Mounds, Illinois
By then, I wasn't worried about getting the ship under way. I was just worried that if they were going to make us sprint again, and not jog, that I wasn't going to make it and I'd fail battle stations. For me, thinking that was the worst part.

Kent and Russell looked on in dismay and disbelief from the bleachers adjacent to the mockup. The clock continued its race to zero, and when the seventeen minutes had expired, the ship was still snugly in port. Division 005 had failed the evolution.

BMC(SW)* Adam Beller is leading chief of the Seamanship Training Division. Interviewed later, he explained, "Actually, it's not unusual for divisions to fail the *Marlinespike* exercise during battle stations. We know we have two major difficulties to overcome. Because of the large number of recruits who cycle through the *Marlinespike*, most divisions get less than a single afternoon of training on board. And because of the heavy training schedule these recruits undertake, that training happens during their fourth week here. By the time they've gone through Service Week, the gas house, firefighting and their PT tests, many of them have forgotten what they've learned. We're aware of the problem, and are trying to move seamanship training later in the training cycle."

Kent and Russell mustered the division in the passageway. "What's the matter with you people!" Kent shouted. "That was the worst thing I've ever seen. I'm ashamed of you, I really am. You guys don't deserve to pass battle stations, you know that? Now get outside. We're going for a little run."

Trenton Kessimakis, 20, Salt Lake City, Utah
When we blew the exercise, Petty Officer Kent was going, like, "Awwww," like he was mad because we didn't know what to do.

Adams *Petty Officer Russell was so mad after the* Marlinespike, *she and the other petty officer made us sprint all the way back to the battle stations building. But I figured it wasn't our fault if people hadn't been there before, you know?*

0200, Building 1312

Rasco *We took off so fast I couldn't even get a cadence or chant going. Petty Officer Russell took off; we took off; Petty Officer Kent was shouting for us to sing, to sing anything, even the "Dog Song" that he hated so much, but we were moving so fast we couldn't get it started. We were flying.*

*Chief Beller is a chief boatswain's mate (E7), with surface warfare qualifications.

The RDCs led the division north on Ohio St., the eastern-most road on base. Adjacent to the perimeter fence, it was unshielded from the 15-mile-per-hour wind blowing in from Lake Michigan. The temperature had dropped below freezing, and the misting rain had changed to sleet.

Mary Smith *It was brutal. I was cold, I was wet, the sleet was blowing in my face, and I was carrying a seabag. My knees were killing me, my boots were rubbing my feet raw. Looking back on it, that was the low point. That was the point where I nearly dropped out and quit.*

Guiterrez *I had a seabag too, and nobody wanted to take it from me. I'm from southern California—we don't get weather like this back there. I just ducked my head down as far as I could and ran. The seabag was riding up on my shoulders hitting the back of my helmet. Some of the females were crying, I know. But we all kept going.*

They arrived once again at Building 1312. Many battle stations events were designed to call to mind the deeds of Navy heroes; the next event was designed to remind them of the mundane tasks that every sailor does each day.

As the recruits gradually got their breath back from their accelerated transit, Petty Officer Bandlow began the story. "As part of the preparations for getting under way, a ship must be loaded with stores, repair parts for equipment, fuel, ammunition, and food. In short, everything must be loaded to support sustained operations at sea. Due to the amount of stores arriving on the pier in large bulk quantities, and often at the same time, loading is frequently an all-hands evolution. The ability of a crew to quickly stow stores is essential to meet underway timelines. Additionally, time is of the essence in preserving perishable food stores. On-loads are critical to a ship's mission accomplishment.

"History provides countless examples of operations hingeing on rapid loading of required stores so that personnel could return to their areas of responsibility to accomplish other critical underway preparations. On 19 August 1994, USS *Stark*, a guided missile frigate, was on patrol off the coast of Haiti in support of Operation Support Democracy. While routinely en route to Guantanamo Bay, for a brief stop for fuel and stores, the ship was directed late at night to proceed at best speed to moor pierside at first light. The ship was to be loaded with required stores and food as rapidly as possible, and depart for the Straits of Florida with all due haste to subsequently conduct Cuban refugee operations. As the ship moored, the pier was filled with stores to support taking aboard hundreds of refugees who were fleeing from Cuba on floating contraptions of all sorts, including rubber innertubes, makeshift rafts, and anything that would float on the sea. Many of these refugees had little chance of completing their escape on those fragile craft. Stores and fuel had to be loaded expeditiously to allow an underway time at the earliest opportunity. The clock was running. Time was of the essence."

Bandlow led the group into the exercise area. Before them stood a large quantity of supplies: ammunition boxes, pipe, rope, timber, spare parts, and other materials common to everyday shipboard life. Many of the boxes were marked "Heavy—two man carry." Between the stores and their final destination lay an obstacle course that simulated the route that sailors might take when replenishing ship. There were ladders to climb, tight passageways, watertight doorsills to overcome, hatches, and scuttles.

Midway through the obstacle course, the recruits would encounter a simulated hangar deck, complete with yellow avaition-support vehicles. The remainder of the obstacle course resembled a hold deep inside a combat ship. Ramps, wooden battens, balks of timber, and a tight U-turn confronted the stores handlers.

Bandlow split the division into two teams. The first team would carry the stores to a watertight doorway halfway through the course, where they would be handed off to the second team. The second group would complete the course and stow the materials in accordance with a printed storage plan. The group was given thirty-five minutes to complete the evolution, and strikes would be assessed for violations such as failing to observe two-person-lift requirements, dropping materials, or committing safety infractions. A siren signaled the beginning of the exercise.

Zuni Robinson, 19, Philadelphia, Pennsylvania

Oh my gosh, I didn't like that at all! My body was so tired, from the run and stuff, and that was our fourth or fifth thing, and I was, like, so tired. And then we had to lift these heavy cans, and my hands were getting callouses, and everyone wanted to double-time, and I couldn't because my legs were so tired.

Leitner *I didn't like that at all! I was tired, and the stuff was heavy.*

Dizon *I think the problem at first was our teamwork. Some people would get stuff, others would just mill around, and we weren't working together very well.*

Joshua Smith, 21, Fort Morgan, Colorado
I was right in front of Russell the whole time, and I knew she was pretty mad about the way things went on the Marlinespike. *So we just hustled the whole time, and really moved.*

Orlando *If the males had listened to us, we would have gotten it done easier and faster. They just jumped in and started carrying stuff. But we figured out that if we went in a circle, and handed stuff to each other, we could do it better. They kept running into each other and us, and that slowed things down some. But they finally listened to us, and then it went lots faster.*

Stamp *I thought that was fun. But then, I was the team leader and all I carried was a clipboard!*

Perhaps motivated by the dismal failure aboard *Marlinespike*, the group performed well during the store-loading exercise. All material was moved and properly stored by the twenty-ninth minute. Petty Officer Russell, who was observing the stowage portion of the event, nodded appreciatively. "You get an additional head call for that, recruits, but make it fast. We're going for a little swim."

0300, Water Safety Training Center

By 0300 things were beginning to go Division 005's way. The aggravating sleet, which had plagued the recruits on the run from the *Marlinespike*, had turned to light snow. The temperature was just 29 degrees—the lowest it would go all night—but conditions had improved overall.

And some respite was in store for the recruits. Building 1312 is just a few yards from the pedestrian tunnel linking

Camps Porter and Moffett. The recruits would have to go through the tunnel to reach the swimming pool in building 1425. And base safety rules prohibited running in the tunnel. They'd make two round trips through the tunnel during battle stations—a welcome break from the jogging or sprinting the facilitators required between other venues.

Scorsone *That tunnel saved me, more than once. I'm not all that fast to begin with, and the weather kept getting worse and worse, and when we came to the entrance of the tunnel and Petty Officer Kent gave the command to break step, it was, like, heaven.*

Leitner *I kept falling farther and farther behind as we ran. I'm thirty-five years old—I'd start out at the front, and keep slipping back as these kids passed me by. But at the tunnel, I'd walk as fast as I could, and get back up into the middle or front of the pack before we started running again. They were able to take it easy through the tunnel, but I kept moving as fast as I could walk, and that's what saved me.*

The division arrived at Building 1425, only to find the main door locked. They had trained at the multimillion-dollar, Olympic-sized pool, which, tonight, was closed for maintenance. After milling about in the gently falling snow, they found the entrance to the smaller, older pool at the eastern end of the building. More surprises awaited them within.

Jones *As soon as we got in there, we changed into our swim suits. They made us put on these old utility pants over our suits— mine were huge! There was no way I could walk in them without holding up the waistband. And they were wet—soaking wet—and freezing!*

HT1(SW)* Jim Lilly set the scene. "Naval history contains many stories of ships that, despite the best efforts of the crew, succumbed to enemy fire and sank. Take the case of the USS *Indianapolis*, a World War II heavy cruiser en route to Leyte Gulf, Philippines, without escorts. Shortly after midnight on 30 July 1944, a Japanese submarine attacked the ship with a salvo of torpedoes. Two ripped into the ship's forward hull, causing

*Petty Officer Lilly is a hull maintenance technician, first class (E6), with surface warfare qualifications.

catastrophic damage and disabling the communications systems. The bridge was not able to send an 'all stop' order to engineering, and the ship continued to plow through the water, accelerating the flooding. The captain was forced to give the 'abandon ship' order. *Indianapolis* sank only thirteen minutes after the initial blast. Of the 1,196-man crew, only 850 were able to abandon ship before the ship went under. These sailors found themselves scattered over thousands of yards, amid an oil slick and small pieces of debris, with only a couple of life rafts.

"Shark attacks commenced early the next morning, and continued throughout the five-day ordeal until rescue forces arrived on the scene. As the days wore on, many sailors began suffering from the effects of shock, dehydration, and delirium. In some cases the crew did everything right: they grouped together, organized, established a chain of command, pooled their resources, and so on. Many of these sailors survived, despite severe injuries and shark attacks. In other cases, crew members did not remember their basic training, and made several critical mistakes. Sailors who drifted away from their shipmates were very susceptible to shark attach. Some refused to follow orders and committed foolish acts, like drinking seawater. Many became delirious and tried to swim to imaginary islands or down to their sunken ship. Those who forgot their training were doomed. The final headcount summarizes the story well: only 317 of the original 1,196 crew members survived.

"Now, recruits, place yourself in a similar situation. Your ship is on patrol in the South China Sea when it sustains extensive hull damage. After a valiant attempt to save the vessel, the captain determines that the damage is too great and gives the order to abandon ship. As you prepare to transit to your 'abandon ship' station, you notice that there are not enough life preservers for everyone in your team—you must decide who gets one and who does not. After donning your life preservers, proceed to the top of the platform and await further instructions."

Hopkins *There was a pile of life preservers on the ground, and they told us to put them on. Someone—I think it was Freeman—yelled out to save the life preservers for the people that couldn't swim too well—those that were NQSs and such. Some people listened to her, and some just grabbed them and put them on. I was going to take one—I was in the front of the line—but I knew that I* *could swim as well as anyone, so I took one and gave it to Gilder-sleeve, who was right behind me.*

The recruits climbed the 10-foot diving platform. At this point, the battle stations facilitators yielded control of the division to a cadre of water safety instructors, headed by Chief Dave Gardner. In addition to their roles as safety monitors during the exercise, the swimming instructors would act as "sharks," making each evolution more difficult by delaying, inconveniencing, and generally harassing the swimming recruits. Some even wore Styrofoam "fins" strapped to their backs, to heighten the effect. Petty Officer Kent changed into his swim suit, and joined in the fun.

Recruits waited at the top of the platform and, when instructed, stepped off and abandoned ship. The recruits knew that sharks were circling below, and that they must swim across the pool and enter a standard Navy life raft, which was tethered at the far end. After entering, they were to exit through the aft end, swim to the side, and exit the pool area. Strikes would be assessed for water safety violations, including entering the raft headfirst, or for those swimmers who could not make it to the raft without assistance. The first recruits stepped off the tower and into the surprisingly warm water below.

Freeman *I liked the swim, that was fun. And I didn't mind the instructors dunking us and splashing water—it was just like being at home in Louisiana messing with the guys and all. But when you put those pants on, geez! They were freezing cold! Even the warm water didn't help much. As soon as I got out I was freezing again, and I stayed cold the rest of the night. And when we went outside and saw the snow was falling harder, it was, oh, man! just our luck.*

Bruce *I thought it was stupid. We had to put on these pants that were a million sizes too big, and they had been used by the last bunch of recruits that went through, and they were wringing wet and they were freezing! And all we did was jump off the tower, swim around for a minute or two, and get into the life raft, and then get out. But as soon as we got out, we were freezing again! And then we had to quickly get dressed and get back outside, and it was snowing harder by then. That's the coldest I've even been in my life!*

Hattrich   *I put on the vest, because it was the last one and no one was going to take it. I could swim, so when I got into the water, I held onto the side of the raft till some of the others got in. I guess the facilitators were picking on the people in the vests, because they kept dunking me, and splashing water in my face for, like, two minutes straight so I couldn't get any air, and I was stressing out.*

Alcazar   *I was the one holding onto the raft, and Hattrich was holding onto my arm, and when the "sharks" were dunking her I was wondering if, like, she could breathe, and the splashing was getting into my mouth and nose. I wanted to yell at them to stop it.*

Leitner   *I had a hard time trying to do an underwater push-up, trying to get into the boat and all.*

Gildersleeve   *When I kept going to the raft, my legs kept kicking and going under the raft, and one of the instructors kept dunking me. He did this, like, three times, and I figured I better get into that boat. And I couldn't get into that boat, and I saw Petty Officer Russell on the deck, and she's laughing at me, cause I was an NQS and she used to rag on me all the time about having to go to swimming classes and all. But it's hard, man, getting into that life raft with three or four instructors grabbing your legs and your arms and trying to drown you and all.*

Johnson   *I got another strike there because the instructor said I went into the raft headfirst, but I didn't, I know I didn't.*

McClellan   *He didn't go in headfirst. I was the team leader on the front end of the raft, and I know he didn't. But the instructor said he did, and there is no way to argue with them in the middle of battle stations, that's for sure.*

Shelton   *I'm swimming over toward the raft, and it's going okay, because all the sharks are off attacking people with life vests on. And as I swim by, I see Petty Officer Kent, just lolling there, doing a backstroke, and he says, "How's it going, Shelton?" I mean— we've abandoned ship, right? And there's all this yelling and screaming and splashing going on, and guys getting eaten up by sharks, and me and him are having a conversation, like two dudes who meet on the street. Awesome.*

Although several recruits did incur additional strikes during the event, no one was disqualified, and after drying off to the best of their ability, the recruits prepared to return to Camp Porter.

0400, Camp Moffett

It was snowing more heavily as Division 005 left the pool and prepared to return to Building 1312. Curiously, even though most of the recruits were cold, wet, and immensely uncomfortable, there was a perceptible change of attitude.

Gildersleeve *We knew we were halfway there, see. From what people had said, the worst part was done. Me, personally, I'd been worried about the pool. I had never been swimming till I came to boot camp. Once that was done, it was, like, we're going home.*

Leitner *I noticed it, too. I think it was because we usually get up at four in the morning. And there's a rhythm your body gets into. From then on it felt like morning to me, even though it was still dark outside.*

The run back to Camp Porter was uneventful. Snow was beginning to stick on the grassy areas, but not on the roadways. Passing Building 1405, the Recruit In-processing Center, Division 005 broke into a heartfelt chant for the first time this evening.

Rasco *I started the chant, and Gildersleeve picked up on it. We usually sing, "PT, PT, good for you and good for me," but Gildersleeve changed it to "Battle stations, battle stations, look at me, look at me." I hope the Smurfs could hear us, in there, on their first night at boot camp.*

14

Battle Stations!
Keeping Faith

Unknown to the recruits, their next two events were to be at Building 1312, and the group would not run again until nearly 0630. Neither of the events still facing the division was particularly physically taxing, although both would call for a great deal of coordinated effort if the group was to be successful.

AD1(AW) Rogelio Velasco joined the division after they had stowed their now dripping outer garments. "As you should remember from your damage-control classes, in July 1967 a bomb dropped on the flight deck of the USS *Forestal*. The resulting fire spread below to the hangar deck and ultimately resulted in the deaths of 134 sailors and injury to hundreds of others. You will remember the footage you saw of the chief who made an early attempt to attack the fire and entered the scene with an extinguisher. Unfortunately, he never came out—he gave his life in the attempt. What you couldn't see was the hundreds of sailors who were trapped below who had to find a way to fresh air and safety. Fire is unforgiving at sea, and any ship can become a floating torch with countless flammable hazards to feed the fire. Even if you aren't directly fighting the fire, you may find yourself cut off and have to rely on your shipmates to help you survive.

"You and your shipmates must get from one compartment to another. The only way to get there from here is through an emergency escape scuttle located in a redhot bulkhead. Each member of the team must make it through without touching the sides or they will be severely burned. Only confidence in each one of your shipmates will make it possible to overcome this obstacle. You must show commitment to the team effort in lending your ideas and accepting those of others. You must display courage in trusting your shipmates to help you get to safety. You must display honor in giving your personal best in order for the whole team to escape harm's way."

The recruits were led to a large compartment, divided by a gray steel bulkhead. A round escape scuttle, about 30 inches in diameter, was cut at the 6-foot level. Black light shone down on fluorescent paint, causing the escape scuttle to glow ominously red. Hot water flowed through pipes within the steel cladding. The wall was noticeably warm, if not dangerously hot, to the touch. Velasco laid out the safety rules for the team, violation of which would result in a strike or disqualification. "If you touch the bulkhead, even for a second, you lose a limb. Anything you do afterwards will have to be minus that arm or leg. Touch it for three seconds, and you're dead. No one may pass another recruit through the scuttle face up, nor may anyone attempt a running jump through the scuttle. Do either of those, and you're done for the night. You have twenty minutes to get everyone to safety."

The recruits began an earnest discussion. For the first time, ad-hoc leaders began to assert themselves.

Fred Atitsogbuie, 19, Bronx, New York
I said, "Let us big guys go through first while there's still enough people to load us through from the front side."

Hattrich   *But we actually had a hint on that one before battle stations. We had a shipmate who had already been through battle stations who told us to put an empty seabag on the hole to protect us against the heat, so that's what we did. I could still feel the heat from the wall as I went through, though.*

Quickly, the team agreed on a plan, and in short order Atitsogbuie, Gildersleeve, and the other six-footers were through the scuttle. The remainder of the division followed in an orderly pattern. The remaining seabags were passed through the hole, and there remained just one person on the other side. SR Teresa Volk was the shortest person in the division. There appeared no way that she could reach the scuttle, let alone clamber through without violating the three-second rule.

Hopkins   *We came up with a way. We took two more seabags, looped the straps together, and protected the wall that way. They didn't reach all the way to the deck, but they gave enough protection for A.T., me, and the MAA to reach through and grab her.*

Petty Officer Kent, standing on the catwalk as the safety observer for the event, chuckled. "I facilitated battle stations for a year," he remarked, "and that's the first time I ever heard that solution. Looks like it might just work." The duty facilitator agreed, and Volk, unscathed, soon joined her shipmates on the safe side of the bulkhead.

Naing T. Kyaw, 19, San Francisco, California

I think we did pretty good. That was like the first event we actually pulled together and did it right.

McClellan *We had thought about losing A.T. somewhere on the run, or breaking his knees or something. [Laughter.] He's so big, they kept using him as the dead guy or victim, and he's huge. But he came in handy that time, rescuing Volk.*

Adams *I didn't get sleepy all night, but that's the one where I did get sleepy. As soon as I got through the hole, it was, like, I'm going to fall asleep right in the middle of battle stations. I leaned up against the wall—after I was safe and on the other side—and I got a strike for it. I had to run around and swing my arms to keep awake. I was so tired I didn't know what I was doing.*

0500, Building 1312

Adams and the others had a wake-up call in store. The first clue came when they saw foul-weather gear—rain pants, rain boots, and hooded parkas—stocked across the passageway from the *Forestal* escape compartment. Quickly, they donned the protective equipment and moved a few yards to the magazine flooding exercise.

C. Williams *I put my foot into a rain boot, and it was soaking wet. I thought, oh no, here we go again!*

Scott Bowser was facilitator and safety observer for this exercise. "During the Persian Gulf war, the USS *Tripoli* (LPH-10) was tasked with clearing minefields to enable the battleships *Wisconsin* and *Missouri* to approach the coast of Kuwait and support ground forces with their 16-inch guns. On the night of 17 February 1991, *Tripoli* found she was being targeted by Iraqi Silk Worm missile batteries and was moving to a different area to operate. The *Tripoli* struck a mine at 0436 on the starboard side in the area of frame 20. The explosion temporarily knocked out all power, caused flooding that disabled an emergency generator and destroyed a paint locker, sending paint and paint thinner through the ventilation system. The fumes overcame some crew members. The forward bulkhead in the magazine used to store 3-inch rounds was damaged, and the flooding that had knocked out the emergency generator was now threatening the magazine with a mixture of seawater, JP-5 (from a damaged tank below the space), and the contents of the destroyed paint locker. GMC(SW) William A. Werley entered the space to assess the damage. He then took charge and 'jumpered' the fire main to enable water to reach the sprinkler system for the magazine, should it be needed. Realizing that the contents of the magazine would be destroyed if the magazine flooded, he communicated the need for additional people to assist in its unloading. Unwilling to allow any more time to pass, he started unloading heavy 3-inch rounds from the magazine until more help arrived. When his shipmates arrived to assist him, they, as a team, moved over one thousand 3-inch rounds and over one hundred cases of small-arms ammunition. Chief Werley's willingness to take great personal risk and ability to organize his shipmates reduced the amount of battle damage and enabled *Tripoli* to remain on station and complete her mission, which was an essential part of Operation Desert Storm. Chief Werley was awarded the Bronze Star in recognition of his efforts and went on to become a senior chief petty officer and an outstanding recruit division commander right here at RTC.

"Now you face the same challenge. As the result of a mine explosion, your magazine is flooding, and the contents are threatened. Your team must display commitment to the mission by relocating the 3-inch rounds in the magazine to another magazine outside of the flooding boundaries. You must show the courage to accomplish the task even when conditions are less than ideal, and honor to avoid shortcuts that may save time but will endanger your ship and shipmates through careless handling of the ammunition. This is the last ammunition your ship has, and you must save it."

Bowser demonstrated the proper procedure for lifting and moving the cylinders. Moving the 20-pound, 3-foot, 14-inch-diameter cylinders was inherently dangerous—a dropped cylinder could do serious damage to a recruit's foot. And the battle stations rules reflected the grim reality that a dropped shell at sea would kill everyone in the compartment. The team had twenty minutes to move a hundred rounds—about a ton of ammunition—through a small escape scuttle to safety.

Bowser left the compartment and mounted the adjacent safety platform. "You will recall that I mentioned flooding, right?" With that, he turned a series of valves, and cold, drenching water began to flow into the compartment from overhead. "It comes in faster than it drains, people, so I suggest you get moving."

Confusion reigned, but only momentarily. The recruits quickly formed two teams, one to remain in the freezing, wet magazine space, and one to cross through to the safe, dry compartment adjacent. Several recruits spotted sound-powered telephones and attempted to establish communication between the compartments. As soon as the receiving team reached the dry magazine area, Petty Officer Kent, who had joined Bowser, turned another set of valves on the observer's control panel. "When the ship sinks, everyone gets wet," he laughed, repeating a time-honored boot camp proverb. Within seconds, everyone in the division was soaked.

Krofta   *I took a strike on that one because I kept pushing ammo through the hole—we had, like, a system going, a chain—and the people on the other side were disorganized, and I pushed one through the hole, and there was no one on the other side to grab it.*

Leitner   *I was the phone talker, and there wasn't anyone on the phone on the other side!*

Wirsch   *They told me to hook up the phone, but I couldn't find the plug. Every time I got near the door, someone would push me out of the way with the ammo canisters.*

K.A. (Bee) Hardison-Porter, 18, San Diego, California
I kind of liked it, though. By that time we were getting pretty hot, because we'd been through the Forestal, and had been in the building for awhile. And the room was small, and we were in a large group, so it was nice to have some water on us to cool us off. I didn't like it when it started going down the back of my rain jacket, though.

Bruce   *I hated it, we had to walk in our sock feet afterwards when we took off the rubber boots, and put on our own, and my socks were wet for the rest of the night and I started getting blisters on my feet then.*

Gildersleeve *I hated that. It was cold, my boots and jacket got totally filled up with cold water, running down my shirt and all, and people kept banging my knees and my elbows with ammo. I just totally hated it, you know?*

The soaked recruits finished the exercise without losing anyone to a "fatality" and with only a few minor strikes assessed for poor lifting technique. The recruits shed their foul-weather gear (ironically, since the weather outside was as miserable as inside the flooded magazine) and prepared for their last round trip through the tunnel.

0545, The Tunnel

The division headed north through the tunnel for the last time. All remaining activities would take place at Camp Moffett. The next time the recruits would transit under Buckley Rd., the sun would be shining, and they'd be on their way to battle stations graduation.

Troeger *I had been keeping count, and checking the time, so I knew we only had a few things left. At that point, all I was doing was putting one foot ahead of the other. I was thinking of my fiancé and little girl back home, and how I wanted to be able to see them at pass-in-review. My body was just, like, numb.*

Hattrich *And I got stuck with the seabag, like, five different times, because nobody wanted to carry it. It slowed you down a lot. And the canteen was bouncing around on my backside the whole time. It was like getting paddled all the way from one event to another. [Laughter.]*

Alcazar *I had the seabag about three times. I failed PT-2 once, so I'm not real fast, and it was really holding me back. People would get it, and carry it for a couple steps, then pass it off. And all the clothes in there were wet, which made it even heavier. I caught up at the tunnel, though.*

At the conference in the RDC lounge earlier that evening, the RDCs and facilitators had agreed that anyone falling behind the trailing (safety) petty officer would fail for the night. As they passed the new construction area just north of the tunnel, Petty

Officer Russell—and a growing group of recruits—was trailing the main body by some thirty yards.

J. A. (Jon) Miller, 18, Las Vegas, Nevada

She saved us. No doubt about it. I asked her afterwards if she was as tired as we were, and was slowing down naturally, and she just looked at me and smiled.

The recruits reached Building 1414, the indoor confidence course. After stowing their snow-covered outer garments, the recruits heard the scenario for the evening's penultimate challenge.

"You and your team have been given the assignment of moving a critically injured shipmate from shaft alley to topside and then to the pier. Your ship has just entered port, and because of recent battle damage there will be no brow available for several hours, and your shipmates must be taken to the hospital ASAP. There are many obstacles you and your team must overcome as a group in order to get your shipmate to safety and proper medical care.

"During peacetime and wartime sailors get injured, usually in the most inconvenient locations. It almost always takes a lot of dedicated sailors to overcome the barriers that are the natural part of a ship's design. During the aftermath of the attack on Pearl Harbor in December 1941, hundreds of wounded sailors had to be removed from what was left of their ships. The ability to do this made the difference between life and death for most. The greatest effort undertaken was the rescue of the trapped sailors in the USS *Oklahoma*. After taking torpedo hits she quickly capsized, trapping many men below. An effort was immediately mounted to cut a hole through the hull to rescue trapped men. This effort saved the lives of thirty-two sailors trapped in shaft alley with no other way out.

"It takes both physical strength and mental agility to overcome obstacles. Can your team meet the challenge and get your shipmates to safety while there is still time? Now you must display commitment to the team by carrying your part of the load and helping to solve the problems you encounter. Now you must display courage by putting yourself at risk to overcome obstacles and save a shipmate. And you must display honor in doing your best to work as part of the team, both giving and taking input to rapidly move your shipmate to safety."

The division watched Petty Officers Robinson and Bandlow negotiate the confidence course. Not every element of the course would be used for the exercise. And because the course required recruits to scale 6-foot obstacles and use rope slides, this evolution was too dangerous for "live" casualties. Instead, the recruits were provided with two 150-pound dummies, each strapped to a standard Miller backboard. The course required teams of four recruits to manhandle the dummy through a series of narrow pipes, simulating the shaft alley of a smaller vessel. They'd negotiate small, twisting passageways, not unlike those aboard ship, and clamber over chest-high and head-high obstacles. The final portion of the course—moving the victim to the pier—would require a climb up a vertical ladder to a 9-foot platform, followed by manhandling the victim to the "pier" below. Stretcher teams were given ten minutes to complete the course.

In the interest of safety, only two stretcher teams were allowed on the course at any time. This proved fortunate for subsequent teams, since the first teams through quickly devised strategies, which the others observed and copied.

Freeman   *The course was pretty easy, but we had trouble figuring out how to get the stretcher and that dummy down to the pier. Then someone figured out that if we took off our canteens, we could use our guard belts to hold the stretcher to the mooring line, and somebody—I think it might have been Guiterrez—shinnied down the rope as a guide. That dummy was heavy, though, so it really slid fast and got away from him.*

Arcia   *I was kneeling on the concrete edge, right where the soft rubber footing for the confidence course starts, so I could see everything that was going on. As soon as I saw what Arty was doing, I knew there was a better way. If we just took more guard belts, we could use them as a rope to slow down the stretcher going down the wire. There was no sense in somebody getting killed this late in the night.*

Gildersleeve   *This time me and A.T. were carrying the stretcher. I'd rather carry a dummy than him, any day. [Laughter.]*

Division 005 completed the shaft alley escape module with no additional strikes. Their fast time surprised the facilitators.

The last exercise of the evening, and the capstone of battle stations, was the damage-control scenario. Because of the inherent risk to recruits, this event was supervised by a full complement of damage control specialists. The Fire Fighting Training Unit would not be ready for the division until 0700. After a brief discussion, the cadre reached consensus. The division would run again.

0700, Fire Fighting Training Unit

Wirsch *When we left the confidence course, I figured we had it made. I had been to Camp Moffett lots of times as yeoman— escorting people to Ship Fifteen and all. I knew the fire station was right around the corner, and we were almost there.*

Hopkins *I knew something was wrong, see, when we came outside, and they made us walk around to the east side of the building. I knew it wasn't to keep us out of the wind—that's the way it was coming. We were standing on the running track—the one that goes all the way around Building 1414, and I'm thinking, Oh no, they can't do this to us. But they did.*

A quarter-mile, eight-lane running track surrounds the confidence course building. The facilitators decided to add two laps of the track to the events to get back on schedule. Fortunately for the recruits, the pace was gentle, and the half-mile "detour" had the division arriving at the Fire Fighting Training Unit promptly at 0700.

Quietly, the battle stations facilitators left the recruits and returned to Building 1312 to wash and change into clean uniforms for the graduation ceremony. DCC(SW) Pam Besaw, chief of the deck at the FFTU, would manage the final exercise. In an interview later, Chief Besaw explained: "The Marines like to say that every Marine is a rifleman. Well, every sailor is a firefighter. There are just a few of us who are rated damage controlmen, but when the ship's in danger, everyone has got to be able to fight fires, shore up bulkheads, and dewater the ship. We try to make our training—and our battle stations exercise—as realistic as we can."

The firefighting exercise is the only event that places recruits in serious risk of life-threatening injury, and for this reason only qualified damage-control instructors are permitted on deck with the recruits. A crew of twelve DC instructors, led by Chief Besaw, met the recruits as they entered. "Take a look at that motto on the aft bulkhead," she told them. "What does it say? It says 'Learn, Don't Burn,' doesn't it? This is the only event where, in addition to failing battle stations and repeating it, you can get ASMOed. And we do it all the time, people. So if you don't want to wind up back on your 6-1 day, you'll do *exactly* what these instructors in the red hardhats tell you, is that clear?"

The threat of a setback—RTC's equivalent of capital punishment—energized the division. "Yes, Chief!"

Rasco *I'm thinking, oh, wow, this is exactly what I need. To make it all the way through battle stations and to strike out on the last event—and get ASMOed in the process. My knees are killing me from all the running, I've been up all night and I can't even think, and I'm saying to myself, "Concentrate, concentrate." It was awful.*

Orlando *It was so bright in there, with the tube lights and all, after we had been outside in the dark, I was having trouble focusing my eyes. But we had just been there, like, a week before, so I knew where things were and stuff.*

Chief Besaw read the scenario for the last event. "You are assigned as a fire party member. Proper use of the damage-control skills you have learned is essential to save your ship. Whenever casualty strikes a ship, it is an unplanned event, and you must be prepared to use teamwork to overcome whatever situation is forced on you.

"On 17 May 1987, while the U.S. Navy was providing security for tankers in the Persian Gulf during the Iran-Iraq war, the USS *Stark* (FFG31) was struck by two Exocet missiles launched by an Iraqi Mirage fighter. The resulting explosion and fire killed thirty-seven sailors, and the ship came very close to sinking, because of the large amount of damage. Because of the dedication of the crew the fires were eventually extinguished, the ship was saved, and was able to be taken to port for repairs. Undoubtedly those on board the *Stark* who survived had gone to great lengths to save their ship. Existing DC party organization had to be adapted to cope with the loss of so many members of the crew. Each and every surviving crew member had to put their lives on the line to try and control the fires and keep the ship afloat while efforts were made to render assistance from other Navy ships in the area.

"Even though you may have specific assignments in your fire party, you must be prepared to take action where there is a casualty. It is probable that in a similar event many shipmates assigned specific duties will not survive and those who do survive must take up the slack. This is why understanding basic damage control is so critical and also why being able to perform as a member of a team is just as critical. Sometimes there isn't enough time to think about it; sometimes you just have to do it. No one individual could have saved *Stark,* but the crew, working as a team, did. Now it's your turn."

The recruits suited up in damage-control equipment—Oxygen Breathing Apparatus, flash protection hoods, fire-retardant gloves, and yellow fire-party helmets. For this event, the division was divided into six fire parties, each responsible for extinguishing a Class A fire, raging behind shipboard watertight doors on the port and starboard sides of the training deck. The location and intensity of these propane-fueled fires was controlled from a safety tower on the second-deck catwalk.

Each team consisted of a fire-party leader, a nozzle man, and hosemen to control the 1.5-inch pressurized fire hose. A pumpman controlled the flow of water from standpipes located amidships. Each team had a DC instructor, standing beside the nozzle man, and a safety observer with the pumpman at the rear of the team. When the traditional RTC command of "Let's go get it!" was sung out by the team leaders, the team leader approached the metal door, examining its surface with an ungloved hand to determine the extent of the fire behind. The doors were then undogged slightly, and shaken to allow super-heated air to escape, preventing backdraft from blowing the door open when the dogs were fully released. With a tap on the shoulder from the instructor, the team leader opened the door fully, and the recruits confronted the inferno inside.

The nozzlemen opened their lines and swung the nozzle, left-right-up-down in the patterns they had been taught. The instructor shifted recruits to various positions, so that each had the opportunity to handle the nozzle of the bucking fire hose. Eventually, each of the blazes was brought under control. At a signal from the deck safety officer, water flow was shut off, and for the recruits of Division 005, battle stations exercises were completed.

Not everyone was fortunate, however. At 0703, SR Zuni Robinson received her third strike of the evening for forgetting to set the timer on her OBA. As she was escorted out of the building for the long walk back to Ship Eight, Petty Officer Russell commented: "I know it seems harsh and brutal, but if someone goes into a shipboard fire and doesn't know how much time he has on his OBA, you'll just wind up having to send others in to rescue him. I don't want any of my recruits putting other sailors in jeopardy out there in the fleet. She's a good recruit, and she'll be able to run battle stations again after a forty-eight-hour rest period, but they have to learn—this is serious business."

Alexis Lopez, 19, Brooklyn, New York

That was the easiest of everything all night. Everyone was telling us that it was gonna be the place where everyone gets all those strikes, and that they were waiting for us, because, see, it was seven o'clock in the morning, and we'd been going all night, and them dudes had just come to work, you know? But it was easy, man.

Johnson *I had two strikes already, so I figured, well, here's where I get "to the rear, march." But it was easy, like he says.*

Division 005 gathered outside the Fire Fighting Training Unit. It was nearly 0800—the sun had risen at 0725—and the only thing between the recruits and the coveted NAVY ball cap was the graduation ceremony. That—and the long run back to Building 1312.

0800, Friday, 01 December

The recruits were exhausted. Counting their full duty day on Thursday, they'd been on the move for twenty-eight hours or more. Those unfortunate enough to draw duty on Wednesday night were approaching their fortieth hour of sleeplessness. They had moved several tons of stores, had had to swim, had fired weapons, carried shipmates, fought fires, and double-timed the length and breath of Recruit Training Command. Now, only a mile run separated them from the chance to exchange their hated "recruit" insignia for a NAVY ball cap, and the right to be called sailors.

Broders *Man, I just wanted to be done. The heat at fire fighting just about did me in. I was sweating under all that gear, and when we got outside and it was cold, it was like a relief. Until I remembered where we were, and that we weren't done yet.*

Kelly *I was actually feeling pretty good right about then. I figured, even if I had to crawl, I was gonna get back to the battle stations building. No way was I going to give up then.*

Starks *I had been through all this before, so I knew what was coming.* I kept telling everyone—particularly the females—keep moving, keep moving. If you stop, you'll never get started again. We were so slow mustering outside, it was, like, it's over, folks! We just need to get back and get our hats.*

Petty Officer Dan Kent took the lead, and the division moved south at a reasonable pace. As the group approached the tunnel, Rasco dropped the running cadence, and, as is traditional at RDC, began the first verse of "Anchors Aweigh."

Wirsch *That really got to me, when Schley started the Navy song. We hadn't sung it when we went through the tunnel earlier. I thought, Oh, wow! That's us she's singing about! We're not recruits anymore! We really are gonna make it! I just closed my eyes and said a prayer of thanksgiving to Heavenly Father for getting me through the night.*

The division cleared the tunnel, turned, and began double-timing down First Ave. To their left, the life-sized replica of Stanley Bleifeld's "Lone Sailor" was lightly coated with snow. To their right, divisions of recruits, en route to class, mustered on the grinder separating Ships One and Two. ETC(SW)** Debbie Reilly, who had pushed eleven divisions through battle stations and was the most experienced division commander at Great Lakes, watched as they approached. "I saw Marty Zeller's division coming out of the tunnel, dirty, freezing, and dog-tired. Some of them looked like they were dragging, not carrying, their seabags. A couple had their Kevlar helmets squashed down on their faces.

*Seaman Recruit Starks, the female MAA, had ASMOed into the division and was the only member who had completed battle stations previously.
**Chief Reilly is a chief electronics technician (E7), with surface warfare qualifications.

It had stopped snowing, but it was cold, and the wind was hitting 'em right on. I figured they needed a little cheering up."

Reilly ordered her division to sound off with three cheers for Division 005. As the recruits made the final turn into Indiana St., the cheers of their fellow recruits echoed off the barracks and battle stations building. Division 005 was coming home.

Scorsone *Right then, I about lost it. I was running on the right side, and saw it was Chief Reilly's division cheering for us. She had been in Ship Eight, back when we were still Smurfs, and she had been really, really tough on us. And she's clapping and her folks are cheering, and they didn't even know us, you know?*

Collins *That was cool, what they did. Petty Officer Kent was shouting for us to get one last chant going, but, to be honest, I don't think anyone had any breath left. We were beat, man, but hearing them cheering for us, and seeing everyone waiting outside the battle stations building, well, it was cool, man, it really was.*

Dizon *I just started to cry when I saw the building at the end of the last run. I was so happy, thinking it was finally done, and I really was going to get out of boot camp.*

Leitner *As soon as I came through the tunnel and made the turn, it was, like, I made it! I made it!*

The division ground to a halt on Indiana St., right in front of Building 1312. Chief Zeller led a small group of wellwishers who greeted the division as they entered the building and prepared for the graduation ceremony. Smelling of soot and smoke—and, well, just smelling—the group took a short head call to clean the worst of the grime from hands and faces, before entering the quarterdeck for the graduation ceremony.

Mary Smith *Seeing Chief Zeller there, that was special, too. I wish he had been able to run with us all night. I knew I was gonna miss him, and Petty Officer Kent and Russell too, when I left. But Chief Zeller—he's my favorite.*

The recruits filed into the assembly area south of the quarterdeck. They were soon joined by the recruits of Divisions 006 and 902. Facing forward, Division 005 was assigned to the starboard side of the central rostrum. Bulkheads surrounding the recruits were decorated with the Navy's core values. Poster-sized photographs told the stories of heroic sailors, whose actions exemplified those values. Hopkins and Rasco quickly dressed the division in parade order, and allowed them to stand at ease as the other divisions paraded in the center and portside positions.

0830: Sailors at Last

ETCS(SS)* Daryl Mullins strode into the assembly area. As leading chief of the battle stations group, Senior Chief Mullins would direct the morning's activities. He called the recruits to attention. Doors opened on the port and starboard sides of the assembly areas. The night's cadre of battle stations facilitators, outfitted in clean, pressed battle dress—with gold ascots highlighting the gold trim on their single-piece coveralls, entered from the starboard side. They marched smartly to the front of the room, halted, and turned to face the recruits.

Nine RDCs—three for each division—entered from the port side. They, too, joined the line facing the recruits.

The morning's reviewing officers followed the RDCs into the auditorium. Capt. Ed Gantt, base commander, and Lt. Erin McAvoy, ship's officer at Ship Eight, would conduct the graduation ceremony. The recruits especially welcomed Captain Gantt's presence. Ever since he had run with them during the Captain's Cup competition several weeks previously, Division 005 had always claimed him as their own. As a former enlisted man, he identified well with the recruits, and they appreciated his candor, openness, and caring attitude toward them and their problems.

The recruits saluted, and held their salute as a recording of the national anthem filled the room. Tears filled the eyes of many of the recruits as they listened to Whitney Houston's rendition of the familiar words. Perhaps never before in their lives had those words held quite the meaning they had this morning.

The recruits dropped their salute as the last bars reverberated around the room. Lieutenant McAvoy began: "Shipmates, this is a time of transition. You entered this room as recruits. For eight weeks—nearly nine weeks—you have studied, you have drilled, you have practiced the skills which we need—and need desperately—in the fleet. You entered recruit training as

*Senior Chief Mullins is a senior chief electronics technician (E8), with submarine warfare qualifications.

individuals. You learned teamwork here. You could not have completed battle stations without exercising that teamwork. There's not one person in this room—not you, nor I, nor Captain Gantt—who can singlehandedly put a ship to sea. Together— *together!*—we can crew any ship, meet any challenge, defeat any foe. You have fought the good fight, you have finished the course, you have kept faith with our core values. And your RDCs have kept faith with you, too. Today you are no longer recruits. You'll not be addressed that way ever again. Today you are *sailors*.

"During battle stations you've heard the stories of sailors who have been tested, and who overcame those challenges with valor. Some have won high awards. Before you leave here this morning, look around you. Count the Medal of Honor recipients whose pictures honor this room. Count the winners of the Silver Star, the Navy Cross, and the Bronze Star. They were once like you, frightened, tired, terrified. They came through when it counted, and you will, too. I'm proud of you—each one of you. Bravo Zulu, sailors!"

The sounds of Lee Greenwood's tribute to the American fighting man filled the room. To the strains of "God Bless the USA," the nine RDCs turned, saluted, and moved to a series of tables near the podium. Kent, Russell, and Chief Zeller each took a handful of ball caps with the word NAVY emblazoned on the front and, with a handshake and a few personal words, presented each new sailor with the symbol of his or her passage through the crucible of military training. "Pass-in-review is for the moms and pops," Chief Zeller remarked a few days later. "This ceremony is for the recruits. Anyone can go buy one of those hats at the NEX—but these kids had to earn theirs. And they'll hold on to that hat for the rest of their lives, I bet."

Alcazar   *I thought I was dreaming. I cried, I was so happy. I never thought I'd make it through battle stations, ever since I got here, you know? I never ran in my entire life. I never did sit-ups or push-ups, none of that. I was surprised, I was shocked. I was just waiting to wake up. And when Petty Officer Kent gave me the NAVY ball cap, that just made me feel so good.*

Hattrich   *I started crying when Petty Officer Russell handed me my ball cap, and she was all smiling, and it was, like, we aren't bad recruits anymore.*

Alcazar *She even gave some of us a hug. I was the last one she gave a hug to, and she's saying, "Stop, stop, or I'm gonna start bawling, too. You're messing up my reputation." And that was kind of heartwarming, because she's known as the mean one, but she's the most respected, too.*

Burger *I was looking at Kyaw, and he was really crying. Especially during the national anthem.**

Alcazar *When we broke ranks, the first person I went to see was Senior Chief Nelson of brother division. When I failed PT-2, he was the person who took me aside and gave me a lot of motivation, and he told me that he'd run with me every day till I passed, and if it wasn't for him, I'd never have passed PT-2 and gotten to run battle stations. Even though he wasn't my RDC, and my RDCs are really great, he was the one that really helped me the most when I needed it.*

Freeman *The best part was looking around and seeing all your shipmates there. Some of them wanted to drop out at different parts of the night, but we kept talking and kept everyone together, and seeing the pride on their faces, it was great.*

Mary Smith *I just wished my dad were there to see me. He was a Navy warrant officer, but he died when I was little. I just wished he was there with me. [Crying.]*

He was, Mary. He was.

---

*Seaman Recruit Naing T. Kyaw is a refugee from Burma, and had been in the United States for only four years. Kyaw also won the division academic award, for the best cumulative written test scores, even though he is not a native English speaker.

15
Dangers, Great and Small

The recruits had not eaten since 1600 on Thursday, and most were famished. The command had arranged a special brunch for the battle stations graduates, and the division, led by Chief Zeller, proceeded to Galley 928. It's difficult to find the proper verb to describe the trip: "marching" doesn't carry the precise connotation; perhaps "strutting" comes closest. Gildersleeve—ever the innovator when it came to cadence chants—was in rare form. They marched as if the word "Navy" on their ball caps were incandescent. They basked in the envy and admiration of the junior divisions they passed. Because it was Friday, civilian guests had begun to gather at MCPON Hall, preparing for that morning's pass-in-review. Hopkins and his team of recruit petty officers made sure the division looked good as they passed by.

Hopkins *It was awesome, just awesome. We passed by an RDC and I said, "Good morning, Petty Officer," like the RPOC is supposed to do. And he looked at us and said, "Good morning, sailors"—not recruits, but sailors! And that was, like, wow! That had never, ever happened to me before.*

The division had another surprise when they arrived at Galley 928. Joined by Captain Gantt and their RDCs, for the first time since arriving at Great Lakes they were permitted to talk during the meal. Several recruits—led by the irrepressible Leah Taylor—rendered impressions of their RDCs, and the resulting laughter filled the dining area. They were sailors now, among sailors, and things would never be the same.

Hattrich *I was just so glad it was over. The only thing that was wrong was that it was Petty Officer Kent's last battle stations* *before he retires, and I don't think we looked all that good for him to the other battle stations facilitators. We maybe weren't as motivated as we could be—we tried singing and chanting, but most of us were so tired and cold and our lungs hurt so bad it was hard for us to sing when we were going between events. But I felt bad for him, and wish we had looked better for him to his buddies.*

Stamp   *I was just relieved that it was over. Every part of my body was hurting.*

Krofta   *I felt that I was finally done, that I was out of here, and all I had to do was pass-in-review and I'd be gone.*

Johnson   *I was just thinking about my daughter, and making her proud of me. See, Gildersleeve had to keep motivating me all night because I'm older, I'm thirty-one, and I can't be doing this stuff like these young dudes, but my man here kept me going, you know?*

McClellan   *We had that big, muscular monster-guy as our facilitator, I don't know his name [Petty Officer Scott Bowser]. When I first saw him, back in the compartment, he scared me, and when he took over as the facilitator for our team, it was, like, okay, I'm going to be back in the rack by midnight, I guess. But he was the coolest and nicest of the whole group, I think. He explained things, and told us the story of each of the events, and he was really, really cool. I went over and shook his hand after the ceremony. I want to go over and see him after pass-in-review if he's around.*

Johnson   *Yeah, I was getting scared, and when we got to that one event [Petty Officer Bowser] took me aside and said, "Johnson, you got two strikes on you, right? You go over there and be the victim this time." And he probably saved me, because if I got three strikes, I'd have been out of there for sure.*

Joseph Schau, 19, Smithfield, Virginia
I was thinking I finally got the cap, because I've been here a long time, and I was glad I could finally graduate and see my family.

Burger   *That song "Proud to be an American" always got to me, but this time it really got me going. And the national anthem too. I nearly started crying, but I didn't want to look like one of the girls.*

Adams *Freeman was crying as soon as we got in there! Petty Offi-cer Russell said, "What are you crying about? You ain't even in there yet." I never thought I'd make it through the night, but the minute that music started, I felt better than I ever had in my entire life.*

Freeman *I felt so relieved that it was over. I felt like I had accom-plished something, I was so proud. And when I went into the room and saw the captain and Lieutenant McAvoy, and when they started playing the national anthem, and we started saluting. And seeing the RDCs that ran all night with us—like Senior Chief Nel-son and he didn't even have to be there, because he had gotten transferred—it was awesome.*

The division returned to Compartment D-01 at 1130. Exhausted, most wanted to fall into their bunks and sleep—for at least a month. But this was still boot camp. Sleep could come later.

"This is a part of the training cycle that worries the com-mand a lot," remarked ETC(SW) Debbie Reilly, the highly expe-rienced RDC who had watched the division pass by during their battle stations exercise. "For weeks, we've been pointing the recruits toward battle stations, and when they finally complete it, there is a natural tendency to slack off. Recruits start doing stupid things, and if they're not careful, they can find them-selves ASMOed so far back that they have to do it all over again. So we do lots of things differently during their last weeks here—for one thing, the RDCs sleep in the compartment with them for several nights during the period. We've had unfortunate inci-dents in the past, and we're determined to do what we can to keep them from happening in the future."

Chief Zeller and Petty Officer Kent were well aware of the dangers. "There's not much really going on after battle stations," remarked PR1 Kent. "There are a couple of important classes, but mostly it's logistics, getting uniforms squared away, practic-ing for pass-in-review, and then weekend liberty. So we have to be innovative to keep the division on-spot and moving. The cap may say 'Navy' but they're not out of here yet, and they need to remember that."

Nevertheless, Kent and Zeller allowed the recruits to muster at forward IG under the guise of debriefing the events of the past twenty-four hours, and many of the recruits were able to nod off during the afternoon. Chief Zeller wisely sequestered himself in the division office, having first taken the prudent step of doubling the fore and aft watch, lest unannounced visitors interrupt the period of reflection. Reenergized, the division marched to evening chow, still inordinately proud of the Navy ball caps that distinguished them from the mass of recruits clogging Galley 928. Later, Chief Zeller granted early taps to the weary recruits, and lights were extinguished promptly at 2000.

Trindade *I was dead. I was out on my feet. I have no idea what we had for chow that night. I'm not even sure we went to chow, to tell the truth.*

Brunney *I ached all over. My legs hurt, my back hurt, my arms really hurt. When we sat down at forward IG, I actually didn't think I'd be able to get back up, I was that far gone. I usually fall asleep right when I hit the rack, but, that night, I think I was asleep even before I got into my bunk. I was zonked.*

The recruits found the weekend relaxing.

Hopkins *Basically, all we did was practice for pass-in-review on Saturday and also on Sunday afternoon. We spent most of the time in Drill Hall 1000, and we must have made the circuit inside that drill hall a hundred times. We'd start on our "spot," listen for the beats of the bass drum, start off and march down the back row, turn, and march back up past the reviewing stand. Over and over.*

Ward *I kept telling him, just keep hanging lefts, man. It's like NASCAR.*

The recruits had a treat on Sunday evening. Petty Officer Kent had rented a few videotapes, and with a little jury-rigging, a video monitor, usually used for training broadcasts, was mated to a VCR cumshawed from the schoolhouse. The recruits spent the evening at forward IG, watching action-packed features. A visitor marveled at the sight of forty adolescent males and forty adolescent females, separated by a 6-foot fire lane patrolled by vigilant adults. It reminded him of eighth-grade dances in parochial school. But no matter—the recruits enjoyed the videotapes, one of which, in tribute to the Coast Guard, was the newly released film *The Perfect Storm*.

Banter among the recruits suggested that they could lick the Hooligans at their own game.

"I don't know where recruits get the idea that the Coast Guard is easy duty," Kent remarked later. "Especially since the closest any of these knuckleheads have gotten to water is when they flew in here over the top of Lake Michigan. They can't even see the lake from here; it's three miles away. So I had to explain to them that, while the Navy trains constantly for disaster and dangerous conditions, the Coast Guard works under those conditions, day and night. These kids ought to know that before one of them pops off in a bar somewhere, and gets a face full of fingers, don't you think?"

By Monday morning, things had returned to normal. The recruits had a full week of morning classes scheduled, and afternoons would be consumed in drill practice or logistic tasks.

Master Chief McCalip explains: "There was a time when recruits might finish battle stations on a Tuesday, say, and graduate on Friday morning. But with conditions in the world the way they are, more and more emphasis has to be placed on terrorism, and how to keep safe, even when you are away from your ship. So the last week is spent mostly in working on those issues. The idea is that this is the last thing they hear in boot camp, so maybe they'll retain it when they get out to the fleet."

The week did start with good news, though. Shortly after completing PT, the division learned that its five members who had "struck out" during battle stations, as well as two additional members who had failed PT-2 the week previously, had passed battle stations with a "straggler group" on Sunday evening. They rejoined their shipmates after the traditional celebration brunch, and the entire division now sported the coveted Navy ball cap.

Hattrich *I was really happy for them and for us. It would be awful for them to watch the division march out of the compartment for pass-in-review, and not be able to go along.*

"I was worried about some of them," Chief Zeller admitted later. "You really hate it when you work so hard to develop teamwork and a feeling of being shipmates, and then some don't get to graduate with the rest of the team. I was particularly concerned about one recruit. She had been with the division since the first day, but was just unable to get her speed up to pass the running portion of PT-2. By some miracle, she really bettered her time on Friday afternoon, so she was added at the last minute to the Sunday battle stations schedule. It took meetings with Senior Chief Tucker, and the intervention of Lieutenant McAvoy, but she wound up finally in the stragglers' group."

After noon chow, the division adjourned to the schoolhouse for the first of a series of lectures on terrorism, personal accountability, and life ashore, both at home and in foreign ports. These lectures would be different than most attended by the recruits so far.

Joshua Haight, 18, Omaha, Nebraska

Well, usually, some old chief or petty officer would get up in class, and start off with some lame joke—really lame jokes—to sort of warm up the class and get us in a good mood. That was usually the signal to look around and, if you were in the middle of the room and nobody could see you, close your eyes and get a nap for awhile. Not this time.

Silently, the instructor (who requested that his name not be used in this context) stepped to the podium and turned on the overhead projector. A wall-sized slide of the USS *Cole* filled the front of the room. The *Cole*, a *Burke*-class destroyer, had recently been attacked by terrorists, while on a routine refueling mission at Aden, in the Republic of Yemen. The instructor quietly progressed through a series of slides, each showing different facets of the damage caused to the port side of the ship. The usual dull roar of recruits moving about the classroom stopped, and all paid close attention as the veteran chief began.

"How many of you ever got into trouble for goofing off in grade school?" Several hands sheepishly went up. "And what happened? Got sent to the principal's office, maybe?" They nodded. "And how many of you didn't pay attention in high school?" A few more hands went up. "Flunked the course, maybe? And in college?" One or two hands went up. "Got kicked out, right?" "Well, listen up, sailors. If you don't pay attention in my class, you are going to die."

Ward *Okay. That got my attention, right there. No nap for me— not in this class. Not today.*

The instructor then read from, and commented on, RTC's Terminal Objective (TO) 6.8: "Terrorism is an indiscriminate crime that comes in various forms of threats and violence and is used primarily to attain political goals. Terrorists generate fear through acts of violence, or try to intimidate and coerce. Acts such as the attack on the *Cole* occur routinely in certain parts of the world, making almost every sailor a potential victim. It's frightening and the results, as the pictures show, can be horrifying. As the attack on *Cole* shows, these people have reached new levels of organization and sophistication. These acts are changing and they challenge the effectiveness of our current security measures. We must increase our level of awareness, because, believe me, it can happen anywhere. It can even happen right here in the United States.

"You and your families are important. You are a target, whether you like it or not. The terrorist may not know you or your wife or your baby. But he will strike at you just the same. Security against terrorism is the responsibility of every member of the armed forces. As a member of the military, you are the most valuable—yet most vulnerable—resource.

"What you will learn over the next few days will assist you in becoming less vulnerable to terrorists. You will not be immune, but you will be safer, if you follow some commonsense precautions. You can protect yourself and your family from terrorists—but only through constant awareness and self-discipline.

"Today, I am going to discuss three steps that every sailor and military family member must take, either overseas or functioning as a member of the armed services:

"You must keep a low profile. Your dress, conduct, and mannerisms should not attract attention. You must make an effort to blend into the local environment. Avoid publicity and don't go out in large groups. And stay away from any civil disturbance and demonstration.

"You must be unpredictable. You must vary your routine to and from work and the times that you leave and return home. Don't exercise at the same time and place each day, and never do it alone, or on deserted streets or country roads. Be sure your shipmates know where you are going, what you will be doing, and when you should be back. And if one of your shipmates is overdue, report that fact immediately. Don't wait, and don't worry about sounding a false alarm. Fifty false alarms—five hundred false alarms—are better than one alarm that doesn't get sounded when it should.

"Lastly, you must stay constantly alert. Watch for anything out of place. Don't ever give personal information over the telephone. If you think you are being followed, go to a preselected secure area. Make sure you report anything that looks the least suspicious. Let the security personnel sort it all out. Your job is to be the eyes and ears of your command. If it makes you uncomfortable, let someone know, and do it immediately."

Assisted by other instructors, he then gave detailed, specific instructions to the recruits regarding threat conditions, and security measures implemented fleetwide. It is imprudent to record specifics here, but the recruits paid rapt attention to the instructors—none took the traditional walk-to-the-rear-of-the-classroom, the usual defense against sleepiness.

> **Broders** *You know, I'm sitting there, and it's like, what is today? December 4 or something? And I'm out of here in like, a week, and then I have two weeks of seaman apprentice school, and, like, oh shoot, man, I can be on a ship before the end of the month, right? That could be me this guy is talking about, you know?*

After returning from a short break, one of the recruits from Division 006 raised his hand and asked about the USS *Cole*. "We know they were bombed and all, but what really happened, Chief? We don't get to read the newspapers or listen to the radio much in here."

"I'll tell you what I know," the instructor replied. "On 12 October, at about noon their time, *Cole* was tying up to a fuel dolphin at Aden in the Republic of Yemen. The ship was at Security Condition Charlie, as it should have been. There were armed men topside, and the fueling was about to begin. One of the small boats—there's some controversy as to whether it was one of the line handlers, or one that didn't belong there—came along the port side, right about amidships, and set off an explosion that blew a hole 40 feet by 40 feet in the portside hull. It was right at the waterline, and adjacent to engineering spaces. One deck above, a messing area ran athwartship, across the entire width of the vessel. The force of the explosion—you can see it from the slides we had up here earlier—tore machinery lose, and dropped part of the messing space down into the engine room, and the engine room down into the bilge. Within seconds, seventeen sailors were dead, and many more injured. If you'll recall, as soon as we got word of the explosion, Captain Gantt set Security Condition Bravo here, and armed guards went up all around our base till we got a better handle on what was happening. You may not realize it, sailors, but you're targets here, just as much as if you were out on the *Cole*, or any other ship that might come under attack."

The recruits nodded. They recalled how they had been called together, shortly after chow on 12 October, the day before their division was placed into commission, and told of the attack on USS *Cole*. Later, Petty Officer Russell recounted the story. "Well, Dan [Kent] had the division all morning, and I was scheduled to go in at 1300. About noon, I turned on the news, and heard about the attack. I called Chief Zeller, and told him to turn on his TV. I recognized the pictures they were showing as a *Burke*-class destroyer, and Chief Zeller had just come from three years on the *Arleigh Burke* itself. So, from looking at the pictures on CNN, and from his knowledge of how the ship was laid out, and my knowledge as a damage control specialist, we pretty much had an idea of what was happening and how bad it was. And it was really, really bad."

The recruits remember their reaction when Petty Officer Russell broke the news.

Caldeira *When we heard, we were all hurt. They were kids, most of them our age, right from here. It really shocked us when Petty Officer Russell told us. She was real beat up by it, and it takes a lot to get her beat up. But they were sailors, and we're all sailors, you know? We're like a team; we're all family. It made everyone quiet for the rest of that day, just staring around in space, thinking what happened, people that young.*

Paes *Most of the people in the division were really terrified. We were so unhappy that that happened. When I heard that, it nearly broke my heart. I feel it heavy in my heart, and I don't know why, but I think it's because we are all the same. I mean, right here on my shirt, it says "U.S. Navy," you know? And I was always asking Pierce and the others what had happened, if there was any more information about it, or what. I just wish that whoever did that would get caught. I think we got a lot more serious about things. I know that I put a lot more attention to what I had to do.*

Scorsone *When I heard about it, my eyes got teary, and I realized that I have to make the best of every day, and I never know when I'll be starting the last day of my life. Everything is a risk, but every day in the Navy is more of a risk.*

Hooton-Hetrick *When we heard about the Cole, I got a real lump in my throat. I was totally saddened by that. I think everybody was shocked that it happened, and that some of the people on board were just as young as we are, and they had just gotten out of boot camp within the last six months. Some people came into the Navy for college money, or to get away from home, but it's not fun and games and you can die, you might die, trying to save your ship-mates, or whatever. It's scary.*

Volk *I was really surprised. It felt like there was going to be a war. We all sat down and prayed that night. I never saw the serious side of anybody until that night. Everybody was saying, what if it had been us? One girl in our division, she got really emotional about it, because her dad is over there somewhere close by.* She was really upset, and all of us chipped in and talked to her, and held her hand, and tried to help her.*

Chief Zeller continues. "The worst part was finding out that one of the fatalities, ENFN Joshua L. Parlett of Churchville, Maryland, had been in our ship, Ship Eight, with Division 453, just a few months before. Senior Chief Tucker knew him well. He was nineteen years old."

After the sobering lecture, the division returned to quarters. A study period ended their training day, and taps sounded at 2200.

Routine varied little over the next few days. The division continued to drill and attend classes, and on Thursday picked up orders to their first duty station.

"That's a major change from when I came in," remarked PR1 Kent. "Twenty years ago, the day that orders came out was a really big day in boot camp. Up to that point, you really didn't know where you were going, or what you'd be doing once you got there. Sure, your recruiter may have promised that you were going to be aircrewman, but chances were just as good that

*The recruit, though often quoted in this book, asked that her name not be revealed, as her father was on assignment in the United Arab Emirates.

you'd wind up in the deck division of a tugboat in the Aleutians. Now, recruits have contracts guaranteeing their next duty, and where they'll be transferred. It makes things better for them, sure, but it does take something out of 'orders day,' doesn't it?"

Orders may have come as no shock, but other surprises awaited the recruits. The weather, which had never been their friend, was about to get worse.

Daniel Smith *Well, during our last week, the RDCs had allowed us to use the radio in their office, provided we kept it down low and there were no fights about what we'd listen to. That wasn't much to fight about. We could only get two or three stations, but it was nice to hear music, news, and the weather reports.*

One unplanned advantage of life without radio or TV was that recruits leaned to forecast weather the same way that sailors have done for ages. The first recruit out the door would quietly pass the word back up the line: "It's snowing," or "It's freezing out there." True, there was a highly formalized system of flags, displayed in front of each ship, to indicate weather conditions. It was a rare recruit, however, who knew how to interpret these flags. Rarer still was the recruit willing to hazard a trip across the quarterdeck—between the Rocks and Shoals of the LCPO's office and the RDC lounge—just to see which way the wind was blowing. Like tradesmen in the Victorian era, the recruits were more comfortable using the back door. Weather reports from WKRS 1220AM in Waukegan were thus eagerly awaited.

Rasco *I started listening to the station in Waukegan and they were predicting snow, lots of snow, beginning Thursday, and continuing through the weekend and into next week. "Big winter storm," "storm alert": those were words I kept hearing. And my mom and grandparents were on their way up from Springfield, Missouri, for graduation, and I was afraid that something would happen to them. I was really worried.*

Wirsch *My family were flying in from Sacramento, and my little brother Matthew—he's just two—was coming along. I was scared that something would happen to them, or their plane, or that they would get stuck somewhere and miss our graduation. And since* *we still couldn't use the phones, I had no way of getting in touch with them. I was just praying to Heavenly Father that they'd be okay, and nothing would happen.*

Two inches of snow had fallen on Tuesday, but the main storm had tracked southward, and no additional snow fell until Thursday morning. The recruits continued practice sessions in Drill Hall 1000, but on Thursday, each time they left the drill hall for chow or classes, they found that the snow had gotten deeper and deeper.

Troeger *My people were coming in from Washington state. I just wanted to see my fiancé and baby. And my family. I didn't care what else was going to happen. That was the only thing on my mind, seeing them safe.*

The recruits busied themselves during the afternoon and evening, putting the finishing touches on their graduation uniforms. Males marveled at their salty appearance in the traditional dress blue "crackerjacks," while, topside, the females made last-minute adjustments to uniforms, and debated just how much makeup Chief Brown and Petty Officer Russell would permit. While in boot camp, all had been treated as "generic" recruits, but now many sewed on the red stripes of the engineering ratings, or green stripes for naval aviation. A few fortunate Seabees even got to sew on the light blue stripes of the construction trades. Many were surprised to find a fair sprinkling of apprentices and seamen in their ranks. Ten percent of the division, including most of the recruit petty officers, had been meritoriously promoted from E1 to E2, while those with six-year enlistments in nuclear programs sported the three diagonal stripes of the E3 pay grade. Everyone was eager to show off at the next morning's pass-in-review.

16
They Make It Happen

"Even with the time pressures we face, I don't know anyone here that doesn't enjoy pass-in-review. With two graduations each week, we spend at least six to eight hours in ceremonial duties alone. But that's the best time of the week, it really, really is. It's a joy to 'Watch Our Mission Marching By' at pass-in-review. Those six to eight hours make the other sixty worthwhile." So says Capt. Pam Tubbs, executive officer of Recruit Training Command. Her boss, Capt. Ed Gantt, certainly agrees.

Captain Gantt *The biggest surprise I found when I arrived here is the sheer number of recruits. When you see the numbers on paper, you have nothing with which to compare them. But attend pass-in-review, and watch recruits marching in, division after division after division. It's great. We have sixteen thousand recruits here every day in the summer. And every night, four hundred more get off the bus. This is a very busy place.*

Captain Gantt has been commanding officer since June 2000. A native of suburban Washington, he enlisted in the Army in 1969 and fought in Vietnam as a helicopter gunner and crew chief. Leaving the military, he graduated from Howard University in 1977. He rejoined the service, and completed Navy flight officer training in 1978. With two thousand hours of F14 flight time and numerous carrier deployments, he has commanded fighter squadrons and served as "air boss" aboard Seventh Fleet carriers. He is highly decorated by the Navy, and highly regarded by his staff. Those recruits who have been fortunate enough to meet him think the world of him.

The executive officer at RTC, Captain Tubbs, entered the Navy in 1977, after graduation from the University of South Carolina. Earning her master's degree in education and training administration from Memphis State University, she has held numerous assignments in personnel, administration, recruiting, and military training commands. A 1998 graduate of the Naval War College, Captain Tubbs left RTC to assume command of the Naval Personnel Support Activity, Norfolk, Virginia, shortly after the events described in this book took place.

Captain Tubbs *You always hear that today's recruits aren't up to yesterday's standards. I think that's unfair and overstated. The naysayers need to come here for pass-in-review and meet the young people being delivered to the fleet. Sure, it's harder to find good recruits. The demographics have changed; in the 1960s we had the baby boomers hitting military age, and there was a huge talent pool to draw from. And now there are fewer folks with military service, so there are not the role models that we had in the past. But look at the parents tomorrow, at graduation. Look at the numbers of career military there, from all the services. Military juniors make great recruits, and one of the golden rules of recruiting is to start with people who understand and appreciate service to the nation. My own youngest son is sixteen, and, I hope, on his way to an ROTC scholarship.*

Commander Bob Rawls can understand that logic. The director of military training (DMT) and third in command is himself a military junior. His father, Cdr. Robert Sherwood Rawls, spent forty-three years on active duty and retired in 1993 as the longest serving military officer. Bob Rawls, who has been around the military since his boyhood, is the kind of guy you'd love to have as a neighbor. Instinctively, you'd know that his yard would be well kept, his car spotless, and that if you ever needed a hand, he'd be there to help. Unfortunately, his job as director of military training often casts him as the "bad cop" in the eyes of the recruits. It was his name that terrified Seaman Recruit Alcazar during Service Week, and the Fleet Quality Assurance organization reports directly to him. A surface warrior, Bob Rawls has served aboard USS *Portland* (LSD37), USS *Caron* (DD970), USS *Mount Whitney* (LCC 20), USS *Lawrence* (DDG4), USS *Josephus Daniels* (CG27), and USS *Stark* (FFG31) in the course of a distinguished twenty-three-year career. In every sense, he has been there, done that—and has the decorations and awards to prove it.

Commander Rawls   *I actually think today's quality is better. Twenty years ago, when I came in, we had a huge problem with drugs. That's why the freedom to refocus boot camp from time to time is important. You take whatever arrives, from wherever society is right then, and still produce the same output. One big change is that we've recently accepted recruits from something like ninety-six other countries, immigrants who join the military out of a sense of gratitude or patriotism. And we've seen no reduction in quality because of that. They are just as smart as any recruits, it's just that the environment they came from is different. And by pass-in-review we've produced a disciplined sailor.*

There is concern in the fleet that the kinder, gentler boot camp is not turning out the highest quality of new sailors. All of the senior staff takes exception to this widely expressed opinion.

Captain Gantt   *Well, I was an enlisted guy in boot camp myself, back in the late 1960s. Most of us would like to look back and say that we were better, but that's just a generational thing. If you talk with today's recruits, you'll find they're not much different. They're just like the sailors who went to the Pacific in the 1940s, or our generation that went to Vietnam. We graduate fourteen hundred very sharp and motivated sailors each week. I'd stack them against any previous generation, any day.*

Captain Tubbs   *For awhile, we might not have been as tough as some would have liked. But we began to tighten up again about three years ago, when we instituted battle stations. In addition to being a crucible for the recruits, it lets us validate our training. Because of it, the curriculum is better standardized, the RDCs and instructors are better trained, and we have high-level interest in getting the best staff training the future of the Navy. So I have every confidence that we'll continue to be rigorous and focused.*

Captain Gantt   *Sure, boot camp is kinder and gentler. We've evolved. Times are different, and people are different. But remember, we reflect society. This is not the nation it was twenty, forty, sixty years ago. Remember fieldstripping cigarette butts? Remember the galvanized butt buckets in the barracks? Now society doesn't tolerate* *smoking, so we don't either. We've decided that profanity, the "cursing like a sailor," is not desirable, so we won't accept that, either. It's the same with violence toward the recruits. We invite groups of senior enlisted and officers up here to see what we're doing, so they can spread the word in the fleet. We'll have a dozen prospective commanding officers from Newport with us at pass-in-review tomorrow. Is it a different boot camp than before? No doubt. Better? I think so.*

Commander Rawls *What we do best now is build the person. On physical, mental, emotional maturity levels. Remember, everything we do here is basic. By pass-in-review it's not finished, but we get the sailor energized to take the next steps. It only works, though, if we provide the right role models for them—guys that walk the walk and talk the talk. When we have senior enlisted who eat, live, and breathe Navy, then we're doing okay.*

Captain Gantt *I personally think our various remediation programs are among the best things we do. We pay tremendous attention to the borderline recruit. My goal is to make sailors. We want the chiefs and petty officers to do everything possible to turn that difficult individual around. We have to see each recruit as an individual, and ask ourselves, what is it that this unique person needs to succeed in the Navy? I believe we have the most complete system in our society for assisting seventeen- to twenty-year-olds, regardless of their backgrounds, who are unsure of themselves, or undecided about the course of their lives.*

Captain Tubbs *And battle stations is the key element of the boot camp experience. It crystallizes what we are about. As Captain Gantt says, they are unique individuals, and sometimes it takes nine weeks, and they still don't get it, but by the time they finish battle stations you can see the transition, and they become a team. While it's the final performance test of the basic naval skills and endurance, more importantly, they begin to internalize our core values. They hear and understand what real sailors have experienced, and what they could be exposed to in the very near future.*

Captain Gantt *We intend to strengthen battle stations even more. We'll build a battle stations building with a realistic mockup, including a near life-sized ship, with full simulation. "Abandon ship" will occur from the deck of that ship, the simulator will be* *surrounded by water. We'll do our seamanship on that mockup. We'll go inside, and fight real fires. Right now we split between facilities, but when we've finally got things the way we want, that will be the closest thing to sea duty you'll ever experience on dry land.*

Other military services run considerably longer initial training. Marine recruits spend up to fourteen weeks before deploying operationally. Resource limitations, however, force the Navy to complete boot camp in less than ten weeks.

Captain Gantt *Well, if we weren't resource-bound, I'd lengthen the time here. We do a lot, but nine weeks is nine weeks. For many, we've changed their behavior, or modified their thought processes, but there are some who just need more time. I'd have more professional trainers, if I could. I'd like to spend more time working with recruits on intelligent life choices. As a squadron commander, I saw it almost daily. Some young sailor goes out, gets drunk, and wraps a car around a tree. That all has to do with intelligent life choices. Kids don't seem to get that now, either from families or from school. We now have a drug-free environment, and these recruits don't have to worry where the next meal is coming from, or getting shot on the way to school. We always talk about the stressors in boot camp—think of the stressors that we don't have here. In this safe, secure environment we'd have the opportunity to help these folks make some intelligent life choices, but we just don't have the time. On 8-5 day, you're out of here.*

Captain Tubbs *There are so many people who want to insert things into the curriculum that the length is being challenged on a monthly basis. The fleet has told us what they want, and we've designed the curriculum to meet those needs. But we need a whole lot more folks. Our student-instructor ratios are high, you might find two hundred recruits in a lecture. It's worse than being a university freshman, sometimes. But it's hard to complain about it, because both service school command and the fleet itself have the same need for those very good people.*

Commander Rawls *Most of the pressure to change is external. It costs us $9.5 million per day to run this command. We actually get pressure to reduce, rather than lengthen it. People say, okay, let's cut off a day. We already are stuffing six pounds in the five-*

pound bag. So what gives? They are talking of reducing Service Week, but in addition to reducing operating expenses by using recruit labor—we're paying them every day they are here, after all—it's a vital part of their exposure to the Navy's way of work. We train the way we fight.

Great Lakes is overcrowded at the best of times. In many ways it is a prisoner of its geography. Much has been written recently about the state of the facilities and the urgent need for recapitalization of the base.

Captain Gantt *We're negotiating now with the Veterans Administration for a parcel of land that will help us expand westward. It's not very big, but it will help, if we can get it. Recapitalization will change our layout considerably. We'll finally separate vehicles and recruits, and the joint-use buildings will reduce transit time significantly.*

Captain Tubbs *It's challenging. This place is not training-centered, it's facility-centered. We use what we have, the best way we can. When the place was designed, no one suspected we'd do sixty thousand recruits annually, well into the twenty-first century. We march more than the Army, just to get where we need to go.*

Commander Rawls *In a perfect world, we would level it and start all over again. We realized that problem long ago. We rehabilitate where we can, but everything is old. As the XO says, we march twenty-five miles per week, and it's all schedule driven. On foot, in formation. Now, marching is good from a lot of perspectives— esprit de corps, motivation, even physical fitness—but the driver is logistics. And right now, it's a bear.*

Perhaps surprisingly, when senior enlisted staff at RTC list their concerns, recruits are fairly far down the list. Time pressures, the off-base environment, family issues all take precedence.

Captain Gantt *I think the time pressures on the enlisted, particularly RDCs, are very real. And, in a sense, that reflects what's happening in the rest of the Navy, with deployments, gapped billets, and what have you. I do know that it's tougher on the female RDCs—PL105 requires us to have male-female pairs on duty at* *night, and with the smaller cadre, each female RDC has a greater share of the watch bill than her male counterparts.*

Captain Tubbs *I know everyone talks about us being in North Chicago, and the situation with the schools. Unfortunately, Navy bases are rarely located in the best part of town. Yes, North Chicago schools have lower results than other districts in the county. Does it keep good people from coming here? I don't want to sound harsh, but this is the Navy. If we need someone here, they are coming. That's why they're called orders, and not suggestions.*

Captain Gantt *Sure, it causes some people to shy away, but scuttlebutt always emphasizes the negative side, and I think things are outweighed by the positive. Watch the RDCs at pass-in-review tomorrow, and watch when they mingle with the parents afterwards. They're two feet off the ground; they're like parents at a wedding. When you turn a kid around, and mom and dad come up and thank you—it's certainly worth it to me, and I suspect it is to everyone who works with the recruits.*

Captain Tubbs *Look, everyone has a boiling point. I've talked to RDCs who have pushed eleven divisions who say "send me back," and those who were nervous wrecks after three. We need more people. But there are so many gapped billets at sea, it's extremely difficult for us to get all the people we need. RTC is holding its own in the allocation of resources, but we are on the cusp of extremis. We're desperately trying to get folks ordered in now to be ready for next year's surge.*

There is amazing congruence between the view from the wardroom and the viewpoint of the recruit division commanders on the street.

Chief Lucas *Well, if boot camp is too soft, I wish someone would show me where. Is it physical training? We're doing PT now six days a week, rather than the three or four days they did before. Is it battle stations? They never had anything like that before. Are we marching less? Letting recruits get away with murder, or what? Show me where it is. Personally, I think that's a copout.*

Petty Officer Russell *Well, I don't know what happened back in the day. These guys that compare us to the old days, like, what did* *happen back then? Did they take them out behind the drill hall and beat the snot out of them? It's like Chief Lucas says, "How do we make this place harder?" We're doing PT six times a week; we march, like, twenty miles a week. What more should we do?*

Senior Chief Nelson *In a sense, the people who are saying that are really accusing themselves. If there's a chief or petty officer in the fleet that can't handle today's seamen or airmen, is that a problem with the sailors or with the supervisor?*

Command Master Chief McCalip *The quality of the sailor in the fleet is determined by the first petty officer or chief petty officer they report to aboard ship, I'm convinced of it. Our mission here is to turn out physically fit, basically qualified sailors. Watch them at pass-in-review. I think we're doing a pretty darn good job.*

Petty Officer Kent *Well, to be honest with you, I used to have that opinion myself, especially when I was at SERE, which is a really tough environment. But I changed my mind when I got here. It's easy to say that the kids today aren't like we were, but it's not true. It's that "I walked two miles through the snow to school" story that you hear from your parents. And the way we run boot camp now is not the way it was two or three years ago, and I suspect it will be different two or three years from now. We've had three commanding officers since I've been here, and each one had his or her own style. Each time we change commands, we change our focus a little. But the changes weren't all that great—boot camp is still boot camp—we just changed some of the hoops the recruits had to jump through. So, the guys that knock us—are they talking about the way things are today, or last year, or when?*

There has been much discussion about the best way to integrate male and female recruits to meet the requirements of Public Law 105, yet still provide the best training for all recruits.

Chief Zeller *I don't think the way we are doing this is the best way, not at all. We absolutely forbid fraternizing, yet everything we do encourages it. We put them in the same spaces, for class or PT or drill or whatever, for eighteen hours a day. We have them take off their sweatshirts, and they do their PT in sweaty, white skivvy shirts—what nineteen-year-old wouldn't get excited? We used to* *keep them apart except for class, but now they mingle, all day, every day. Then we expect that they won't flirt. I'll give you one real-life example that happens three times a day. Because of the thousands of recruits trying to get through the mess halls for every meal, we make them line up, heel-to-toe, at the galley portals. Heel-to-toe, male to female. I've had female recruits in here, crying—not that the male tried to do anything, don't get me wrong—but because it's so, well, degrading. It's really not the best way to do this, at all.*

Petty Officer Kent *I don't see the reason for all the fuss over integration, to tell you the truth. I never saw much difference in output between integrated and nonintegrated divisions. Look, all these kids have been through integrated education since kindergarten. They've all worked with members of the opposite sex at their civilian jobs. So how is two months away from the opposite sex going to screw up their idea of how to work together? But, like Chief Zeller says, when you put them together, you are automatically setting up fraternization problems. You get note passing, you ignite everybody's raging hormones, and you have people getting jealous of each other. It ruins morale, it really does.*

Petty Officer Russell *I don't know what's the best way to do it, but I bet it isn't this. I think this way causes us more problems than it solves. Integrating, deintegrating, having them into two separate houses: we don't really spend as much time with them as I'd like. Right now, I'm in my own house, and I don't know what my females are doing topside. Sure, there is an RDC there, but she's working with her own people, just like I would be, and my people could be goofing off for all I know.*

Senior Chief Nelson *I look at it like this. Having males and females in one division, but having two berthing spaces, is like having a home and your summer place. When you're at home, you are always wondering what's going on at your summer place—is the water turned off? Is the sump pump working? And when you're at your summer place, you wonder if the neighbors are breaking into your house in town and walking away with everything. That's what it's like when you have your recruits spread into two compartments. I trust Zeller's crew with my males down below, but I don't really control what half my recruits are doing, part of the time.*

Senior Chief Tucker *No doubt about it, I'd have them totally separate during boot camp. Sure, you'd make everyone adhere to the same standards—PT, training, classroom, whatever—but keep them separate for two months. Right now, you have guys looking at girls, with all that entails. What we need to do is to have it so that they look at everybody as their shipmate, someone that has a job to do, either here or in the fleet. As the LCPO, I wind up as the "judge" here a lot. Some poor guy is caught talking to a female out in the passageway or whatever, and it gets written up as fraternization, and we ASMO them back a couple weeks. It's not necessary, and it screws things up.*

Senior Chief Atkinson *I think they need to separate them. Let them meet up for training or drill or whatever. But the other way is too hard for everyone. The thing is, you need to be able to train recruits, and not worry about the male-female interaction. The bottom line is we need to get them basically trained and physically fit. After eighteen years, they know each other, right?*

Educational requirements for recruits have been lowered, to help alleviate manpower shortages. The Navy will accept up to 10 percent of its recruits lacking a high school diploma. There has been some controversy as to the wisdom of this solution.

Petty Officer Kent *Well, the percentage of non–high school grads that get here is not all that large. And when they get here, they get separated to ACE or whatever. When they get to the fleet, a lot get their GEDs and move up, and even go to college, some of them. I personally think they make better sailors, lots of times. They know that, hey, they started at a disadvantage, and the Navy took care of them, and they find a home in the Navy.*

Chief Zeller *I don't think it has a real impact here in boot camp. They wind up in an ACE division, where we teach a little bit more by example and less by reading. Believe it or not, non–high school graduates must have a higher minimum ASVQB test score [50, as opposed to 31 for high school graduates], so they aren't necessarily dumb. The big problem is that they weren't a success in high school, and so they develop a quitter attitude. And there still is a reluctance to separate nonperformers. I worry that sometimes we send people on who really should be bounced. But there are tools that we use that can turn someone around, and I think we try* *everything we can to get them straight before we either pass them onward or send them home.*

Petty Officer Russell *These recruits have two problems that I can see. One is that they have trouble taking tests, and probably will have trouble making rate once they get to the fleet. You have a lot of studying to do. For example, I'm studying for chief right now. We damage controlmen are a "go out and do it" rating, but there's still lots to read and remember. And the other thing is the quitter attitude, as Chief Zeller said. Their attitude seems to be, "Hey, if I don't like it, I'll walk out the front gate." Those RDCs at Ship Fifteen, where we have the special programs—they have the toughest motivating job of anybody on the base.*

Command Master Chief McCalip *We're on the right track, I think. We've finally figured out the right way to handle non–high school graduates. But what would really make a difference for them would be to strengthen the Delayed Entry Program [DEP]. When we get to the point where they can work a little while with the recruiters, they'd be better prepared when we get them, and we'll be better off. There's not a single recruit that walks through that gate planning to fail when they get here. So our job is to give them every opportunity we can to succeed. Some we identify immediately as having too many problems for us to handle, and those we send home. Others just need a little kick to move them in the right direction. Because, even if we set them back three or four times, and finally have to let them go, we've at least made them better citizens than they were when they got here.*

Chief Lucas *Captain Gantt said it best. He said that in society today, there are not very many regimented programs that develop good solid values. So it's not unusual to get kids who don't match, or even understand, our Navy core values. We've had to develop programs like PASS for anger management, ACE for non–high school graduates, and training to give every recruit some coping skills. Lots of these kids didn't have parents to motivate them, but they have to get it somewhere. And, as Master Chief points out, even if they are only in the Navy for four years, they will leave as better people.*

Senior Chief Tucker *The Marines have the right idea. The real big difference is that the recruiter doesn't get credit for his recruits until* *they finish boot camp. We don't do that, but if we did, I bet we'd see a lot better caliber of recruits, real quick. The other thing is that the Marine recruiter is held accountable for the physical fitness of the recruits. When we get one who's not physically fit, it screws up everything else; you spend all the time trying to get them ready to pass battle stations, and you downplay academics and seamanship training and all the other stuff. And if I think my folks need a run, I want to be able to run on the streets, and we can't do that here. Because of our location, we have to PT indoors six months of the year. You have them running around in circles, and you can't motivate and monitor, when they are strung out all around a quarter-mile track like a Slinky toy. Why they closed down San Diego I'll never know; you could be outside every single day in the fresh air. Go to any military base anywhere in any country—watch any Army or Marine movie about boot camp, for that matter—and you see people running in groups, building esprit and motivation. We just can't do that here because of our facilities, and that's a great loss.*

One of the main reasons why senior petty officers resist orders to Recruit Training Command is the perceived impact on family life. Time pressures, weather, and difficulty with the local schools all combine to make the assignment less attractive than many would like.

Chief Zeller *There's a lot of time pressure. We now have three RDCs in each division, which helps. But then again, they've changed the rules so that we have to be with the recruits a lot more than we used to. We're with them from reveille to taps, 0400 to 2200 each day. And there are lots of times when there have to be at least two RDCs working with the division. Inspections, or some other events, require at least two and sometimes all three of us here at the same time. There are periods when you are here for eighteen or nineteen hours, for maybe ten days in a row. Sure, there are times when you can get down to the lounge for awhile, but problems usually follow you wherever you go. Now, when you drop the division off at the schoolhouse, you might get a little time to unwind. But you have paperwork to do; you might have to walk someone around if they have to go on emergency leave, or things like that. We try to schedule it so that we don't kill ourselves, but on average we do about eleven or twelve hours a day, six days a week. That's average. During the first days of a push there's no down time whatsoever.*

Command Master Chief McCalip *The time pressures are real. We are working very hard with the chief of naval personnel to get the right number of people here, as well as the right caliber. It's a challenge to get people to Great Lakes, no doubt about it.*

Petty Officer Kent *Both the weather and the time pressures are murderous. It's a killer for families. You give much more time to this job than in any other one I've ever had. And many of the time requirements are stupid. We have to be with them every waking hour. That's stupid—they develop no self-control whatsoever. When I first got here, we could at least let recruits go from the school-house to the chow hall with the RPOC in charge. That's, what? Two hundred yards? Now, they can't free-steam as a division till their seventh week. By then, they are almost out of here. Otherwise, we are with them every single moment, except when they are actually in class. That's really stupid.*

Senior Chief Nelson *I'm a family man, but I tell my wife, "When I have a division, you have to treat it like I'm on a two-month deployment." If you have recruits for nine weeks it's about the same thing. Now, my wife has been with me for sixteen years, and she's a strong woman. But my kids are getting to an age where I'd like to spend a little more time with them, because you don't want them hanging around with the wrong crowd. But I knew what I was getting into before I got here.*

Command Master Chief McCalip *It's true. You can have more down time aboard a deployed ship than you do here. It takes a very special type of person to want to come here; you have to be truly committed to the future of the Navy to do this job. You know what you are facing here. But there are huge benefits to coming here. There's proficiency pay, and the probability of early promotion to chief or to senior chief for the guys that are chiefs already. Last cycle, we had the highest CPO selection rate, about 40 percent, of any command in the Navy. We had about 35 percent for selection to master chief, and that's unheard of anywhere else. And we are the largest source of command master chiefs or chief of the boat anywhere in the fleet. So there's a payback, but this isn't a nine-to-five job, by any means.*

Senior Chief Tucker *All this is true. But the RDCs should really be better screened before they get here. And that's the sending com-*

mand's responsibility. The command master chief needs to talk to the guy and his family, because this place is really hard on families. The screening process really has to be done on the ship, and maybe better than it is. I think we are getting mostly the right guys, but there are a percentage that probably would be happier, and doing a better job, somewhere else. And I'll tell you another thing that really makes it hard on families. The school system in North Chicago is probably the worst at any duty station I've been at in fifteen years. When I was here the first time, I brought my kids. Now they are down in Missouri. That's another reason why we can't get good guys up here. There are no secrets in the Navy. You think that people in the fleet don't know about the school system outside these gates?

Comprehensive statistics, published in the *Lake County News-Sun* on 2 November 2000, showed North Chicago School District 137, which serves the Great Lakes Naval Base and surrounding communities, rated dead last among all school districts in the county. For example, Katzenmaier Junior High School, located just north of the base, showed 45 percent of all students below the state's minimum acceptance levels for seventh-grade science, 50 percent below state minimums in seventh-grade math, 35 percent below standards in eighth-grade reading, and 77 percent below state minimum competency levels in eighth-grade math. By the tenth grade, things are even worse. At North Chicago High School, 48 percent were below standards in tenth-grade reading, and a whopping 80 percent in tenth-grade math.

Chief Zeller *North Chicago has a really poor reputation. And it's well deserved. That's the main reason that I'm a geo-bachelor. When I was here at service school command, we thought it was so bad that we yanked our kids out of public school and sent them to private school at our own expense. That's why we decided that I'd come up here single this time, and my wife and family would stay at home in Kansas City. Every minute I can get, and there aren't many, I'm down I-55 heading home.*

Senior Chief Atkinson *He's right. The schools here are terrible. You can't afford to pay for a place in town, babysitters for after-school time, and still pay for private school. And I'm making E8 money. I have three kids: eight-year-old twins, and a six-year-old. I'm a single, custody parent. You don't have the energy to look after your* *own kids. You know you can fix your kid's problems, but you just don't have the energy. I'd be up at 0300 to make reveille here on the base, and push recruits till, maybe, 1800 or so, and that's only if I could get away and let my partners handle it. I'd go home to help my kids with their homework. There were days—and I'm not exaggerating—when all of us fell asleep at my kitchen table, me with my head down, and them on the floor. And then I'd get up at 0300 and do it again. It's murder.*

Petty Officer Russell

I have two kids in North Chicago schools, and I don't think it's as bad as other people suggest. I know one thing, you have gangs and drugs and all that stuff wherever you go, even in the most expensive schools. In a way, it's better here. When they had those shootings out in Colorado, the first thing they did afterwards was put in metal detectors and security and stuff. Well, North Chicago has been dealing with that for years, so all that is already there and protecting the kids. My oldest daughter, in particular, is not a follower; in fact, she'll go up and counsel these other kids about right and wrong. You just have to be sure your own kids are law-abiding. My daughters say, "Hey, mom, you ain't our RDC, you're our mom." I have to turn it off when I go out the gate.

Command Master Chief McCalip *I think things are changing. Everyone in this command is aware of the school problem, but, in the last couple years we've gotten much more involved with the schools. The flag officers, other officers, senior enlisted, every level. We even have a liaison team of military parents who work with the school board. They know that we're paying attention to the problem, and in the two years that I've been here I've seen huge changes.*

Chief Lucas *You want to know what the schools are really like? Okay, go find out where the senior officers are sending their kids. Gurnee, Lake Forest, wherever; it's sure not North Chicago. Then check and see how many home-school parents we have among the enlisted. I bet there are a hundred, at least. My wife home-schools our kids. Check out the number of guys that live up in Wisconsin—up above Kenosha, some of them. These are RDCs that get up at 0200 to make 0400 reveille here. It's nothing but the schools.*

Petty Officer Kent *Between that and the base layout, it takes a lot out of you, for sure. I can tell you how bad it is. I did a push out of*

Ship Thirteen, down at the south end. In that first few weeks when you are going back and forth through the tunnel all the time, it's murder. When those kids first get their seabags, its like the Bataan death march, it's that bad. When you are centrally located, like at Ship Eight, it's not so bad. But from Ship Thirteen to the Fire Fighting Training Unit? A good thirty-minute march. Unfortunately, your schedule will read the same as a guy's in Ship Two, so you had better walk faster, leave earlier, and if you try to follow the schedule, you'll never make it. So you're always thinking, "How can I save time, or how can I cut a corner to stay on schedule?" when you're at the ends of the base.

Senior Chief Atkinson *It's fun in the summer. But in the winter it's bad. Marching is one of the things that RDCs enjoy the most. But in the winter it is atrocious. Ice, snow, people slipping, potholes, you name it. March from swim call back to Galley 1128 in the wintertime—how many sick recruits will you get out of that?*

Senior Chief Nelson *In the winter, it does get bad. If you march recruits from one end to the other, it's hard. Here's something that nobody else told you, I bet. You get out there in the traffic pattern, the first thing you look at is the guidons of other divisions heading your way. If you get behind a division that just got here, and hasn't learned to march, it's like being behind a truck on the Dan Ryan Expressway. It really slows you down.*

Senior Chief Atkinson *Well, if they were only going to keep one, it should have been San Diego or Orlando. All our bases are on the coasts, the weather is better. It's all politics. I think they ought to put things right next to the fleet. We get days here, like right now, when the weather keeps us from doing much of anything.*

Senior Chief Tucker *Having the base here is just dumb. You have guys who won't come here, good guys who would really make fantastic RDCs—because they are settled on one or the other coast, and why come here for just three years? You know you'll have to move back to one of the fleet homeports when you are done. But, more than that, we need to have these young people around the military, they need to see sailors just going about their business, day after day. This place is artificial, all they see are those jobs that are necessary to run this training center, and they never see a machinist mate working on a ship's engine, or a storekeeper running a forklift, or anything like that.*

Command Master Chief McCalip   *Great Lakes was the wrong deci-sion. I would have kept San Diego, and I would have built a new boot camp right next to Norfolk. We'd be in fleet concentration areas, and sailors will stay in the Navy if you can keep them in the same place. Families get 51 percent of the vote about staying in— and if you keep them in one place and not move them unnecessar-ily, we'd be lots better off.*

Petty Officer Kent   *At surge, when the June high school graduates all hit, things are bad. It's worst at the galleys. You can get to the galley, and have six or seven divisions ahead of you. If you have an event you have to get to, and it's all the other way across base, you are in a world of hurt. What do you do? You can't buck the line, the other guy has the same problem, and you can't be late for the event, because there are two or three divisions coming over after you. So what do you do? It's eat up and get out, folks. Dinner becomes five minutes. The other problem is putting ninety-four people in a compartment. When you have racks down the middle, you can't see what's going on in the back. The kids back there get away with murder.*

Petty Officer Russell   *The last division we had was a ninety-four. The grinders were so bad you couldn't get them out of the way to get into class. And the chow lines were bad. Everywhere there were lines. And it tears up the barracks. I'm the ship's building mainte-nance and supply petty officer, in addition to pushing a division. The wear and tear is bad when we have twelve eighty-person divi-sions in the building. With twelve ninety-fours . . . [Shaking her head.]*

Chief Lucas   *And lots of the stuff that we need, we have to buy ourselves. The Navy doesn't issue irons to press uniforms, so the first thing we do when a new division arrives is pass the hat and buy enough for the division. At the end, when they graduate, we put all the dogtags into a hat, and the winners get the irons, and spare cleaning gear, and whatever else we bought. Our cleaning supplies—the soap and polish and everything—is so watered down to meet HazMat requirements, that it's just better for us to run over to the commissary and buy our own supplies. Every RDC here has a load of stuff in the back of his car. Any one of us could open up a janitor's service, with what we carry around in the trunk.*

Command Master Chief McCalip *But, you know what? There are over seven hundred recruit division commanders on this base. And I bet you every single one of them would do it all over again. Fifteen of them will march into that pass-in-review tomorrow. And they wouldn't trade that moment for anything.*

17
Bravo Zulu, Young Sailors—
Well Done!

Reveille sounded early on graduation day. Chief Zeller hit the lights at 0330, but for once no one felt like dawdling in their racks. After early chow, they returned to their compartment for showers and, for the female recruits, that long awaited moment when they could wear makeup again. All three RDCs worked with the recruits, ensuring that each uniform fit perfectly and—with judicious use of tape, pins, and (in at least one case) staples—perfecting the work of the contract tailors who had last altered the uniforms.

Petty Officer Russell explains: "Recruits—mostly female recruits—are constantly complaining about how their uniforms don't fit. They really bad-mouth the tailors. But what they don't realize is that they aren't the same people who took the uniforms over to the tailor shop during their fourth week here—they've lost twenty pounds, or moved it around or whatever. So how can they expect the uniform to fit perfectly the first time they get into it? Any RDC who has been here awhile brings a sewing kit on pass-in-review day."

After a last-minute inspection, the division left the compartment at 0750. The holding area, because of the inclement weather, had moved to Drill Hall 800.

Hopkins *I figured, typical boot camp. There's snow all over the ground, it's freezing cold, we're going to Drill Hall 1200, which is way north of our ship, and the first thing they do is send us south, to Drill Hall 800. The guys on the front are yelling to me, "You're going the wrong way, Hump," but that's where Chief told me to go, so that's where we went.*

While the recruits were mustering at Drill Hall 800, twelve hundred visitors had arrived and checked in at MCPON Hall. Because of the snow, and the danger of accidents, Senior Chief Atkinson held the visitors there until just before 0900. A cadre of Service Week recruits then escorted the visitors to Drill Hall 1200. They were entertained by the Great Lakes Navy Band, founded in 1917 by LCDR John Philip Sousa. Conducted today by MU2* Alan Miller, the band played traditional holiday tunes and then broke into a rousing military cadence, echoing that of the recruit band leading the 412 graduating recruits through the double doors at the south end of the cavernous drill hall.

McClellan *We could hear them cheering as the other divisions went in before us, and as we hit the door, we could hear the applause and cheers coming from our left. I tried to look around and see where everyone was sitting, but, being next to last, we only had a real short time before we stopped and dressed to attention. It seemed like the people that were there for our division were off to our left slightly, though.*

Wirsch *I wanted to see my little brother Matthew so bad! After we dressed right, and came to parade rest, I was looking around a little to see if I could spot him. When the chaplain gave the invocation, I could hear a baby crying, but it didn't seem to be him. But I just knew, somehow, that everyone had made it okay, and that they were in that crowd somewhere.*

Hopkins *Well, my dad uses a wheelchair, so I spotted him right away. They had the disabled guests up on the front row. I couldn't see anyone else, but I knew if he was there, then everyone else was, too. I just wanted to get my drill commands right, so that I'd make him proud.*

The command takes great pride in the recruit graduation ceremonies. Every element of Navy protocol is on display during the ninety-minute pass-in-review. A formal quarterdeck is permanently established at the far north end of the fifty-year-old drill hall. Sideboys manned the rail, as six bells, followed by ruffles and flourishes, signaled the arrival of Rear Adm. David

*Petty Officer Miller is a musician, second class (E5).

Polatty, commander, Naval Training Center. Four bells and bosun's pipes marked the arrival of Captain Gantt, accompanied by Capt. David O'Brien, the day's reviewing officer. In honor of the fifty-ninth anniversary of Pearl Harbor Day, two guests of honor, both Pearl Harbor survivors, joined the entourage as they moved toward the reviewing stand. Joseph Triolo, BMC, USN (Ret.), and Ambrose Ferri, PNC, USN (Ret.), would take the recruits' salute today.

The recruits stood at attention, heads bowed, as the base chaplain invoked divine blessing on them and their families. They stood at parade rest as the recruit performance division —their battle stations comrades from Division 902—sang, marched, and drilled for the assembled guests. Captain O'Brien rose to speak.

Rasco *Oh, man, I was feeling bad, standing there at parade rest. The FQA inspector behind us kept coming up to me and telling me to unlock my legs, or I'd pass out. I must have looked white as a sheet. I know I was sweating and feeling pretty bad, but I kept my military bearing throughout it.*

Leonard *It must be the big moment for the guy that gets to speak. He thanks everybody that's there—the admiral, the captain, the whatever—and finally gets around to talking to us. Meanwhile, we've been in that hot drill hall, surrounded by smelly shipmates [laughter] in those hot uniforms for, like, forever. I'm thinking, why doesn't he just get on with it?*

Captain O'Brien was mercifully brief. After a quick weather report from San Diego, where he commanded both Naval Air Station North Island and Naval Base Coronado, he spoke of his own memories as an aviation officer candidate years ago. "Wherever you go, and whatever you do," he said, "you'll always remember your recruit division commander. And even when you leave the Navy, after four years or forty years, you'll mark significant anniversaries and events by where you were serving, and who your shipmates were, when they occurred." He ended with the traditional Navy word of praise: "Bravo Zulu for a job well done."

Commander Mary Kolar, who had relieved Captain Tubbs as executive officer, took the podium and identified recruits worthy of special accolade. Two were from Division 005, the only division to have more than a single honoree. Seaman Eric Hopkins, the recruit chief petty officer, received the Retired Officers Association Leadership Award as the outstanding RPOC in the graduation group. The irrepressible Jared Ward, whose sardonic optimism had so enlivened and encouraged the division, received the Navy League Award for exhibiting those characteristics best summed up by the word "shipmate." The division's four operational flags: athletic, academic, drill, and STAR (for compartment readiness) dipped in honor of these two outstanding recruits.

The band struck up "Anchors Aweigh," and the crowd rose, cheering. The divisions kicked off, and marched the length of the drill hall, turned, and marched before the west side bleachers. As Division 005 passed the reviewing stand, an entire section of the bleachers broke into sustained and enthusiastic cheers. Division 005, eighty-one young men and women, from cities large and small, in thirty states, was going to the fleet.

Pandemonium erupted as liberty call was announced, and parents and other family members rushed onto the drill deck to seize, hug, and kiss their recruits. An old sailor, standing in the shadows, served as a willing surrogate for several members of Division 005 whose families had been delayed by the winter storm. It was the least he could do.

Afterward, the recruits and their families spoke of the past few months.

Captain Frank Moll, USN (Ret.), is SR James Troeger's grandfather. A World War II veteran, he stayed on active service through the 1960s. "I was very happy when James decided to join the Navy, but apprehensive. I'm still apprehensive. Even the best-laid plans can go wrong."

Ms. Susan Markley is James Troeger's mother. "Well, we had heard from him only once the day he got to Great Lakes, and then it was several weeks till his first letters arrived. And we were so worried—what are they doing to him up there? And then, when they marched in, we weren't able to spot him in the crowd."

Melissa Burns is Troeger's fiancée. "I was trying to use the viewfinder of my camcorder to spot him, but I couldn't see him in the crowd. We were seated off to his left, so we really didn't have a good angle to see him when they first marched in."

Troeger *I saw my grandparents as soon as we walked into the drill hall, but I didn't see anybody else. I kept moving my head during formation, figuring everybody would be together, but I couldn't see them from where I was standing.*

Melissa Burns *It's funny, but the first thing I noticed is how much hair he has now! [Laughter.] His head was shaved before he went to boot camp, so it looks really different now.*

Captain Moll *I noticed a substantial change in his bearing. Much more confident, and a real change in the person from two and a half months before.*

Melissa Burns *He looks good in his new uniforms, that's for sure!*

Some recruits had practical things in mind as soon as liberty call was announced, while others were more philosophical.

Hopkins *The first thing I want when I get off base is a hot shower, and a big steak. In fact, I want the steak so much that I thought of eating it in the shower.*

Buki *It's like a burden is off my shoulders, finally. It's gone by really fast, but now I'm going to miss a lot of the people that were here. For a while, I wanted to wring their necks, but now I'm happy that we stuck together and everything.*

Rasco *I'm scared. We're getting ready to go out to the fleet, and start another whole part of this career, you know? Boot camp was hard, and I'm excited about leaving, don't get me wrong. But we don't know what's going to happen to us. I have a two-week school, and then I'm out to an aircraft carrier or a squadron or whatever. Like, I know I'll have two weeks of Airman Apprentice School at Pensacola, and then I have no idea where we'll go.*

Wirsch *I have six months of school, to be an electrician's mate, but still, I don't know what that is going to be like or what is going to happen afterwards, like Rasco says.*

Rasco *I'll miss everyone. We'll probably never see each other again, you know?*

Wirsch *I thought boot camp was going to be a lot harder than this, though. When we were doing battle stations, or when we were doing PT, it was, like, okay, okay, it hurts already, stop it. But the rest of the time, it wasn't all that bad, really.*

Freeman *Except for the sleep. I don't care where I go next, for the first two weeks there, I'm going to sack out. Y'all come wake me if something happens, okay? [Laughter.]*

Wirsch *I'm scared that the same thing that happened to the Cole will happen to whatever ship I'm on. We hear all the time, the world is just waiting for us out there, and it could happen anytime.*

Freeman *I know that going to war is what the Navy is there for. My dad is an ex-Marine, so I knew that coming in.*

Rasco *Yeah, but you think about that stuff, and then you don't, really. You don't think about death all the time. You don't think your cousin is going to get killed in a car wreck or anything bad is going to happen. It just does.*

Freeman *I think being on the ship is going to be fun. It's going to be hard work, sure, but it's going to be first you work, and then you play. But I'm going to experience so many things that I'd never experience back in Dequincy [Louisiana] or if I stayed in college just to play softball.*

Buki *The best memories that I'll take out of here will be the weird things that happened to us. Like, when we are on watch at night in the female compartment, there's always someone who sits up at attention, right in her sleep, and it's so funny. I know we got cycled the other day, and we had to do lots of arm circles, and I woke up in my sleep and my arms were going around and around. [Laughter.]*

Freeman *Well, the best memories I'll have are Wirsch singing in the shower! [Laughter.] When I first got here, and we had eighty females, trying to shower in three minutes, I was so nervous, I didn't know what I was going to do. And then Wirsch thinks she's Madonna, it helped me chill out. And I'm going to miss those little* *things like how we all say good night to each other at lights out, and always having someone to lean on.*

Wirsch *I'm not going to miss reveille. But what I'll really miss is when I'm having a really, really bad day, and someone comes up to me and says, "Smile, we only have twelve days or six days or whatever left."*

Rasco *My favorite memory was battle stations ceremony. I felt like I was twenty feet tall. I felt like we were in a huge stadium and there were thousands of people looking down on us. I felt so proud that day.*

Wirsch *I always like it when I'm downstairs in the office, and it's time to deintegrate, and I yell, "Good night guys," and all these guys yelling, "Good night, Wirsch." That's going to be my favorite memory.*

Buki *That was something that I hadn't thought about at all. Living with eighty other girls for, what, nearly three months now? I figured that I'd just sit in the corner somewhere, and do PT and stuff when they said so, and have my nose to the grinder and stuff. I never figured it would be like this at all.*

Rasco *I've come so far in the last few months, but there's so much farther to go. Like, I didn't even know who I was when I came in here. And I still don't, really. It's so confusing.*

Wirsch *I'll tell you something that you might not understand. For me, all my life I've felt like I've been competing with all the cheerleaders and beauty queens and stuff at school. And to have guys say good night to me, and having never, ever seen me with any makeup on, well, that was really special to me. I thought that guys would never even breathe my way if I didn't get all made up before I set foot outside the house at home, you know?*

Buki *They had no choice! [Laughter.] No, I'm serious! These guys saw us females as people for the first time in their lives, I bet! Like, I used to be a high-maintenance person—it took me an hour and a half to get ready if I was going out or something. But after a couple days in the division, it was, who cares?*

Wirsch *Insecurity—that's something else I had to deal with while I was here. Like, battle stations! I wanted to die after that first run. We were all trying to motivate each other all night.*

Cari Williams *Well, if it wasn't for Freeman, I'd have quit, sure. She kept me going.*

Freeman *And y'all helped me when we were in the search and rescue, and all.*

Rasco *We all learned to help each other.*

They did, indeed. Captain Tubbs was right. That's what boot camp is all about.

The recruits knew that liberty would expire at 2100 inside their compartment. The division would also have liberty on Saturday and Sunday. Each recruit was assigned to a duty section; their duty day had to be spent on base, but on the other days, they were free to leave. There were several restrictions. They must remain in uniform at all times, stay clear of the off-limits area in North Chicago, and remain within fifty miles of the base at all times. Regardless of age, no recruit could consume alcohol, nor were they permitted to drive automobiles while on recruit liberty. Other than those minor restrictions, their time was their own, and most headed off to Chicago or Milwaukee. A surprisingly large number headed off to Gurnee Mills Shopping Center, one of the largest discount shopping centers in the United States, just a few miles west of the base.

Those in the duty section were required to be aboard Ship Eight only during their scheduled watches. The rest of the time could be spend with visitors, either at MCPON Hall or the adjacent branch Navy Exchange. This branch exchange—"Ricky Heaven" to the recruits—had plenty of video games, food shops, concessions, telephones, and other things to make the time pass quickly. The stress relief was obvious in the demeanor and voices of the recruits.

Gildersleeve *I sat there in MCPON Hall with my mother and father, and just talked about what had happened to me since I left home, and they told me all about what was happening back in Birmingham. It was nice, you know, just chillin' there. They got to meet some of my crew, and it was a great way to spend some time* *together. My father, see, was in the Air Force, so we talked about how it was for him, and how boot camp was for me.*

Morale, Welfare, and Recreation (MWR) had provided a few tickets to the Sunday Chicago Bears game. A few lucky recruits watched the Bears beat New England, 24-17, in the last game scheduled to be played at Chicago's famous Soldiers Field. And some of the recruits—well, sailors are sailors, even if they just graduated from boot camp. Chief Zeller recounts the story: "I had the duty Sunday night, and all the recruits got back on time, and in a really good mood. Some were in a *really* good mood, you know what I mean? The guys in particular were laughing and joking around. You can't keep any secrets in the Navy, so pretty soon I heard the story. One of our more decorated recruit petty officers led a detachment of his fellow recruits to a strip joint up on Route 41 in Antioch, just north of the base. That was perfectly legal, the area is not off limits or anything. It's a wonder he didn't run into a bunch of off-duty RDCs—that would have been awkward, wouldn't it? But apparently, it's totally nude on Sundays, and sailors get in free. One of his shipmates, a sheltered kind of kid who had never been exposed to that kind of thing before, dropped two hundred dollars or more on lap-dances before they left." He shook his head. "They must have seen these kids coming."

All present and accounted for, and tucked in for the night, the recruits knew that they had it made. Nothing could stop them now. Except, of course, the weather.

Adams *I was in the office, sorting the mail, when I first heard the radio. It said, like, two feet of snow was possible on Monday, and that they were declaring all kinds of emergencies. I heard them mention Lake County—I had no idea where that was, so I asked Chief. He just laughed. We're in Lake County.*

Guiterrez *I'm from southern California, out in the dessert below the Imperial Valley. I thought Adams meant two inches. I figured, hey, we've got more than that right now. No big deal, right? Wrong!*

The situation was indeed bad, and deteriorating by the hour. By Monday morning, it had begun to snow heavily, with winds gusting to 30 miles per hour.

Chief Zeller continues the story: "I stayed in the compartment with them, as we're required to do for the last few days that they are here. I hit the lights at 0400 on Monday, for the recruits' last full day of boot camp. It was bitter cold, and snowing to beat the band. It looked like we were in the worst blizzard the area had seen in quite awhile. Horizontal snow, and the wind chill was way below zero. The CDO declared it a Black Flag Day, which meant no training, and the only time the recruits could leave the ship was to make it to chow, if we could. I was glad, once again, we're in Ship Eight—I'd have hated to have to march to the galley from Ship Thirteen or Fourteen or one of those down that end.

"The plan was that Russell would come in and split the day with me, but she had an accident leaving her house, and wound up with six stitches in her foot. And I didn't think that either she or Kent would make it in, anyway, that's how bad it was snowing. They said we had fifteen inches by the middle of the afternoon. I tell you—getting to noon chow was a real trip. I was about ready to look around the ship, to see if we had any MREs (Meals, Ready to Eat) around. Or maybe C-rations from World War II up in the attic somewhere. But we finally went outside, and it was comical, it really was. I watched Zaragoza, who's from California and had never seen snow before, and she was having a ball, trudging along over to the galley. She's tiny, and the drifts were almost over her head. Naturally, they gave us a south side line again, so we had to trudge through the snowdrifts all around the galley to get in. Meanwhile, south end divisions were passing us, heading to north side chow lines. They really ought to fix that system.

Things got so bad that the skipper closed down the base by 1300. That really screwed things up for us, because I had a few recruits who had to stay behind in the holding unit, or for medical or legal reasons, and I couldn't get their paperwork through ASMO Central. Some stuff just didn't get done. We hung around the compartment all day—we couldn't do anything else, and every hour or so I'd send someone out to see if things had gotten any better. My car was completely covered by 1400, so it was good that we weren't going anywhere. I sat around and told sea stories to help fill the time. We'd gotten reamed a few days before because of the videotape escapade, but it didn't matter, I guess. Kent had shown *The Perfect Storm*, and now we were in the perfect storm.

"I held reveille on Tuesday at 0330. It was still snowing, although it was finally tapering off. The radio said that O'Hare was shut down, and that everything was a complete mess. I called over to the CDO, and he said to move the division over to 1405 on the chance that the buses would get through later that morning. I can't describe what it was like moving two divisions all the way across the base. Russ Redekop from 006 came down below and told me, 'Wherever you go, we'll go, because if we go alone, they might not find us till spring.' We slogged all the way across base, in at least a foot and a half of snow, in dress uniforms, dress shoes, and carrying seventy-five-pound seabags. Right before we left the ship at 0430, Russell made it through with her truck, and we managed to load it with about twenty-five garment bags, but most of the division carried the thirty-five pounds of dress uniforms, along with their seventy-five-pound seabags. It made battle stations look easy.

"We had the division strung out all the way from the ship over to Building 1405. Talk about a freezing morning! I even started singing the 'Dog Song' to help motivation, though it's not an approved street song, and we were still two hours before the time when we're allowed to sing on the streets. It took us well over an hour to move a mile and a quarter. That had to have been the coldest—the most uncomfortable, anyway—that any of us had ever been, even Pankratz from Montana, or Taylor from Alaska. But everyone was in great spirits, and we kept on skidding and sliding and slogging along.

"We finally made it to 1405, although after we'd gone inside and warmed up a little, someone came and told me we still were missing one or two. So I slogged back outside to rescue 'em. We finally got them inside, and warmed them up. Nobody knew when the buses would arrive, or even if they would. I kept thinking to myself, 'Whatever happens, I do not want to march this division all the way back over to Ship Eight, not at all.' I figured I might have a mutiny on my hands if I did. I'll tell you how bad it was: it took Russell almost as long to drive that mile and a quarter with the garment bags as it did for us to march over. The plows had not been out, and because we were still in Black Flag, the shovel brigades were still confined to their quarters.

"Finally, hours later, one bus made it through. It was for the folks going to Pensacola. Talk about a cheer going up! Except, once they got on, it got stuck in the snow, so it took about fifty of us to rock and push it till it got moving. The rest of the buses got stuck on the way in, and two of them skidded and collided as they turned into the base from Buckley Rd. We finally said the heck with it, and marched out to meet the buses. Two of them had to back all the way out onto the road surface, before they could get going again. What a mess. All I could think was, man, I hope they get out of O'Hare. Whatever they did, I didn't want anyone bringing them back to me! Not after that morning!"

Jared Ward, as usual, had the last word. "There's just one thing I want to know, and nobody can tell me. With big Navy bases in California, and Florida and Hawaii and all, whose goofy idea was it to keep boot camp up here?"

And that, young sailor, is a good question, indeed.

18
A Sailor Remembers

The old sailor stepped out of the shadows. The last buses had finally left, and the sailors of Division 005 were on their way to the fleet.

After thanking the Public Affairs staff for their many kindnesses over the three months he had shadowed Division 005, he turned to leave the base for the last time. Crossing the snowdrifts that lined Illinois St., he saw a division coming through the tunnel to his left. They were Smurfs, of course—the tightly bound guidon and the unpracticed cadence identified them even if layers of foul-weather gear covered their brand new Navy sweat suits. He recognized the tightly bundled chief petty officer as one whom he'd seen at Ship Eight during the months he'd accompanied Division 005. "What's your new division number, Chief?" he called. "082—picked 'em up last night, and taking them over to the ship." "What compartment, do you know yet?" "D-01— Zeller's old house." Life goes on.

The old sailor stepped into the small park just east of the tunnel entrance. There stood a life-sized replica of the Navy Memorial in Washington, Stanley Bleifeld's statue of the Lone Sailor, seabag at his side. Three granite pillars stood to the right. Brushing away the snow and ice with a gloved hand, he read: "The founders of the Navy Memorial envisioned this Lone Sailor as 25 years old at most, a senior second class petty officer who is fast becoming a seagoing veteran. He has done it all— fired his weapons in a dozen wars, weighed anchor from a thousand ports, tracked supplies, doused fires, repelled boarders, typed in quadruplicate and mess-cooked, too. He has made liberty call in great cities and tiny villages, where he played tourist, ambassador, missionary to the poor, adventurer, souvenir shopper and friend to new lands. His shipmates remember him with pride and tell their grandchildren stories, some of which, like him, are seven feet tall."

He smiled to himself. Twenty-five years old, he thought. Well, most of the kids have a chance to make second class by the time they're twenty-five. Their average age is what, twenty? Twenty-one? They've got a lot on the ball, the sailors of Division 005. Every one of them will have a petty officer's crow before too long, I bet.

He brushed the snow off the rest of the plaque. He knew what was written there, of course. Marty Zeller had asked him to tell the story one night, when the kids were downhearted and dejected about finishing dead last at Captain's Cup. He'd stepped out of the shadows that time, too, and told them a story about a kid named Jeremy—a kid, well, a kid just about like them. Jeremy wasn't the biggest guy in boot camp. As a matter of fact, at 5 feet, 6 inches, he looked more like a jockey than a sailor. He wasn't the fastest recruit, or the strongest, or the smartest, either, but he kept on going, and when he needed a hand, his shipmates helped him, just as he did when they needed him. Just like the kids of 005, he thought. Like Mike Shelton, who gave the last sip from his canteen to Maria Alcazar, the night of battle stations. Like Becky Freeman, lost and disoriented in the smoke-filled room, but who bounced back to motivate and energize the others on the long, freezing runs to the pool and to fire fighting. Like Schely Rasco, whose first thought when she heard of the disaster on the USS *Cole* was not of her own safety when she went to sea, but how the mothers and fathers must feel when they heard the tragic news. Just like three kids named Smith, and two named Williams, and Jones and Johnson and Jackson, and kids named Gray and Grayer. He read the simple dedication:

> Respectfully dedicated to the memory of
> Jeremy "Mike" Boorda
> Who Trained at Great Lakes
> March to May, 1956
> From Seaman to Admiral
> A Sailor's Sailor

Admiral Mike. That's what his sailors called him. A mustang, up through the hawsepipe, from seaman recruit to chief of naval operations. From the bottom to the very top—no one else had ever done that, before or since. He was a guy who loved his sailors, everybody knew that, and they loved him in return. He fought, and fought *with valor*, for the kid on the messdecks, and the petty officer on the flight line, and for every chief in every goat locker, on every ship afloat. For every sailor, everywhere.

Sailors like the kids of 005. For Gildersleeve, who kept his painful knees a secret so that he could run battle stations with his "crew." For Mary Smith, who missed her dad so much. For Megan Wirsch, the ever helpful and preternaturally competent yeoman, who practiced her "aye-aye, sir" to the point of distraction. For every single one of them.

The old sailor reached into his pocket. Buried down beneath the tape recorder, beneath the reporter's notebook and the pencils, beneath the orders giving him access to every nook and cranny of the command, he found what he was looking for. He took out the small square of Melton wool, the navy-blue square with a single white diagonal stripe. He had carried it, like a talisman, every day that he worked with the division. He looked at it again in the fading winter light.

He remembered the pride he had felt that day in 1966 when, before another pass-in-review, he had sewn it on his own dress blue uniform. Thirty-five years ago, he thought. Where have the years all gone? In his mind's eye he saw them yet again: his own shipmates, marching through the tunnel in the howling gales of a winter long ago. For many, as for himself, graduation from boot camp had meant orders to Vietnam. He was one of the fortunate ones. He came home to a loving family, a long civilian career, and the honor—for honor it was—of telling the story of today's recruits.

He fingered the rating badge yet again. With his free hand, he scraped away the accumulated snow and ice from under the left foot of the Lone Sailor. Gently, reverently, he placed it there, a votive offering for sailors everywhere. As the last notes of retreat sounded in the distance, he turned, saluted, and walked away.

By now, I suppose, the rains and snow may have caused that woolen square to decay, or the wind may have blown it to some far corner of the base. Or the birds may have taken it to make a nest for their young. Or, who knows? It may be there, still.

Appendix:
Division 01-005 Recruit Roster

Eighty-one recruits formed Division 005 on 3 October 2000. Because of illness, reassignment, training deficiency, or disciplinary action, twenty-three of these recruits were cycled to other divisions during their training period. Twenty-three other re-cruits rotated into the division; the first on the division's 1-2 day, and the last on the 8-3 day of training. These recruits marched under the Division 005 guidon at pass-in-review on 8 December 2000.

Rating	Name	Age	Hometown	Divisional Assignment
Seaman Apprentice	K. L. Abbott	19	Pensacola, FL	
Airman Recruit	K. R. Adams	18	Hillsborough, NC	Recruit Mail P.O.
Airman Recruit	M. T. Alcazar	20	Los Angeles, CA	
Airman Recruit	J. M. Arcia	18	Silt, CO	Recruit Education P.O.
Airman Recruit	F. K. Atitsogbuie	19	Bronx, NY	
Seaman Recruit	N. A. Broders	19	Tigard, OR	
Seaman	S. A. Bruce	18	Social Circle, GA	
Seaman	K. C. Brunney	19	Foxworth, MS	
Seaman Recruit	J. M. Buki	19	Erie, PA	
Seaman Recruit	J. J. Burger	19	Holmesville, PA	Recruit Ship's Yeoman
Airman Recruit	V. L. Burrell	18	Painesville, OH	
Airman Recruit	D. T. Caldeira	19	Brooklyn, NY	Guidon
Fireman Recruit	D. P. Callahan	22	Fort Worth, TX	
Airman Recruit	W. D. Carpenter	23	Lebanon, MO	
Seaman Recruit	J. A. Castillo	19	Gardena, CA	
Seaman	M. J. Collins	25	Amarillo, TX	
Seaman Recruit	S. L. Courtheyn	19	Minerva, OH	
Seaman Recruit	C. J. Crist	18	Westland, MI	

Rating	Name	Age	Hometown	Divisional Assignment
Airman Recruit	R. L. Cumpson	20	Inglewood, CA	
Seaman Recruit	R. R. Davis	17	Chicago, IL	
Seaman Recruit	K. G. Dawson	18	Mt. Vernon, NY	
Seaman	K. C. Dizon	20	Hayward, CA	
Seaman Recruit	T. A. Fletcher	17	Bridgeport, CT	
Airman	R. A. Freeman	21	DeQuincy, LA	Ship's Master at Arms
Seaman Apprentice	T. L. Gamble	19	Mounds, IL	
Airman Recruit	R. D. Gildersleeve	24	Birmingham, AL	Recruit Master at Arms
Seaman Recruit	M. J. Gray	19	Baltimore, MD	
Airman Recruit	A. J. Grayer	19	Orange Park, FL	
Airman Recruit	A. Guiterrez	18	Imperial, CA	
Fireman Recruit	J. D. Haight	18	Omaha, NE	
Seaman Recruit	M. Y. Hardin	24	Springfield, TN	
Seaman Recruit	K. A. Hardison-Porter	18	San Diego, CA	
Seaman	J. L. Hattrich	19	Fort Mill, SC	Recruit Section Leader
Airman Recruit	J. E. Hebert	21	Leland, MS	
Airman Recruit	S. M. Herring	18	Chino Valley, AZ	Recruit Section Leader
Airman Recruit	J. B. Hooton-Hetrick	22	Colorado Springs, CO	
Seaman	E. A. Hopkins	18	Shelbyville, IN	Recruit CPO (RPOC)
Fireman Recruit	S. M. Jackson	18	New Brunswick, NJ	
Fireman Recruit	D. E. Johnson	31	Lubbock, TX	
Airman Recruit	J. L. Jones	19	Claremont, CA	
Seaman Apprentice	T. E. Kelly	25	Pueblo, CO	
Seaman Apprentice	T. R. Kessimakis	20	Salt Lake City, UT	
Fireman Recruit	A. J. Krofta	22	Cleveland, OH	
Seaman	N. T. Kyaw	19	San Francisco, CA	Recruit Religious P.O.
Fireman	E. L. Lee	25	Mazee, MS	
Airman	L. L. Leitner	35	Detroit, MI	
Fireman Recruit	S. E. Leonard	19	Morenno Valley, CA	
Airman Recruit	A. Lopez	20	Brooklyn, NY	
Seaman Recruit	K. L. McClellan	18	Phoenix, AZ	
Seaman Recruit	J. A. Miller	18	Las Vegas, NV	
Seaman Recruit	D. S. Mills	18	South Daytona, FL	
Seaman Recruit	S. D. Nance	17	Southlake, TX	Ship's Mail Petty Officer
Seaman Recruit	L. M. Orlando	20	Selden, NY	
Airman Recruit	M. Paes	18	Rialto, CA	

Rating	Name	Age	Hometown	Divisional Assignment
Seaman Apprentice	A. E. Pankratz	18	Great Falls, MT	
Seaman Recruit	P. J. Parker	18	Coffee Springs, AL	
Fireman Recruit	X. Pasillas	26	San Bernardino, CA	
Seaman Recruit	S. J. Pierce	19	Swainsboro, GA	
Airman Recruit	S. Prosper	18	Vista, CA	Recruit Section Leader
Airman Apprentice	M. R. Rasco	25	Springfield, MO	Assistant Recruit CPO (AROC)
Fireman Recruit	Z. Robinson	19	Philadelphia, PA	
Seaman Recruit	E. W. Ryan	22	Waynesboro, PA	
Seaman	J. R. Schau	19	Smithfield, VA	
Seaman Recruit	D. A. Scorsone	18	Fort Gibson, OK	
Seaman Recruit	M. L. Shelton	19	Marlow, OK	
Seaman	J. A. Sison	20	San Diego, CA	
Seaman Apprentice	D. W. Smith	22	Vancouver, WA	Recruit Athletic P.O.
Airman Apprentice	J. C. Smith	21	Fort Morgan, CO	Ship's Master at Arms
Seaman Recruit	M. A. Smith	21	Denison, TX	Medical Yeoman
Airman Recruit	M. M. Stamp	21	Englewood, CO	Ship's Yeoman
Seaman Recruit	D. T. Starks	18	Chicago, IL	Assistant Master at Arms
Seaman Recruit	L. L. Taylor	18	Anchorage, AL	
Seaman Recruit	M. J. Trindade	19	Edison, NJ	Recruit Religious P.O.
Seaman Recruit	J. P. Troeger	21	Mountlake Terrace, WA	Dental Yeoman
Airman Recruit	T. S. Volk	19	Manayunk, PA	
Airman Apprentice	M. L. Walls	20	Aikoi, WV	
Seaman Recruit	J. A. Ward	20	Taylorville, IL	Section Leader
Seaman Recruit	C. L. Williams	19	Lake Charles, LA	
Seaman Recruit	S. L. Williams	18	Brooklyn, NY	
Seaman Recruit	M. A. Wirsch	20	Auburn, CA	Yeoman
Airman Recruit	J. Zaragoza	18	Riverside, CA	

Glossary

Aft Behind, or to the rear.

AFVAB Armed Forces Vocational Aptitude Battery. A series of screening tests that determines the recruits' aptitude for particular skill fields (ratings) in the Navy.

AROC Assistant recruit chief petty officer. The acronym is a carryover from a previous title, assistant recruit officer in charge.

ASMO Assignment memorandum. The form on which setback to a junior division is recorded. A fate worse than death for the average recruit, since it significantly adds to the stay in boot camp.

Attention on Deck The traditional Navy alert that an officer is entering the space.

Battle Flags Competitive flags won by a division. They include Drill, Academic, STAR (Compartment Readiness), Athletic, and so forth.

Below In civilian terms, "downstairs."

Berthing Space Sleeping quarters.

Black Flag Day A day when weather conditions are so bad as to preclude any outdoor activity.

Boondockers Navy work boots. About the closest civilian approximation would be a pair of reinforced, steel-toed Wellington boots.

Bravo Zulu The traditional naval commendation of "well done." From the signal flags B and Z, hoisted to send this message to the fleet.

Brother Division Two divisions at RTC are always linked, and complete all training events together. Divisions 005 and 006 were brother divisions.

Bulkhead A wall or partition.

Cadence Numerical beats, sung to keep a marching unit in step. At Great Lakes, the "official cadence" approximated "1, 2, 3, ah, 4" with alternate sequences ending on a rising, and then falling, note.

Camp Moffett The area of RTC north of Illinois Route 137. It houses the in-processing, confidence course, fire department, and swimming facilities.

Camp Porter The area south of Illinois Route 137. It houses the recruit living areas, schoolhouse, galleys, and three of the four drill halls. Linked to Camp Moffett by an underpass called The Tunnel.

Caterpillars A division not yet commissioned. So named for the tightly bound guidon and ship's flag, which look like antennas, leading 160 legs, which sometimes are even in step.

Chant Cadence call other than the official "1,2,3, ah, 4." Generally called by the AROC, a good chant relieves the drudgery of long, boring marches.

Chit A small slip of paper, giving permission to attend a certain function, or noting a deficiency. Chits of all sorts keep the Navy afloat.

Chow Navy food. Remarkably good, sometimes, too.

Chuckhugger One who coddles recruits or is overly sympathetic to their problems. The worst pejorative in the mind of an RDC.

Chuckie RDC slang for recruits. Rarely heard from recruits themselves, who prefer to call themselves "Rickys."

C.O. Commanding officer. Informally, the Skipper, but never addressed that way by his juniors.

Compartment A room. "The Compartment" usually refers to the barracks space where the recruits live.

Cookie The enamel medallion worn on the left breast pocket by each RDC.

Corpsman Hospital corpsman; in other services, a medic.

CPO Chief petty officer. Incapable of error when confronted with contradictions, chiefs simply belay orders and act on information newly received. The human race at its best. Honest.

CS Gas O-chlorobenzylidenemalononitrile, a common, nontoxic tear gas or harassing agent. Hard to spell or pronounce, and worse to inhale.

Cumshaw To beg, borrow, or steal. Similar to *promote* in the other services. Usually pronounced "comm-shaw."

Cutlass A short, curved ceremonial sword; the badge of office of the RPOC.

Deck The floor.

DEP Delayed Entry Program. Individuals can enlist in the Navy and remain at home for up to a year, to complete school, work with recruiters, and so on.

Ditty Sock A sweatsock, into which recruits stuff wallet, watch, and other valuables when exercising. Knotted, it's worn tucked into the waistband.

DMT Director of military training, third in command at RTC. This officer has the unfortunate duty to be the "bad cop" to recruits; the very initials send chills of fear throughout a division.

Dog Song A chant that begins, "My dog is a vegetable, now he's in the hospital." Beloved by the recruits, loathed by some of their superiors.

Drifty Spaced-out, or nonprofessional. From *adrift,* as in "gear adrift."

Dropped Made to do pushups, ad infinitum—or, often enough, ad nauseam.

FFD Fit for full duty. You may still feel terrible, but the corpsmen say you're ready for action.

Forward Ahead, toward the front; opposite of aft. The forward watch is usually the recruit upon whose unfortunate head the wrath of the FQA inspectors or the roving OOD usually falls. Not an enviable position to hold.

Forward IG Forward instructional guidance. Recruits are mustered in the forward half of the compartment and sit on the deck, legs crossed, for periods of RDC instruction.

FQA Fleet quality assurance; senior petty officers who ensure that RTC is operating as intended. The name strikes even greater terror into the hearts of recruits than that of the DMT, to whom they report, mainly because there are more of them.

Freakin' The most profane word permitted of RDCs. "Freakin' knucklehead!" bawled out by an irritated RDC is a sure precursor of bad things to come.

Galley Mess hall. Technically, the galley is the kitchen area of the mess hall, but the term is used loosely to describe the entire building, including the dining areas.

Gedunk Junk food, and the place or machine that sells it.

Gig Line The straight line formed by the buttons of a recruit shirt, a tie (if worn), and the edge of the belt buckle.

GQ General quarters. At RDC recruits stand at attention at the foot of their racks when GQ is called.

Grinder Large open areas (paved at Great Lakes) where drill is performed and where cars are parked during public access periods.

Guidon Small, blue flag with white numerals, the "license plate" of a division.

Gundecking To claim to have performed a task or duty without having done so. Equivalent of "pencil whipping" in the other services. The term takes its origin from the gundeck of sailing ships, where young midshipmen used to stand in inclement weather while claiming to take star sights by sextant. One cannot see the sky from the gun deck, but one can see the navigator's signal of the noon position transmitted from the flagship.

Heads Restroom facilities, including showers, sinks, and toilets.

Hooligans From "Hooligan's Navy." Navy term for the U.S. Coast Guard. (Coast Guard slang for the Navy is unprintable.)

House Recruit term for the compartment. Officially discouraged by RTC staff, the term is used by everyone, including RTC staff.

Integrate/Deintegrate To move the male and female elements of a division together, or to separate them. In most cases, only sleeping and hygiene functions require deintegration of the division.

ITE Instructional training exercises. A very energetic workout, used to discipline or motivate recruits. To be avoided at all costs.

Johnny Cash Navy slang for the attractive and comfortable winter working uniform. Black, with a narrow tie, it resembles the famous country singer's outfit.

Knucklehead The second worst pejorative permitted to the RTC staff, second only to "freakin' knucklehead."

Ladder The staircase. Recruits usually wait under the main staircase when summoned to the LCPO's office. Not an enviable place to be.

LCPO Leading chief petty officer. An E7, E8, or E9 chief petty officer, second in command to the ship's officer. If you want something done, see the LCPO.

Liberty Freedom to leave the base, at least for a short period.

Liberty Cuffs Officially forbidden by uniform regulations, these ornate dragons, snakes, or—for the truly daring—naked images are sewn into the inside cuffs of the dress blue (crackerjack) uniform. Junior sailors think the cuffs make them look salty, senior sailors think they make the juniors look silly.

LLD Light or limited duty. Not sick enough for SIQ but not well, either.

1MC The general public address system in the barracks. The term is taken from the circuit designation for the general all-hands intercom aboard ship.

MAA Master at arms. The internal police force of the Navy. While there is now a formal rating for masters at arms, in many cases it is a temporary, out-of-rating assignment. The MAA is responsible for maintaining good order and discipline. The recruit MAA is generally chosen for size, strength of personality, and common sense.

Mainside That part of the Naval Training Center, Great Lakes, not occupied by recruits. Service School Command, the Naval Hospital, and the administrative offices of the base are all located at Mainside, east of Sheridan Road, about two miles east of Recruit Training Command.

Master Chief Senior enlisted E-9 rating. The best of the best.

MCPON Master chief petty officer of the Navy. The highest ranking enlisted member of the U.S. Navy. Serves as the enlisted adviser to the chief of naval operations. MCPON Hall is the visitors' center at RTC Great Lakes, named in honor of these extraordinary sailors.

MEPS Military entry processing station. One of sixty-five joint service processing centers located in major cities.

Muster Roll call. To "make muster" is to be where you need to be, when you need to be there. Also used in the sense of "to gather" as in, "Hey, Chief, muster your recruits, so that the LCPO can talk to them."

NEX The Navy Exchange System. Similar to the PX in other services.

NQS Nonqualified swimmer. One who has not yet passed the third-class swim test.

OBA Oxygen breathing apparatus. A fire-fighting appliance with a self-contained oxygen generator and face mask.

OOD/JOOD Officer of the deck or junior officer of the deck. At RTC, the ship's OOD is a rotational assignment for RDCs; the JOOD watch is manned by recruits.

Passageway A corridor or hall. In speech, often abbreviated to "P-way."

Petty Officer Enlisted member, in pay grades E-4 through E-6. The petty officer is a noncommissioned officer, similar to a sergeant in the other services; the backbone of the Navy.

PL 105 Public Law 105, which mandates gender integration of many military functions, including recruit training.

PT Physical training, or exercise.

Push To lead a division of recruits. Used as a verb and as a noun. Each RDC is expected to complete nine "pushes" before leaving RTC.

Quarterdeck A sacred, ceremonial space found on all navy ships and stations. Usually highly polished, and surrounded by naval artifacts.

Quartermaster Enlisted member responsible for the navigation of a ship at sea, and not for the issuance of stores, as in other services. (Storekeepers handle material issue in the Navy.)

Rack Bunk or bed.

RDC Recruit division commander.

Red Rope Another name for the RDC, from the red aiguilette worn on the left shoulder.

Rick on a Stick Injured recruit using crutches.

Ricky Recruit nickname for anything recruit-related. Probably from the name "Ricky Recruit," often used as an exemplar for filling out forms, chits, and so forth.

Ricky Bug Juice Kool-Aid, or something similar. The chemical composition is unknown, and unknowable.

Ricky Crud Anything that ails you in boot camp. May be as mild as a case of the sniffles, or as severe as double pneumonia.

Ricky Heaven The branch NEX, off limits except to the liberty party after pass-in-review. By extension, any place in the known universe other than RTC, Great Lakes.

Ricky Lawnmower Fingernail clippers, the utility of which is amazing. They are used to trim threads, cut dog-tag chains, and for a host of other applications never envisioned by the inventor.

Ricky Ninja A mythical character who invades berthing spaces after Taps and creates havoc. Well, maybe not so mythical.

Ricky Sunday Relaxed routine from 0600 to 1300 on Sunday and holidays. By long established custom, RDCs do not visit the berthing spaces during this time, except under extraordinary circumstances.

Roadguards Recruits, wearing bright orange fluorescent vests, who stand on either side stripe of a crossing zone, to further protect recruits as they march in formation across the street.

RPOC Recruit petty officer, chief. A recruit, selected for leadership ability, who acts as an assistant to the RDCs and serves as a surrogate leader in those rare times when an RDC is not present.

RTC Recruit Training Command, an element of the Naval Training Center, Great Lakes, Illinois.

Scuttle A small hole in a bulkhead, deck, or hatch, used as a pass-through.

Scuttlebutt A drinking fountain, after the "water butts" used on sailing ships. By extension, rumor or gossip, which usually had its origins while sailors were standing around the scuttlebutt.

Seabag Same as duffel bag or barracks bag in the other services. Formerly carried by sailors on the left shoulder, it now sports two arm straps, and is worn like an oversized backpack. The old way was saltier.

SEALs The Navy's elite Special Forces Branch. Recruits are screened for SEAL, Underwater Demolition Teams (UDT), and other special units while in boot camp.

Senior Chief Chief petty officer in the E-8 rating. Everything defined about chief petty officers is doubled for senior chiefs.

Service Week Generally, the fifth week of training. Recruits are assigned to assist in various jobs required to keep the base operational. Also, a generic term for those who are in their fifth week of training; e.g., "Chief, ask your Service Week to make copies of these documents, please."

Ship RTC's preferred word for barracks. While each is named after a famous warship, most are referred to by their number, with Ship One at the northernmost end of Camp Porter, and Ship Fourteen at the south. Ship Fifteen, the special programs barracks, is located at Camp Moffett.

Ship's Crew Each division assigns about five recruits to the maintenance of common areas within the ship. Ship's crew act as watchstanders, handle mail, perform maintenance, and also shovel snow when needed.

SIQ Sick in quarters. Ill or injured recruits who are confined to bed in the barracks.

Skivvies Underwear. The Navy issues six pairs to each male recruit; female recruits bring their own from home.

Small Stuff Small cotton rope (line), the uses of which are infinite. The Navy's historical answer to duct tape.

SMART Card Combination identification and debit card, carried by every recruit in a shirt pocket during boot camp.

Smurf Newly arrived recruit, from the blue sweatsuit issued immediately upon arrival. Named from the resemblance to the 1980s cartoon characters.

Special Boats The extraordinarily courageous special assault teams that man small, fast watercraft to deliver SEALS on their missions. Descended from the heroic Riverine Patrol Forces in Vietnam.

TAD Temporarily assigned for duty. A short assignment to complete a specific task away from one's home unit.

Topside Upstairs.

UA Unauthorized absence. The Navy equivalent of AWOL (absent without leave). Thirty days of UA equate to desertion, a federal crime.

Watch A particular duty. "On watch" equates to "on duty" in the other services. At RTC, each berthing compartment has two watchstanders at all times, one to guard the front door, and one the back.

Watch Cap Navy-blue knit cap, worn during cold weather. Replaced, during really bad weather, by a navy-blue ski mask.

XO Executive officer, second in command.

Yeoman Navy clerical rating. Equivalent to "writer" in the Marine Corps. Division 005 was blessed with an extraordinarily efficient yeoman, who, strangely enough, was then assigned to electrician mate's school upon departure.

Index

Abbott, Katie, 123
academic capacity enhancement (ACE).
    See special programs
Adams, Katie: at battle stations, 124, 133,
    137, 139, 141; on sleeplessness, 152
Alcazar, Maria: at battle stations, 133, 136,
    148, 155, 165–66; and phone call home,
    64; on physical training, 118; at service
    week, 85–87; and Thanksgiving liberty,
    99–100
anxiety, recruit: upon arrival, 18–19; at gas
    chamber, 102–9
Arcia, Jennifer, 10, 85, 90, 157
arrival at RTC, recruits': bus trip, 9–10;
    clothing issue, 21; commissioning
    ceremony, 42; and first haircuts, 22;
    stress upon, 18–19
assignment memorandum (ASMO), 26;
    recruit reaction to, 66
Atitsobuie, Fred, 137, 151
Atkinson, Jeff: background of, 20; on
    facilities, 80–81; and gender
    integration, 188; on boot camp
    haircuts, 20; and LCPO duties, 77; and
    off-base schools, 192; and RDC
    marching, 194; on service week, 83;
    and special liberty, 96; on impact of
    weather on recruits, 80

Bandlow, Mike, 135, 142, 143, 157
barracks: berthing compartments, 27;
    conditions of, 58; field day, 65; ship
    names of, 12
battle stations: activities following, 169;
    alert beginning, 123; celebration, 167;
    ceremony completing, 164–66;
    criticality of, 182; damage control

exercise, 158–61; disqualification from,
    133, 138; Division 005's participation
    in, 121–66; emergency sortie exercise,
    138–41; escape scuttle exercise, 150–52;
    final transit from, 162–63; investigate
    and rescue exercise, 133–37; letdown
    after, 169–70; lifeboat exercise during,
    126–48; magazine flooding exercise,
    152–55; mass causality exercise,
    126–29; RDC reactions to, 137, 141,
    158, 162; RDC roles during, 123, 155;
    recruit reactions to, 128, 132–33,
    136–37, 140–41, 143–44, 147–52,
    154–59, 161–69; rules, 122; running
    during, 126, 129–30, 141–42, 145, 155,
    158, 161; safety concerns, 130; shaft
    alley rescue exercise, 156; small arms
    exercise, 130–32; stores loading
    exercise, 142–44; stragglers group
    following, 171; team composition for,
    123; uniforms during, 125
Beller, Adam, 141
Besaw, Pam, 104–5, 107–8, 158–59
Betton, Arron, 31, 39, 50, 57
Black, Christopher, 106
Bluejacket's Manual, 104–5
Boesel, Julie, 96
bonus, enlistment, 5–6
Boorda, Mike, 210–11
boot camp: kinder, gentler, 181, 185–86;
    navy, other locations, 13, 14, 69, 194–95
Bowser, Scott: and battle stations kickoff,
    122, 125; emergency sortie exercise,
    139; magazine flooding exercise, 154;
    recruit respect for, 168; weapons
    simulation exercise, 131
Broders, Nick, 65–67, 162, 174

225

Rivero, Rowland, 34–38
Robinson, Ed, 123, 126, 134–36, 157
Robinson, Zuni, 143, 161
Russell, Lela: background of, 14–16; at battle stations, 121, 125, 133: on building conditions, 58, 86; at Captain's Cup competition, 109; on female haircuts, 22; at graduation exercises, 165; on gender integration, 187; recruit makeup and, 178; aboard USS *Marlinespike*, 141; personal motivation, 17; on non–high school graduates, 189; regarding physical fitness, 118; on quality of recruits, 94–96, 185; regarding off-base schools, 193; on seamanship, 68; and sea stories, 77, 79; summer surge, 195; swimming, 48; and terrorism, 175; and weather, 82; on weight control, 21
Ryan, Edward 40

Santa Barbara, (AE-28) USS, 13, 15
Schau, Joseph, 168
Scorsone, Dayna: at battle stations, 145, 163; while marching, 30; at physical fitness tests, 118; on terrorism and military duty, 176
schoolhouse (Building 1127), 46, 68, 85, 129
schools, North Chicago, difficulties with, 185, 192–93
screening, specialized careers, 24
seabags, difficulty carrying, 21, 125, 130, 142, 155, 207
seamanship training: history of, 69–70, 72; and *Marlinespike*, 69–73; recruit reactions to, 70–71
sea stories, RDC, 76–78, 206
self-help programs, RDC, 70, 72
separation and segregation, 24
service week: description of, 83–84; recruit reactions to, 84–90; perceived value of, 184
setback, training. *See* assignment memorandum, ASMO
Shelton, Mike, 64–67, 117, 148, 210
Ship Fifteen (special barracks), 62
Sison, James, 84, 89, 130, 133
sleeplessness, impact of: at battle stations, 124, 129, 152; during arrival processing, 20, 24; during class, 68; at gas chamber, 106; during service week, 87, 89
smart cards, 20, 29

Smith, Daniel, 53, 177
Smith, Joshua, 144
Smith, Mary: and battle stations graduation, 163, 166; as medical yeoman, 33; at military entrance processing station, 6; at seamanship training, 73; and Thanksgiving liberty, 99, 100
special programs: academic capacity enhancement (ACE), 60–61; fundamental applied skills training (FAST), 60; personal applied skills system (PASS), 61; physical fitness training unit (FIT), 61; recruit evaluation unit (REU), 48, 62–63; recruit holding unit (RHU), 61–62, 206
Stamp, Melissa, 104, 129, 136, 139, 144, 168
Starks, Demitrus, 73–74, 86–87, 162
Stevenson, Fines, 70–72
summer surge, 86, 118, 195
Survival, Escape, Resistance, Evasion school (SERE), 14, 132
swimming: and fear of water, 48; qualifications and training, 47

Taylor, Leah, 19, 98–99, 207
teamwork, development of, 65, 182, 204
telephone calls home, 19–20, 64, 100, 109
terrorism: recruit attitudes toward, 175–76; training to reduce, 172–74
time pressures, RDC, 190, 192
tradition and folklore: caterpillars, 45; ghosts, 27–28; guidon, importance of, 45; Ricky ninja, 45, 64–65
traffic, on base, 82, 111, 112, 113
training: communications, 71; classroom logistics, 30, 46; fire fighting, 93, 119–20; housekeeping, 45, recruit opinions of, 46, 68; staff reactions to, 47; schedules, 26; weapons, 91–93
Trindade, Marcia, 111–12, 170
Triolo, Joseph, 199
Troeger, James, 119, 155, 178, 201
Tubbs, Pam, 179–85, 204
Tucker, John: background of, 12–13, 15–17; and battle stations, 172; commissioning ceremony, 44–45; gender integration, 188; comparison to Marine Corps boot camp, 189–90; RDC selection and screening, 191; recruit motivation, 94
tunnel, (Buckley road underpass), 27, 80, 104, 110, 144–45, 155, 162, 194

uniforms: initial issue, 20, 31; fit, 197; recruit reaction to, 97, 99
United Services Organization (USO), 7

Velasco, Rogelio, 123, 134, 150
Vogt, Tom, 23–24
Volk, Teresa, 98–99, 108, 119, 176

Wagner, Mike, 56–57
Walls, Mark, 45
Ward, Jared: and barracks field day, 65; as division honor graduate, 200; and navy food, 41; at pass-in-review practice, 170; and seamanship training, 71; as section leader, 66; service week, 86, 90; and Thanksgiving liberty, 101; and uniforms, 97; on weather and location, 208
warrior weeks, 91–93
weather, impact of: on battle stations 121, 125, 129, 142, 149; on departure, 205–6; when marching, 80, 82; on pass-in-review, 177–78
Werley, William, 153
Williams, Cari, 74–75, 97, 152, 204
Williams, James, 130–31
Williams, Stacy, 117
Wirsch, Megan: background of, 28; at battle stations, 154, 158, 162; at divine services, 116; and food preferences, 39;

letters home, 31, 116; aboard *Marlinespike*, 71; illness of, 33; and music, 75; at pass-in-review 198; reflections concerning training, 201–4; relating with shipmates, 73; at reveille, 74; on Ricky Sunday, 76; and weather, 177
Wisch, David, 87–88
Witcher, Mike, 129

yeoman, recruit, 33, 85–87
Youell, Timothy, 56

Zaragoza, Jeanette, 20, 108, 132
Zeller, Martin: background of, 13–14; at battle stations graduation, 169; on conditions in barracks, 58; at division departure, 205; on fire fighting, 119; at gas chamber, 107; on gender integration, 186; at *Marlinespike*, 73; personal motivation, 17; regarding non–high school graduates, 188; on processing week, 29; on physical fitness, 54, 118; on recruits, 78, 94–95; selecting recruit petty officers, 28; and school system of North Chicago, 192; and service week, 83; and shipboard communications, 71; time pressures upon, 190; and warrior weeks, 91

About the Author

A veteran of the Vietnam War (USN MCB-1, Phu Bai and Danang, 1969–70), Leahy graduated from Recruit Training Command, Great Lakes, in 1966. After his honorable discharge from the Navy, he returned to school and completed his baccalaureate and graduate education and served as a civilian contractor in a number of intelligence-gathering programs overseas. Leahy recently retired as a senior manager in international operations after a long career with the Western Electric Company (now Lucent Technologies—Bell Laboratories). He is currently an adjunct professor of business at the Ross School of Leadership and Management at Franklin University.

Leahy resides in Columbus, Ohio, with his wife, the former Margaret Agnes McGraw. They are the parents of three grown sons.